T0319751

Social Capital in Europe

To Giuditta Levato, Napoleone Colajanni and all who fought to defend a lost cause. I learned from you there is a south everywhere, a south to struggle for.

Social Capital in Europe

A Comparative Regional Analysis

Emanuele Ferragina

Research Fellow, Oxford Institute of Social Policy, University of Oxford, UK and Fellow, Green Templeton College, University of Oxford, UK

Edward Elgar

Cheltenham, UK • Northampton, MA, USA

Published by
Edward Elgar Publishing Limited
The Lypiatts
15 Lansdown Road
Cheltenham
Glos GL50 2JA
UK

Edward Elgar Publishing, Inc.
William Pratt House
9 Dewey Court
Northampton
Massachusetts 01060
USA

A catalogue record for this book
is available from the British Library

Library of Congress Control Number: 2012939106

MIX
Paper from
responsible sources
FSC® C018575

ISBN 978 1 78100 021 2

Typeset by Servis Filmsetting Ltd, Stockport, Cheshire
Printed and bound by MPG Books Group, UK

Contents

Preface

Some books present fresh evidence; others make arguments that urge the reader to see old problems in a new light. This work is decidedly of the latter sort.
Theda Skocpol

A friend of mine, having listened to my complaints about the complexity and apparent unfairness of finding post-doctoral research opportunities pointed out that I should not forget where I came from. This homily aroused my deep curiosity, and implied cliché, namely the suffocating difficulties which confront émigrés coming from a backward environment, in my case Southern Italy, with its limited social mobility and academic aridity. I was reminded that I have been armed with a unique geographical DNA to undertake a comparative assessment on the nature of different macro-systems, implicit in my friend's comment, and to form an outlook on the nature of social relation.

Two important studies, *Tracce di Comunità* (Bagnasco 1999) and *Making Democracy Work* (Putnam 1993), and Professor Nicola Negri's lectures on economic sociology at University of Turin, were inspirational sources, the building blocks needed to construct a general review of social networks and trust in society. But it was only after leaving my homeland that, with a different perspective, I have been able to elaborate my interest for these issues, and to distil my focus to a few key variables.

I have turned my interest in social ties into the measurement of social capital, have fashioned quantitative models supported by general theory, and have analysed the nature of social relations with a comparative historical analysis. Refining my research questions has allowed me to reach a provisional synthesis between my theoretical understanding of social capital and the application of a comparative method geared on empirical analysis.

PART 1

The Methodological Toolbox

1. Introduction

Social capital theorists have renewed the old interest in the importance of active secondary groups in supporting well run political institutions in modern democracies (see Bourdieu and Passeron 1970; Bourdieu 1980; 1986; Putnam 1993; 2000). Putnam (1993) unified quantitative and historical analyses, arguing that the lack of social capital in the South of Italy was more the product of a peculiar historical development than the consequence of a set of contemporary socio-economic conditions. This conclusion has sparked a lengthy debate and received fierce criticism (see Ferragina 2010a).

Criticism has hitherto mainly focused on the lack of awareness of the structural socio-economic conditions of society (see Skocpol 1996; Skocpol et al. 2000; Thomson 2005), as for example, the level of income inequality (Knack and Keefer 1997; Costa and Kahn 2003; O'Connel 2003), and the excessive determinism of the historical analysis (Lupo 1993; Lemann 1996; Tarrow 1996). These two criticisms are integrated by analysing 85 European regions, revisiting Putnam's hypothesis and contributing to the debate on the determinants of social capital. More specifically, the scope of the book is to: (1) test the impact of four socio-economic predictors (that is, income inequality, economic development, labour market participation and national divergence) on social capital through a causal model, and (2) integrate rather than simply juxtapose socio-economic and historic-institutional explanations of social capital variation with the analysis of two deviant cases.

Following Tocqueville, Putnam argued that nations need strong social participation in order to guarantee the functioning of democratic institutions. However, Putnam (1993) did not take into account Tocqueville's (1961: 8) main explanation about the high level of social participation in 1830s America; the widespread condition of equality. In accordance with Tocqueville's argument and following a large bulk of empirical work (Knack and Keefer 1997; Costa and Kahn 2003; O'Connel 2003; Beugelsdijk and Van Schaik 2005a; Ferragina 2010a) this book tests the effect of income inequality and economic development on social capital. It has also been argued (Gorz 1992: 182) that the ability to work provides a sense of participation and membership in societal activities among citizens. Hence, we test the effect of labour market participation on social capital. Finally, strong regional differences within nations might also impact on social capital (see Chapter 3).

Revisiting medieval history, Putnam explains the contemporary lack of social capital in the South of Italy as the result of there being no medieval towns in the twelfth and thirteenth centuries. This explanation was simply juxtaposed to the lack of present day social capital but not in fact connected to it (Lupo 1993; Tarrow 1996). Unlike Putnam, we propose to assess the impact of historic-institutional evolutions on social capital starting from the interpretation of the general socio-economic conditions and observing what the causal model leaves unexplained. The integration between these two levels of analysis helps to sharpen and refine the general findings emerging from the socio-economic model (Lijphart 1971) and at the same time, gather additional information from the in-depth comparison between regular and deviant cases.

Wallonia and the South of Italy are regions which deviate from the general pattern identified by the regression model because of extremely poor social capital scores accompanied by positive residuals.[1] The concomitance of low social capital scores and positive residuals indicates that according to the socio-economic model, Wallonia and the South of Italy should have even lower social capital scores than observed. Reversely, in the other regions where social capital scores are below the average, the socio-economic model predicts higher levels of social capital than observed.

These findings challenge Putnam's hypothesis because from a comparative perspective, in the South of Italy and Wallonia, the adverse socio-economic conditions seem to be more important than the negative influence of historic development in explaining the present lack of social capital. Starting from the comparison between Wallonia and the South of Italy with Flanders and the North East of Italy, two regions in which higher social capital scores are accompanied by positive residuals, the book proposes an alternative historical explanation: the *sleeping social capital theory*. This theory is complemented by an institutional comparison between Belgium and Italy.

1.1   THE FOUNDATIONS OF SOCIAL CAPITAL THEORY

Certain ideas emerge from the intellectual debate seeming to promise a solution to all fundamental problems and clarify all obscure issues (Langer and Knauth 1942). The strength of these new paradigms overwhelms all other theories for a while, but after gaining familiarity with them, we realize that they cannot solve our puzzles and we see that even excessive popularity progressively ends (Geertz 1973: 3). Only at this stage is a more settled assessment of a new paradigm possible. Without doubt the social capital concept falls into this category of ideas. After two decades of intense debate, we may analyse it without overemphasis, discussing the significance of its emergence and its main determinants.

Social capital with its ambiguous nature, an elixir to revitalize democracy for many (see Cusack 1999; Freitag 2006; Knack 2002; Ostrom and Ahn 2003; Paxton 1999; Rothstein 2001) and a poison that brings back dangerous concepts for others (see Fine 1999; 2008; Lemann 1996; Ferragina 2010a; Smith and Kulynich 2002; Thomson 2005), enabled Putnam to rediscover traditional elements of sociological theory (see Portes 1998) and propose a call for the renewal of democracy. Putnam (1993) transformed social capital from an academic concept (see Hanifan 1916; Jacobs 1961; Bourdieu and Passeron 1970; Loury 1977; Coleman 1988; 1990) to a practical tool to (re)*Make Democracy Work*, generating a tremendous interest among politicians and the general public.

This tremendous interest is grounded in the extraordinary ability to connect policy making and traditional sociological theory (Table 1.1):

(1) discussing the possibility of reconciling the dichotomy individualism versus communitarianism;
(2) merging Tocqueville's enthusiasm for participative democracy and the concern of the founding fathers of sociology about the effects of modernization on social cohesion;
(3) reflecting upon the importance of accumulating social capital for community building;
(4) integrating micro and macro foundations of social science in proposing a general theory;
(5) shifting from socio-economic to cultural explanations in investigating the lack of social capital and its impact on the quality of democracy;
(6) internalizing social science into economic discourse and by the same token broadening the scope of economics beyond its boundaries.

First, the social capital concept is linked to an old debate and proposes a synthesis between the values contained in the communitarian approaches and the individualism professed by rational choice theory. Historically, the power of community governance has been stressed by many philosophers from antiquity to the eighteenth century, from Aristotle through Thomas Aquinas to Edmund Burke. Putnam bridged the polarity between individualism and communitarianism, highlighting the importance of

Table 1.1   Social capital from Tocqueville to Making Democracy Work

Social capital theory (1) is an attempt to bridge the polarity between communitarianism and individualism		
The 19th and 20th Century Origins (2)		
Comparative Politics	Sociological Theory	
Tocqueville Equality, decentralization and participation in civil society foster the continuous improvement of democratic institutions	Tönnies, Durkheim, Simmel, Weber Industrialization and urbanization transformed social relationships irreversibly Modernization Theorists Contradiction between modernity and traditional communities	
The Predecessors		
Community Building (3)	Micro/Macro Foundations (4)	Culture (5)
Hanifan & Jacobs Importance of the layout of rural communities and cities to accumulate social capital	Manchester School and Social Network Theorists Focus on networks at individual and aggregate levels	Banfield, Almond and Verba, Inghlehart Social capital and culture to explain the lack of institutional development
Integration of Sociology and Economic Theory (6)		
Bourdieu	Loury	Coleman
Social capital is one of the three forms in which capital appears: economic, cultural and social	Social capital to explain the acquisition of the standard human characteristics	Discussion of the forms of social capital; integration of social capital in the utility functions of the individuals
Social capital and Democracy		
Putnam From social capital as an academic concept, to social capital as a practical tool to (re)make democracy work		

Source: Author's elaboration.

social engagement to face the crisis of liberal democracy (Bowles and Gintis 2002). This sociological line of enquiry strikes a balance between individualism, the engine of economic growth, and the function of secondary groups, the glue that prevents social disintegration (see Tocqueville 1961).

Second, closely following the founding fathers of sociology, Putnam investigated the idea that industrialization and urbanization transformed the social relationship. He observed the breakdown of traditional bonds and the exponential development of anomie and alienation in society. In this sense he re-kindled the debate of the founding fathers of sociology focusing on: (1) the distinction between formal and informal social networks, (2) the necessity of secondary groups for the functioning of society, and (3) the importance of exclusivity to generate a competitive advantage for restricted clubs.

The distinction between *Gemeinschaft* and *Gesellschaft* (see Tönnies 1955) illustrates the difference between the type of solidarity generated by old communities and those existent in modern societies; the attributes of the first term[2] differ from the less bonding attributes associated with the second term. Putnam called this distinction to mind in his discussion of bonding (which is similar to Tönnies' *Gemeinschaft*) and bridging (which is similar to Tönnies' *Gesellschaft*) relations.[3] The fear of social disintegration in the transition from a *mechanic society* to a *modern society* was already current at the end of the nineteenth century (Durkheim 1893). In this vein, at the turn of the twenty-first century, social capital theorists emphasized the importance of social networks in preserving the fragile equilibrium between individual and social needs.

A nation can work properly only through the mediation of secondary groups, which are necessary bodies in grafting atomistic individuals to the life of a nation; the denial of this model would transform society into a 'veritable sociological monstrosity' (Durkheim 1893: 29). Closeness and exclusivity are important characteristics that allow groups to create club goods like social capital (see Bourdieu 1980). Weber (1946), observing the structure of religious sects, emphasized this aspect illustrating the importance of robust informal networks to enforce rules and create relationships among members.

In the 1950s and 1960s modernization theorists (Bell 1962; Nisbet 1969; Stein 1960; Whyte 1956) placed a pessimistic emphasis on this debate, arguing similarly to Putnam and Fukuyama that modernization leads to the destruction of communitarian values and institutions. Nisbet (1969: 10) emphasized the need to defend the forgotten traditional values of community from the powerful emphasis of modern societal concepts like progress, reason and freedom. According to him, the lack of certitude connected with freedom generates disenchantment and alienation.[4] However, modernization scholars have not been able to support their propositions on the decline of participation and trust with empirical evidence (see Thomson 2005). For this reason the debate slowly died down, only to re-appear in a new guise within Putnam's social capital theory.[5]

Third, Putnam borrowed from Hanifan (1916) and Jacobs (1961) the idea that social capital can be accumulated or destroyed according to the appropriateness of the social investment made by communities. Communities are like corporations; before starting large-scale activities, they need to accumulate capital from all their components to reach a critical mass of resources before expanding activities. In the same way, the constant contact between neighbours increases social capital that in turn improves collective social productivity (Hanifan 1916: 130).

Fourth, Putnam took from social network theorists (Berkowitz 1982; Burt 1992; Laumann 1973; Wellman and Leighton 1979) and in particular from Mark Granovetter (1973; 1985) the idea that social capital theory can be helpful to bridge individual and macro level analyses to explain the evolution of democracy (Barnes 1954a and b; Bott 1957) and the necessity to overcome the simplistic claim that only present social structure matters for the analysis (Piselli 1997; Knox et al. 2006).

Fifth, Putnam affirmed that the decrease of social engagement needs to be explained mainly at the cultural level (Jackman and Miller 1996: 634). This consideration builds on contributions from Banfield (1958), Almond and Verba (1963) and Inglehart (1988), suggesting that countries with a high level of civic culture are more likely to sustain democracy over time than countries with low levels, independently of their socio-economic development (for a critique see Muller and Seligson 1994).

Sixth, Putnam's contribution transformed the debate launched by Bourdieu (1980), Loury (1977) and Coleman (1988; 1990) into one of the hottest topics in social science.[6] Over the last two decades, Putnam's theory has gained a large consensus upon the notion that social engagement is the only way to revive democracy. Bourdieu (1980) considered social capital theory a valid tool to complement the analysis of class stratification based on human and economic capital. Loury and Coleman reversed Bourdieu's perspective arguing that social capital was useful to broaden the scope of economic theory rather than a way to introduce economic theory into sociology. Loury applied social capital theory to explain the income gap between white and black people and Coleman argued that social capital was part of the utility function of individuals.

From a neo-classical perspective, Coleman inaugurated a broad discussion on the importance of social capital to create public goods. Putnam expanded Coleman's work, and affirmed that the creation of public goods via social engagement was the most productive investment for society. This was because in secondary groups people institutionalize the spirit of community by going beyond the current interests of their members. The dropping membership rate in this type of association is the starting point of *Bowling Alone*. Putnam turned this negative phenomenon into a general theory that looks at the role of civil society as strengthening democracy and he proposed a political strategy to reverse the negative trend. Similarly to Marx in *Das Kapital* (Aron 1967), Putnam merged scientific and moral elements together, providing quantitative evidence to rationalists and a Tocquevillian call to social engagement to idealists.

Summing up, Putnam's social capital theory concords with the conclusions of the founding fathers of sociology, emphasizing the importance of community building and renews the interest in the impact of cultural factors and modernization over communitarian spirit and democracy. It also reconciles micro- and macro-institutional analyses by suggesting that participation in secondary groups is the only antidote to the crisis of liberal democracy.

These foundations together with much empirical support conferred a strong authority to Putnam's work. However, its discussion about the determinants of social capital has raised many criticisms, notably the disregard of socio-economic factors and the role of public powers (Skocpol 1996; Costa and Kahn 2003) and the excessive determinism of the historical analysis (Lupo 1993; Tarrow 1996; Lemann 1996). For this reason the aim of this book is to re-kindle the debate on the determinants of social capital, integrating the socio-economic and historic-institutional perspectives more closely. This integration is approached by bridging the gap between quantitative comparative and comparative historical analyses.

1.2   RESEARCH DESIGN AND THE COMPARATIVE METHOD

The research design unifies synchronic and diachronic approaches, linking deductive and inductive reasoning; thereby revisiting the debate on the determinants of social capital. The main features of the research design are illustrated in the light of the development of the comparative method in social science (Table 1.2). We argue that different socio-economic and historic institutional configurations contribute to explain why a healthy civil society blossoms in certain regions and not in others (following in this respect a long-standing line of enquiry from Aristotle [1997], Montesquieu [1914], and Tocqueville [1904; 1961] to Putnam [1993]). This investigation causes us to face the perpetual tension between deductive and inductive reasoning (Mill 1882) by fully exploiting the potential of comparative analysis, integrating quantitative and historical approaches.

Many researchers have studied civic engagement and trust in different countries relying on survey data (Almond and Verba [1963] being the first); however they often failed to develop clear deductive frameworks to guide their statistical modelling (Sartori 1970; Przeworski and Teune 1970). For this reason we explore the potential impact of income inequality, economic development, labour market participation and national divergence on social capital from a theoretical point of view before embarking on the empirical model (Chapter 5). Furthermore, in order to sharpen the results of the quantitative model (Lipset 1960; Lijphart 1971), this synchronic analysis is complemented by an historic-instructional analysis of Wallonia and the South of Italy in relation to another two Belgian and Italian regions, Flanders and the North East of Italy.

We follow the logic of the comparative historical method by (Mahoney and Rueschemeyer 2003): (1) discussing why historical evolutions do not explain the low level of social capital in Wallonia and the South of Italy; (2) discussing historical sequences that overcome the staticity of the quantitative model; and (3) systematically comparing Wallonia and the South of Italy to Flanders and the North East of Italy; two cases that share a similar institutional configuration and high residuals in the regression model but present a much higher level of social capital.

The use of comparative method has a long history (Table 1.2) that can be traced back to Aristotle's discussion on the nature of political regimes (1997). Montesquieu (1914), Tocqueville (1904; 1961) and Mill (1882) extended the use of comparative method and contributed to the development of innovative analyses. Montesquieu asserted that political and legal institutions mirror the social character of each national community, Tocqueville isolated the factors that were fostering the success of American over European institutions and Mill systematized the use of quantitative methods bridging the tension between deductive and inductive reasoning.[7]

Social scientists continued to emphasize the potential of comparative methods from different angles. On the one hand, from an historical perspective Barrington Moore[8] (1966: XIII–XV) highlighted that the understanding of a specific country helps to bring to the fore obscure details of other countries. He argued that comparisons serve as a rudimentary control model for new theoretical explanations. On the other hand, from a quantitative perspective Almond and Verba showed the potential of large scale comparative analyses, measuring civic participation across five countries.[9] Despite the shortcomings of their methodology (for a critique see Benjamin 1965), the application of large scale

Table 1.2   The logic of the Comparative Method

The research design bridges synchronic and diachronic approaches,
linking deductive and inductive reasoning to re-kindle the debate on the determinants
of social capital

The Founding Fathers			
Aristotle	Montesquieu	Tocqueville	Mills
He compared political regimes starting with the social context	He asserted that political and legal institutions mirror the social character of each community	He isolated the factors that were fostering the success of American institutions	He defined the method of agreement and difference and discussed the tension between deductive and inductive processes

The Potential of the Comparative Method		The Importance of Theory-Driven Approaches	
Barrington Moore	Almond, Verba	Sartori	Przeworski, Teune
Comparative analysis brings to the fore obscure details of countries and serves as rudimentary control model	They collected and codified quantitative items to measure civic participation in five countries	He warned against the reduction of critical thinking fostered by the dominance of quantitative analyses	They argued the importance of theoretical frameworks before the formulation of empirical analysis

The Necessity to Introduce a Diachronic Perspective to Quantitative Studies	
Lipset	Lijphart
He lamented the absence of historical depth in the prevailing sociological work of his time	He emphasized how the selection of deviant cases was the best way to generalize conclusions and produce theory

The Revival of Comparative Historical Analysis
Adorno, Horkheimer, Bloch and Polanyi They helped the discipline to survive during totalitarianism
Development during the 1950s, 1960s and 1970s Anderson, Bendix, Eisenstadt, Giddens, Marshall, Tilly, Thompson
Profound dissatisfaction with the overwhelming presence of sociologists and political scientists who looked at reality only from a synchronic perspective

Table 1.2   (continued)

The Main Characteristics of the Comparative Historical Analysis
(1) Concern for the 'identification and explanation' of casual configuration that produces certain outcomes;
(2) The analysis of historical sequences to avoid static explanations of reality;
(3) Systematic and contextualized comparison of similar and contrasting cases

---

Main Strength of the Comparative Historical Analysis
It helps to overcome the absence of diachronic perspective in quantitative studies

The Main Shortfalls of Comparative Historical Analysis
(1) The problem of case selection;
(2) The potential theoretical weakness;
(3) The overemphasis on narrative and path dependency approaches

---

Source: Author's elaboration.

empirical models to cross-national studies became standard practice in political science.

However, the excessive reliance on quantitative studies without sufficient theoretical background was criticized by some scholars. Sartori (1970) and Przeworski and Teune (1971) underlined the importance of the elaboration of deductive frameworks to guide and discipline empirical research. Sartori (1970) warned against the reduction of critical thinking fostered by quantitative research, and highlighted the importance of maintaining the theoretical and deductive keystone of comparative research:

> Most of the literature introduced by the title 'methods' (in the social, behavioural or political sciences) actually deals with survey techniques and social statistics, and has little if anything to share with the crucial concern of 'methodology', which is a concern with the logical structure and procedure of scientific enquiry. In a very crucial sense there is no methodology without *logos*, without thinking about thinking. (Sartori 1970: 1033.)

In the last 40 years the lack of logical structure jeopardized the ability to design and analyse issues in social science, often turning quantitative work into pure statistical modelling, without any awareness of the underlying philosophical logic necessary to undertake comparative studies. 'We seem to embark more and more on comparative endeavours without comparative method' (Sartori 1970: 1052). Przeworski and Teune (1970) complemented Sartori's discussion, showing the importance of establishing theoretical logical frameworks before embarking on any sophisticated statistical analysis.[10]

Lipset (1960; 1996) and Lijphart (1971; 1975) discussed the necessity to introduce a diachronic perspective in comparative studies to complement the lack of historical depth of quantitative studies. With his all-embracing mindset, Lipset was not yoked to any set of theoretical and methodological assumptions (Jesus Velasco 2004: 599) and for this reason regretted the absence of historical depth in the prevailing sociological work of his time: 'I have felt that one of the major weaknesses in contemporary sociology has been its tendency to ignore historical factors in attempting to analyse relationships' (Lipset 1958: 13). Lijphart (1971; 1975) defined the domain and the characteristics of comparative politics against the experimental and the statistical method. He emphasized how the selection of deviant cases was the best way to sharpen conclusions and produce theory (Lijphart 1971: 692).

As already emphasized, after the 1960s, the quantitative comparative paradigm became dominant in political science and sociology (see Sartori 2009). In reaction to this pre-eminence comparative historical sociology progressively re-emerged.[11] During the 1950s, 1960s and 1970s many sociologists (Anderson 1964; 1974; Bendix 1964; Eisenstadt 1963; Giddens 1979; Marshall 1950; 1963; Barrington Moore 1966; Tilly 1964; 1978; Thompson 1968) revived the interest in this discipline recalling the work of Hume, Marx, Tocqueville, Durkheim, Weber, Adorno, Horkheimer, Bloch, Polanyi and others. This is what Smith defined in *The Rise of Historical Sociology*[12] (Smith 1991). The importance of this tradition[13] and its modern revival influenced comparative scholars who were dissatisfied by the prevalence of quantitative synchronic approaches in the literature (Mahoney and Rueschemeyer 2003).

However, historical comparative sociologists[14] are not a homogenous group of scholars. They use various methodologies and analyse different types of cases (nations, regions, departments) sharing only three main common characteristics (see Mahoney and Rueschemeyer 2003: 11–13): (1) the concern for the 'identification and explanation' of causal configuration that produces certain outcomes of interest; (2) the analysis of historical sequences to avoid static explanations of reality; and (3) the systematic and contextualized comparison of similar and contrasting cases.

Skocpol (1979) proposed applying this methodology to overcome the absence of a diachronic perspective in quantitative studies. *States and Revolutions* is a manifesto for the renewal of comparative historical analysis. However, comparative historical analysis also has some important shortcomings.

Firstly, comparative historical methods alone cannot help to select an appropriate unit of analysis[15] (Skocpol 1979). To face this limitation we melt the boundaries between quantitative and historical methodologies.

The reconciliation of the two methods is proposed by selecting Wallonia and the South of Italy, looking specifically at the residuals of the quantitative model.

Secondly, comparative historical methods may be theoretically weak, as highlighted by Kiser and Hetcher[16] (1991), from a rational choice theory perspective. They lamented that in comparative historical analysis the inductive process completely overtakes theoretical reflection (Kiser and Hetcher 1991: 24). This position raised an interesting debate; Quadagno and Knapp (1992) argued that comparative historical sociologists did not forsake the importance of theory,[17] subsequently, Somers[18] (1998: 739) replied by proposing the integration of theory and historical induction: history can help to construct general knowledge and it is not only useful for illustrative and descriptive purposes but also to generate causal inference. In this work the general theoretical explanatory power of the comparative historical analysis is derived from the comparison between the South of Italy and Wallonia with Flanders and the North East of Italy (see Lijphart 1971).

Thirdly, comparative historical methods often rely on the widespread use of narrative logic and path dependency approaches without adequate support for sequential problem solving (Haydu 1998: 353–4):

> Advocates of narrative tales fail to clearly identify the mechanisms that link events into overarching tales. Path dependency identifies some of these mechanisms but fails to provide the overarching tales. [. . .]. One way of meeting these needs is to link facts from different periods into larger sequences of problem solving. Periods are demarcated on the basis of contrasting solutions to recurring problems, not different values of a causal variable or diverging outcomes between historical turning points.

By describing both the continuity and discontinuity of historical evolutions, it is possible to connect the historical and institutional development of a region without being deterministic. A sequential approach, in this sense, can provide a fuller sense of past causal experience and a way to integrate multiple registers of historical time (Haydu 1998: 358). This approach will be illustrated and applied in Chapters 7 and 8 in opposition to deterministic theories.

1.3   SUMMARY OF THE BOOK

The book is articulated into three parts. The first (Chapters 1, 2 and 3) clarifies the methodological tool box, the second (Chapters 4, 5 and 6) investigates the socio-economic model and the third (Chapters 7 and 8) compares the divergent cases emerging from the socio-economic analysis at the historic-institutional level. Chapter 9 provides concluding thoughts.

More specifically, Chapter 2 defines social capital and describes its measurement. The objective is not to provide a new conceptual framework or a new definition, but to explain the theoretical and technical arguments that contributed to the construction of the index used in this work. The first section reviews the measurements proposed in the previous litera-ture. The second clarifies the need for a new indicator, the methodology adopted to define the indicators and the dimensions of social capital, the characteristics of the regional units of analysis and the limitations of the new index.

Chapter 3 proposes historical, institutional and empirical reasons to shift from the national to the regional level of analysis. From an historical perspective, the regional analysis helps to account for the particular evolu-tions of certain areas, namely the South of Italy, Flanders and Wallonia, Eastern Germany and so on. From an institutional perspective, the regional analysis takes into consideration the impact of the European inte-gration process and the progressive decentralization of competences from the central states to the regions, which have become more pronounced in the last decades as demonstrated by the Regional Authority Index (RAI). From an empirical point of view, the regional analysis is the most suited to capture the evolution of social capital because the Europeans that identify themselves with their region, rather than their local community or nation, tend to have stronger social networks and more generalized trust.

Chapter 4 presents the social capital scores for the European regions. The regional measurement is introduced by the theoretical debate between the Manchester school and the social networks theorists and by national measurement. In the theoretical debate, the necessity to bridge the gap between the use of individual observational data to measure social capital and the use of macro-independent variables is discussed. The national measurement has the function to show that the results gathered from the new index are consistent with the previous comparative literature. After this introduction, the new regional scores are compared to Beugelsdijk and Van Schaik's (2005a) scores and subsequently the 85 regions analysed are grouped into seven categories, according to the scores in the three social capital dimensions (formal social networks, informal social networks and social trust).

Chapter 5 clarifies the relevance of the socio-economic predictors and the technical arrangements adopted to measure their impact on social capital. The nexus between these variables and social capital is approached looking at: the theoretical debate on the rise of income ine-quality in Western European countries; the evolution of activation labour market policies and the opportunity to introduce a universal basic income; the previous study on the relation between economic development, culture and social capital; and the relevance of national fragmentation.

Chapter 6 discusses the effects of the socio-economic predictors on social capital and connects the quantitative model to the historic-institutional analysis. The relative impact of the four independent variables on social capital and its three dimensions is tested using an ordinary least square regression (OLS) model. The model indicates that income inequality, labour market participation and national divergence are the most important predictors of social capital, while economic development is not significant. This result is refined in four ways: establishing a hierarchy among the predictors of social capital, investigating the impact of each variable on the three social capital dimensions, proposing different empirical models by dropping variables in turn, and testing the impact of the predictors on regions with different social capital rankings. Finally, the results of the quantitative model and the historic-institutional analysis (that is undertaken in Chapters 7 and 8) are connected through the selection of two divergent cases. The selection process is based on the residuals of the OLS model.

Chapter 7 discusses the relation between historical evolutions and social capital in the South of Italy and Wallonia. Vico's philosophy of history serves to introduce the results from the socio-economic model and the comparative historical analysis. The characteristics of the deviant cases are highlighted by comparing two control cases (Flanders and the North East of Italy). It is argued that, in the divergent cases the value of historical legacy is curtailed by the negative impact of the socio-economic factors; it is as if social capital 'sleeps'. The image of a historically passive South is critically re-assessed using the example of the *fasci siciliani*.

Chapter 8 integrates the historical discussion with an institutional perspective. The analysis is framed according to North's theory of institutional change and the use of a problem-solving approach. In both countries social fragmentation has been handled by political parties distributing public resources among their clientele. The high level of corruption and the strong control of public life by political parties has reduced the incentive for citizens to create secondary groups (outside the party's system) progressively eroding social trust and horizontal ties. The collapse of this system in the 1990s accelerated the decentralization process. Federalism was conceived as a way to increase accountability and social participation. However, the effects of the decentralization process on social capital in asymmetrical countries are not always positive.

NOTES

1. The positive residuals do not undermine the condition of normality (see Chapter 6).
2. He considered kinship, neighbourhood and friendship as part of the *Gemeinschaft* which constitute the pillars of the social capital dimension labelled in this work (see Chapter 2) as informal social networks.
3. We will allude to this difference in our measurement of social capital with the distinction between formal and informal social networks (Chapter 2). However the distinction between formal and informal social networks cannot be fully assimilated to bonding and bridging social capital. The formal social networks dimension largely corresponds to what Putnam defined bridging social capital, but there are elements of the informal social networks dimension (such as meeting colleagues outside work) that cannot be considered bonding social capital.
4. He looked with nostalgia at the image of the man in the past. The idea of 'natural and political man', an image which provides a positive idea of social connectedness, was substituted in the twentieth century discourse by concepts like 'inadequate man', 'insufficient man' or 'disenchanted man'.
5. The first appearance of the concept, with the exception of Hanifan (1916), is in 1961 with Jane Jacobs' *The Death and Life of Great American Cities*. She criticized the artificial development of American cities and suggested putting social capital at the centre of city planning. Some authors adumbrated the impact of social relations on social structure and public policies without using the words 'social capital', but by describing similar phenomena (see Bott 1957; Banfield 1958; Mitchell 1969; Granovetter 1973). However it is only with Bourdieu (1980) that the concept gained academic recognition in the sociological debate. The main contemporary approaches to social capital analysis originate from differing points of view in many important aspects: the role of the individual in society and their duties (Fukuyama 1995; Pizzorno 1999; Sudgen 2000); the capacity of individuals to make rational choices and the impact they receive from different groups (Coleman 1998; 1990; Becker 1996); the evaluation of the institutional role (Woolcock and Narayan 2000; Rothstein and Stolle 2003) and the Welfare State (Van Oorschot and Arts 2005); the importance attributed to strong and weak ties (Granovetter 1973); the perpetual tension between community and society (Bagnasco 1999); the possible negative impact of this tension (Portes 1998); and the evolution of a neo-capital theory that postulates the shift from a class-based to an actor-based perspective (Lin 2000).
6. *Making Democracy Work* has been cited 21,068 times and *Bowling Alone* 19,043 times (Google Scholar http://scholar.google.it/scholar?q=robert+Putnam&hl=it&btnG=Cer ca&lr=, accessed 26 December 2011).
7. Mill proposed to enhance comparative studies on the basis of the methods of agreement and difference (1882: 278–80). This methodological distinction is still widely used in the literature (Skocpol 1979; King et al. 1994).
8. Barrington Moore was largely inspired by the work of Brinton (1938); in *The Anatomy of Revolution* he compared the similarities between four major revolutions (English, American, French and Russian).
9. Almond and Verba tested a theory based on Lasswell's work (1948) with comparable empirical data collected in the United States, Germany, Mexico, Italy and the United Kingdom. In the words of Stein Rokkan (1964: 676): 'This book represents an innovation in the literature of comparative politics: it opens up new perspectives on the theory of democratic politics; it demonstrates the potentialities of a new method of data gathering and analysis; it points to a series of problems for further research and theorizing on the sources of national differences in the character of the relationship between government and the governed.' Another cross-national comparison largely influential in the literature has been proposed by Wilensky (1975).
10. They are especially famous for the proposition of two alternative research designs: 'the most similar and the most different system design'.

11. Comparative historical sociology is an old discipline; its roots can be traced to the work of important political philosophers, such as Hume and Marx, and the founding fathers of sociology, Tocqueville, Durkheim and Weber. The expansion of the discipline has been threatened largely by the advent of totalitarianism, and has survived only through the work of outstanding intellectuals (Adorno 1950; Adorno and Horkheimer 1979; Bloch 1954; Polanyi 1957).

12. Between 1958 and 1978, the number of American doctoral dissertations in the broad field of social history quadrupled (Smith 1991: 2).

13. On the connection between the comparative historical analysis and the work of the 1950s, 1960s and 1970s see Skocpol (1984). A more recent systematization of comparative historical sociology has been published by Mahoney and Rueschemeyer (2003).

14. A broad definition of historical sociology has been provided by Skocpol (1984: 1): 'Truly historical sociological studies have some or all of the following characteristics. Most basically, they ask questions about social structures or processes understood to be concretely situated in time and space. Second, they address processes over time, and take temporal sequence seriously in accounting for outcomes. Third, most historical analyses attend to the interplay of meaningful actions and structural contexts, in order to make sense of the unfolding of unintended as well as intended outcomes in individual lives and social transformations. Finally, historical sociological studies highlight the particular and varying features of specific kinds of social structures and patterns of change. Along with temporal processes and contexts, social and cultural differences are intrinsically of interest to historically oriented sociologists.'

15. Skocpol highlighted two other limitations of comparative historical analysis. The impossibility to control for all potential dependent variables: 'often it is not possible to find exactly the historical cases that one needs for the logic of certain comparisons. And even when the cases are roughly appropriate, perfect controls for all potentially relevant variables can never be achieved' (Skocpol 1979: 38), and the assumption that each case is independent: 'another set of problems stems from the fact that comparative historical analysis necessarily assumes (like any multivariate logic) that the units being compared are independent of one other. But actually, this assumption is rarely if ever fully valid for macro-phenomena such as revolutions. [. . .] These phenomena occur in unique world-historical contexts that change over time, and they happen within international structures that tie societies to one other' (Skocpol 1979: 39).

16. Another interesting criticism has been proposed by Goldthorpe (1991; 1997). Without denying the importance of history in sociological analysis he rejected the idea that the two subjects cannot be separated. He used different instruments to collect empirical evidence to show the divergence between the inquiries carried out by historians and sociologists.

17. Also authors like Tilly (1984), Ragin (1987), Abbott (1990), Bonnell (1980) and Skocpol (1984) highlighted the importance of theoretical interpretations in comparative historical analysis.

18. Their discussion is integrated by the contribution of: Boudon (1998) on the limitations of rational choice theory; and Goldstone (1998) and Calhoun (1998), on the recognition of the importance of Kiser and Hetcher's criticism. However, they take a distant position from the generalization of their judgment. According to them not all historical sociologists undermine the role of theory. Nearly an entire issue of the *American Journal of Sociology* (Vol. 104 (3) 1998) is dedicated to this discussion.

2.   Measuring social capital

Social scientists from different disciplines have proposed a wide range of definitions and methodologies to measure social capital. Adler and Kwon (2002) collected the most influential, yet this accurate review did not clarify the terms of the debate. Thus, the definition and measurement of social capital remain contested issues. Two factors explain this lack of consensus. The first is the possibility to overstretch a vague and historically rich concept. All indicators used to measure social capital try to quantify an intangible reality, which eludes every attempt to clarify (Durlauf 2002). The second factor is the typical lack of communication within the academic world (Paldam 2000: 632), as new definitions and measurements that are hard to compare are proposed by all and sundry.

For these reasons a new definition is not tendered. Instead, this chapter will illustrate the reasons that contributed to the selection of Putnam's definition. We will focus on the concept in operation, showing how the proposed index is suitable for investigating social capital at the regional level. Putnam defined social capital as a combination of networks, social norms and trust: 'social capital refers to features of social organizations such as networks, norms, and social trust that facilitate coordination and cooperation for mutual benefit' (Putnam 1995: 67).

Social capital is a multidimensional concept and for this reason, we will measure it by combining three separate dimensions: formal social networks, informal social networks and social trust. The formal social networks dimension is defined as the involvement of people in formal associations; the informal social networks dimension is defined as the involvement in social life and the importance attributed to friends and family; social trust is defined as the willingness of individuals to discuss current affairs and trust other people and institutions.

The chapter is divided in two sections: the first introduces the main elements of the new social capital index by illustrating the previous measurements; the second discusses the reasons for proposing a new measurement, its dimensions, the modality of selection of the regional units of analysis and its potential limitations.

2.1 PREVIOUS MEASUREMENTS

The new index is constructed using the dimensions defined by Putnam and taking into account several methodological contributions proposed in the literature (see Table 2.1). Putnam clarified and put into operation the measurement of the different dimensions of social capital, mixing empirical evidence and historical research. Paxton innovated measurement tools, shifting from output to survey data. Hall and Rothstein showed the importance of considering survey in connection with archival data to compare the trend delineated by Putnam in the United States with the situation in the United Kingdom and Sweden. Knack and Keefer extended social capital measurement to a large number of countries. After them Van Oorschot and Arts, starting from Putnam's definition, discussed the influence of different welfare state systems on social capital in Europe. Finally, Beugelsdijk and Van Schaik undertook a comparative regional analysis of the relation between social capital and economic development.

In *Making Democracy Work*, Putnam (1993) explored the different institutional performances of Italian regions. Firstly, he considered institutional performance as an independent variable, to illustrate how institutional change affects the identities, the power and the strategy of political actors. Secondly, he considered institutional performance as a dependent variable, to highlight how their performance has been driven by historical events (Putnam 1993: 9).

The model used to predict institutional performance shows that socio-economic development and civic engagement are the two main explanatory factors in the different regional performances. However, according to Putnam, too much emphasis has been placed on the classical socio-economic argument; in reality, the large difference between the North and the South of Italy is mainly explained by civicness. Therefore one needs to prioritize the study of cultural rather than socio-economic factors to explain the variance of social capital and the success of political institutions.

After measuring social capital in the Italian context, Putnam applied similar logic to the United States, to see if the crisis of American democracy could be explained by the decline of social capital (Putnam 1995; 2000). 'Solo bowling' (Putnam 2000) became a metaphor to describe the decline of associationism and civic spirit in the United States in the last 40 years. This analysis generated a germane debate, a mixture of admiration and bellicose criticism that fostered the development of new methodologies to explore this elusive concept.

Paxton (1999) revisited the social capital decline hypothesis and argued that Putnam used misleading indicators to measure it. According to

Table 2.1   Previous measurements

Authors	Aim of the Study	Type of Indicators
1. Social capital and Quality of Democratic Institutions		
Putnam (1993, 2000)	Causes of different institutional performances across Italian regions and causes of the decline of social capital in the US	Output Indicators (1) Number of associations (2) Newspaper readership (3) Electoral turnout (4) Preference vote
2. The social capital Decline Hypothesis		
Paxton (1999)	Verification of Putnam's hypothesis	Survey Data (1) Associationism (2) Trust individuals (3) Trust institutions
Costa & Kahn (2003)	Verification of Putnam's hypothesis and extension of the conclusions to Europe	Survey Data (1) Volunteer activity (2) Formal membership (3) Daily activities (4) Entertaining and visiting friends
3. Social capital Decline Hypothesis in European Countries		
Hall (1999)	Verification of Putnam's hypothesis in United Kingdom	Survey and Historical Data (1) Voluntary organizations (2) Levels of trust
Rothstein (2001)	Verification of Putnam's hypothesis in Sweden	Survey and Archival data (1) Voluntary organizations (2) Levels of trust
4. Social capital in a Comparative Perspective		
Knack & Keefer (1997)	Discussion of the relationship between social capital and economic development	Survey Data (1) Social trust (2) Social norms
Van Oorschot & Arts (2005, 2006)	Discussion of the relationship between welfare state generosity and social capital	Survey Data (1) Social networks (networks, sociability) (2) Social trust (trust) (3) Social norms (civism)
Beugelsdijk & Van Schaik (2005)	Measure of social capital at regional level and its impact on economic growth	Survey Data (1) Group membership (2) Trust

Table 2.1   (continued)

Authors	Aim of the Study	Type of Indicators
5. Social Capital and Income Inequalities in European Regions		
Author's study	Improvement of social capital measurement at regional level and exploration of social capital predictors at quantitative and historic-institutional level	Survey Data (1) Formal social networks (2) Informal social networks (3) Social trust

Source: Author's elaboration.

Paxton, Putnam overstretched the social capital concept and suggested a theoretical explanation not adequately supported by his empirical work. The use of outputs rather than opinion data in *Making Democracy Work* and *Bowling Alone* generated a great deal of confusion.

The electoral turnout for example, one of Putnam's indicators,[1] was an output of social capital and not one of its components (Paxton 1999: 90). Paxton extended this argument to all Putnam's empirical models suggesting institutional performance and social capital indicators were not clearly separated, invalidating the theoretical framework. Paxton proposed overcoming this problem by using observational data. After her seminal work the use of survey data progressively became a standard choice to measure social capital.

Paxton constructed the social capital index combining two dimensions: associationism and trust. The assocationism dimension was based on three indicators: evenings with neighbours, evenings with friends and membership in voluntary organizations. Increasing scores in these three indicators showed a higher involvement in society (Paxton 1999: 107). People who were more involved in their community and social activities tended to be more satisfied with the services offered by their city and in general with their friends (Argyle 1992). The trust dimension had two components: trust in individuals and trust in institutions. The first measured the willingness to trust others and the fairness of their actions, the second considered the trust in organized religions, the education system and the government (Paxton 1999: 105–6).

Paxton argued that overall social capital did not decline during the period 1975–94, with the exception of the component trust in individuals. However, she suggested careful consideration of Putnam's theoretical argument rather than its dismissal. Social capital had remained stable in the country, argued Paxton, but decreased among marginalized people; therefore Putnam's alarm has to be refined and focused on poor and socially excluded individuals rather than the entire society.

Costa and Kahn (2003) proposed an approach similar to Paxton. They revisited the hypothesis of social capital decline and tested the explanations proposed by Putnam.[2] Social capital was measured using four components: volunteer activity, membership in political associations, time spent in specific activities and social activity.[3] Basically only Paxton's associationism dimension was considered.

They confirmed Putnam's decline hypothesis, but proposed a different explanatory model; that the rise of income inequalities and the growing community heterogeneity[4] were the main causes of social capital decline in the United States. Their findings also had implications for European countries. High income inequalities and low ethnic homogeneity predict lower degrees of membership and involvement in European societies. According to Costa and Kahn, the high level of social capital in Scandinavian countries was fostered by the egalitarian structure of their societies and their ethnic homogeneity. They suggested that, with the progressive increase of immigration and the rise of income inequalities, Europe will follow a similar trend to America (Costa and Kahn 2003: 41).

Hall (1999) and Rothstein (2001) tested the social capital decline hypothesis in the United Kingdom and Sweden; respectively similar and dissimilar cases to the United States. The United Kingdom had been characterized by strong civic engagement during the nineteenth and twentieth centuries, an engagement similar to the one described by Tocqueville in the United States. Hall justified this claim using the evidence provided by Almond and Verba's comparative study (1963). They argued that during the 1950s, both the United States and the United Kingdom had a highly developed civic culture,[5] with a high level of social trust, good civic organization and strong political participation (Hall 1999: 419).

The United Kingdom, for this reason, constituted a crucial case in testing Putnam's social capital decline hypothesis.[6] Hall suggested that in the United Kingdom, despite this historical similarity to the United States, an erosion of social capital was not yet taking place. He offered three factors to explain its current social capital stability: the increasing educational level (brought about by the transformation of its educational system) that encouraged a greater propensity to be involved in community activities; the change in class structure and the emergence of a growing middle class, which tended to be more socially active than the working class; and governmental policy, which helped the development of the voluntary sector. Nevertheless, despite this stability of social capital, a new generational trend marked its reduction amongst a younger age cohort, as traditional forms of mechanical solidarity disintegrated.

Rothstein (2001) investigated Putnam's hypothesis in a different context by measuring the variation of social capital in Sweden. Sweden is a peculiar case among Western European countries, because its high public expenditure and ambitious Welfare State programmes have been generated in the context of a very healthy society: '[t]he combination of democratic stability and popular legitimacy, considerable economic growth, a collaborative system of industrial relations, and a uniquely universal and generous Welfare State were the central parts of this model' (Rothstein 2001: 209). For this reason a comparison with the United States followed the most different design approach.

Rothstein showed, using archival and survey data, that social capital in Sweden had increased since the 1950s. The synergy between high state involvement and civic engagement, according to Rothstein, was explained by the universal social programmes adopted by Swedish institutions; these were not likely to produce negative effects on social capital because they avoided stigmas and fostered cohesiveness through the redistribution of economic resources.

Knack and Keefer (1997), Van Oorschot and Arts (2005), Beugelsdijk and Van Schaik (2005a and b) proposed cross-national and cross-regional comparative measurements of social capital. Knack and Keefer tested the importance of trust in enhancing economic development thereby empirically supporting Arrow's hypothesis (Arrow 1972: 357) and argued that much economic backwardness can be explained by the lack of mutual confidence. Two dimensions were used to measure social capital: trust, defined as general trust in other people, and civic norms, defined as the propensity to not perpetrate opportunistic behaviours, that is, claiming government benefits which one is not entitled to or avoiding a fare on public transport (Knack and Keefer 1997: 1256–7). In their empirical test, trust was considered to be the primary source of social capital and this choice was propelled by the high correlation between trust and economic development and by the attention attributed to this relation in the literature (Fukuyama 1995).

They explored the relationship between social capital and economic performance by looking at three types of relation: the relationship between interpersonal trust, as in the norms of civic cooperation and economic performance; the relationship between the density of associational activity and economic growth, by exploring the divergent hypothesis of Putnam (1993) and Olson (1982); and the relationship between trust and associational activity with formal institutions (Knack and Keefer 1997: 1251).

Social capital appeared to be significantly correlated to economic growth and lower inequalities. In societies where governments are perceived as more trustworthy, people can adopt appropriate long-term investment decisions, drastically reducing the prisoner's dilemma problem. Where trust is lower, political leaders are more inclined to direct revenue windfalls towards consumption rather than productive investments. Political coalitions are more unstable and trust relations among individuals are more fragile. Knack and Keefer concluded that trust and civic norms are stronger in the more egalitarian nations and where institutions are able to restrain predatory actions.

Van Oorschot and Arts (2005) discussed, using a similar approach to Knack and Keefer, whether the existence of generous Welfare State provisions had negative consequences on social capital levels in European countries, replacing the sense of communal duties with formal and bureaucratic ties. This issue had been the object of much ideological controversy[7] (Etzioni 1995; Fukuyama 1995), but no empirical work had tested the theoretical propositions before Van Oorschot and Arts (2005).

They tested empirically the so called crowding out hypothesis in European countries by using three dimensions of social capital: social networks, social norms and social trust (following Putnam's definition). The social networks category included passive and active participation in 14 types[8] of voluntary[9] organizations: time spent with friends, relations with family and friends and two indicators measuring political engagement.[10] Social norms referred to particular attitudinal or behavioural characteristics[11] (Van Oorschot and Arts 2005: 12). Social trust had two sets of indicators: trust in individuals and trust in institutions.

They concluded that there was no empirical evidence[12] to suggest the crowding out hypothesis and supported the theoretical arguments advanced by Skocpol (1996) and Rothstein (2001) in defence of the synergic role of the state in the creation of social capital (Van Oorschot and Arts 2005: 19). Their empirical construction of social capital index largely inspired the measurement which is proposed in this work (see next section).

This review is concluded by the regional perspective of Beugelsdijk and Van Schaik (2005a and b). They tested the existence of a relation between economic development and social capital, extending Putnam's analysis of Italian regions to 54 other European regions and formulating the first comparative cross-regional analysis.[13] However, despite the originality of their approach, their methodology has two shortfalls. First, the choice of the dataset; the selection of the European Values Study (EVS) (1990) wave instead of the EVS (1999–2000), reduced the potential number of regions in the sample.[14] Second, in some regions social capital was measured by aggregating very few individual observations, namely Bremen 26, Hamburg 25, Saarland 35 and Sardegna 20. These two limitations made the regional ranking questionable (for example the South of Italy and Sicily ranked higher than Lombardia and the North West; this is completely opposite to Putnam's results). The next section discusses the need for a new regional measurement and some technical arrangement to overcome the limitations of Beugelsdijk and Van Schaik's work.

2.2 THE NEW REGIONAL INDEX

This section illustrates: (1) why we need a new regional index; (2) the methodology used to construct the new index; (3) the constraints in the selection of the regional unit of analysis; and (4) the limitations of the index.

2.2.1 Why We Need a New Regional Index

As illustrated in the previous section, the need for a new regional index comes from the lack of reliability of Beugelsdijk and Van Schaik's measurement. The new index deals with the shortcomings of the previous measurement by: (1) using two more-recent datasets, (2) increasing the number of regions sampled, and (3) accruing the number of observations for each region considered in the analysis.

First, the EVS (1999–2000) and the Special Eurobarometer 223 (2005)/273 (2006) replace EVS (1990). 'The European Values Study is a large-scale, cross-national, and longitudinal survey research program on basic human values. It provides insights into the ideas, beliefs, preferences, attitudes, values and opinions of citizens all over Europe.'[15] Standardized questionnaires are proposed every nine years in European countries. Eurobarometer questionnaires were created by the European Commission in 1973 and have the function of monitoring the evolution of public opinion in the member states.[16] The combination of these two datasets (EVS and Eurobarometer) increases the reliability of the overall measurement because each regional score is calculated twice. The rankings obtained using the two datasets are quite similar, indicating a good consistency of the scores despite the non-representativeness of the sample at the regional level.

Second, the number of regions sampled increased from 54 to 85[17] (Table 2.2). This larger sample allows one to test the effect of five predictors on social capital (see Chapter 6). Third, Beugelsdijk and Van Schaik (2005a) included in their sample four regions with less than 35 observations: Hamburg (25 observations), Bremen (26), Saarland (35) and Sardegna (20). In this work, instead, the aggregate score for each regional unit is based on at least 100 observations.

Table 2.2 Regions discussed in the study

Regions Considered in the Study	EVS 1999 Number of Observations	Euro 2005 Number of Observations	Regions Considered by Beugelsdijk & Van Schaik (2005)	EVS 1990 Number of Observations
AT Ost-Osterrich	380	251		
AT Sud-Osterrich	329	203		
AT West-Osterrich	504	328		
AT Wien	309	248		
BE Brussels	497	95	BE Brussels	497
BE Vlaams Gewest	821	571	BE Vlaams Gewest	1560
BE Region Wallone	594	345	BE Region Wallone	735
DE Baden-Württemberg	160	134	DE Baden-Württemberg	286
DE Bayern	181	178	DE Bayern	380
DE Berlin	135	81	DE Berlin	164
DE Brandenburg	170	90		
DE Bremen*	24	5	DE Bremen	26
DE Hamburg*	20	22	DE Hamburg	25
DE Hessen	103	95	DE Hessen	191
DE Mecklenburg-Vorpommern	115	71		
DE Niedersachsen	126	126	DE Niedersachsen	249
DE Nordrhein-Westfalen	289	263	DE Nordrhein-Westfalen	626
DE Rheinland-Pfalz	54	75	DE Rheinland-Pfalz	125
DE Saarland*	16	18	DE Saarland	35
DE Sachsen	290	147		

Table 2.2 (continued)

Regions Considered in the Study	EVS 1999 Number of Observations	Euro 2005 Number of Observations	Regions Considered by Beugelsdijk & Van Schaik (2005)	EVS 1990 Number of Observations
DE Sachsen-Anhalt	175	94		
DE Schleswig-Holstein	23	46	DE Schleswig-Holstein	92
DE Thüringen	155	88		
DK Hovenstansomradet (Copenhagen area)	262	354		
DK Sjaelland, Lolland-Falster, Bornholm (excl. Hovenstadomradet)	174	127		
DK Fyn (Syddanmark)	171	222		
DK Jylland	416	308		
ES Noroeste	132	116	ES Noroeste	267
ES Noreste	123	113	ES Noreste	283
ES Comunidad Madrid	151	129	ES Comunidad Madrid	329
ES Centro	161	132	ES Centro	371
ES Este	330	293	ES Este	717
ES Sur	254	211	ES Sur	532
ES Canarias	49	51	ES Canarias	103
FI East Finland (Ita)	155	151		

Region		
FI South Finland (Etela)	406	463
FI West Finland (Lansi)	288	288
FI North Finland (Pohjois)	189	126
FR Bassin Parisien	324	190
FR Centre Est	209	128
FR Est	100	90
FR Ile de France	299	153
FR Méditerranée	235	110
FR Nord	84	74
FR Ouest	201	144
FR Sud ouest	163	115
UK E. Mids	61	59
UK Eastern	46	111
UK London	90	116
UK North East*	56	43
UK North West	138	107
UK Scotland	84	107
UK South East	187	169
UK South West	79	86
UK W. Mids	99	104
UK Wales	59	69

Region	
FR Bassin Parisien	140
FR Centre Est	123
FR Est	107
FR Ile de France	185
FR Méditerranée	105
FR Nord	91
FR Ouest	142
FR Sud ouest	109
GB E. Mids	63
GB Eastern	75
GB London	56
GB North	269
GB Scotland	291
GB South East	169
GB South West	83
GB W. Mids	139
GB Wales	282

Table 2.2 (continued)

Regions Considered in the Study	EVS 1999 Number of Observations	Euro 2005 Number of Observations	Regions Considered by Beugelsdijk & Van Schaik (2005)	EVS 1990 Number of Observations
UK Yorks & Humbs	60	88	GB Yorks & Humbs	57
UK Northern Ireland	1012	307		
GR Voreia Ellada (Northern Greece)	nd	343		
GR Kentriki Ellada (Central Greece)	nd	232		
GR Attiki	nd	370		
GR Nisia aigaiou, Kriti	nd	55		
IT Nord-Ovest	218	100	IT Nord-Ovest	292
IT Lombardia	320	148	IT Lombardia	247
IT Nord Est	235	137	IT Nord Est	259
			IT Emilia Romagna	110
IT Centro	355	147	IT Centro	208
IT Lazio	181	89	IT Lazio	156
			IT Abruzzo-Molise	59
			IT Campania	313
IT Sud	466	261	IT Sud	163
IT Isole	225	123	IT Sicilia	200
			IT Sardegna	20

LX Luxembourg	1211	510	
NL North Netherlands	100	130	NL North Netherlands 76
NL East Netherlands	238	188	NL East Netherlands 156
NL West Netherlands	475	464	NL West Netherlands 501
NL South Netherlands	185	234	NL South Netherlands 281
PT North	355	364	
PT Center	185	239	
PT Lisboa and Vale do Tejo	365	279	
PT Alentejo and Algarve	95	118	
SE Gotaland (including Malmo and Goteborg)	507	452	
SE Svealand	385	362	
SE Norrland	123	195	
IE Connaught/Ulster	nd	179	
IE Dublin	nd	293	
IE Munster	nd	281	
IE Rest of Leinster	nd	247	

Notes:
* Not considered due the small number of observations.
Euro: Eurobarometer.

Source: Author's elaboration from EVS 1990; EVS 1999–2000; Eurobarometer 2005.

2.2.2 The Methodology

Social capital is a multidimensional concept and has to be measured taking into account all its different components. After Putnam's definition, Van Oorschot and Art (2005) measured social capital using the EVS dataset (1999–2000), combining social networks, social trust and social norms dimensions (as discussed in the previous section).

They measured social norms dimension through the question: 'Please tell me for each of the following statements whether you think it can always be justified, never be justified, or something in between . . . claiming state benefits you are not entitled to . . . cheating on tax if you have the chance . . . lying in your own interest.' It is suggested that the reduction of opportunistic behaviours described in this question is a direct consequence of a high degree of participation and trust in society and not something that can be considered a social capital dimension; therefore, the social norms dimension is excluded from the analysis.

In addition to the exclusion of the social norms dimension, three other changes have been introduced in comparison to Van Oorschot's and Art's (2005) study. Firstly, two distinct dimensions of social networks have been considered (formal and informal social networks); secondly, the variable 'time spent with colleagues' has been added in the dimension of informal social networks;[18] and thirdly, interest in politics is considered as an indicator of social trust rather than one of social networks: people are interested in politics if they think they can improve or change their society, and as a result they are more involved in collective actions. Our social capital measurement includes: formal social networks, informal social networks and social trust dimensions.

The formal social networks dimension is defined as the involvement of people in formal associations, a measure of the official engagement in social activities. Simple membership is distinguished from active participation in associations. This distinction plays an important role in the literature. Putnam (2000) described the decline of social capital in America through the reduction of participation in associations. The corresponding increase of membership in new types of associations, that is, green/environmental ones, according to him, was not able to generate the same links and connectivity among people. This distinction has been contested and many empirical models have shown how Putnam's explanation was not convincing[19] (Paxton 1999).

The informal social networks dimension is defined as the involvement in social life and the importance people attribute to informal networks. Four items are considered: the frequency of meetings with friends and the frequency of meetings with colleagues outside of work, the importance attributed to friends, and the importance attributed to family.

Finally, the social trust dimension is defined as the capacity of individuals to discuss current affairs and trust other people and institutions. This dimension captures the attitude of people in the public sphere: their willingness to discuss political issues of general interest, the propensity to trust other people without knowing them and the trust towards different types of institutions (Table 2.3).

In order to measure these three dimensions of social capital, the nine basic components of each dimension (membership, participation, meeting colleagues, meeting friends, importance of family, importance of friends, discussing politics, generalized trust, and institutional trust) have been standardized and summed up to create the compound indicator in five steps.

1.   The average value of every dimension has been calculated; taking into account separately the percentages obtained from the EVS and Eurobarometer datasets for every region.
2.   The distance from the average for every region has been calculated according to the formula $(Xn-Xm)/Xm$, where Xn represents the regional value and Xm represents the average value.
3.   The values obtained from the previous operation have been divided by the standard deviation of the distribution, in order to produce standardized scales, according to the formula: standardized value = value/ standard deviation.
4.   Informal/formal social networks and social trust scores have been calculated through a weighted average of the single dimensions considered (for each dataset).
5.   The final social capital score has been calculated through the weighted average of the three dimensions. The regional aggregate scores are presented in Chapter 4.

2.2.3   The Selection of the Regional Units of Analysis

In this work 85 regions are considered. Two main constraints have influenced the selection of the units of analysis. First the obligation to use the Nomenclature of Territorial Units (NUTs) formulated by the European Union and second the need to take into account the regional units set up in the three datasets used for the study: EVS (1999–2000), Eurobarometer (2005; 2006) and Luxembourg Income Study (Table 2.4).[20]

Comparative regional analyses have been traditionally based on the NUTs (Boldrin et al. 2001; Dunford 1993; Magrini 1999) because all macro-data available are collected according to this standard nomenclature.

Table 2.3 Social capital components

Eurobarometer	EVS	Eurobarometer	EVS
	Formal Social Networks		
1. Membership		2. Participation	
(1) Recreational,	(1) Welfare,	(1) Recreational,	(1) Welfare,
(2) Cultural,	(2) Cultural,	(2) Cultural,	(2) Cultural,
(3) Professional,	(3) Political,	(3) Professional,	(3) Political,
(4) Consumer,	(4) Local community action,	(4) Consumer,	(4) Local community action,
(5) International,	(5) Dvp/Human rights,	(5) International,	(5) Dvp/Human rights,
(6) Environment,	(6) Environment,	(6) Environment,	(6) Environment,
(7) Charity,	(7) Professional,	(7) Charity,	(7) Professional,
(8) Elderly,	(8) Youth work,	(8) Elderly,	(8) Youth work,
(9) Leisure,	(9) Recreational,	(9) Leisure,	(9) Recreational,
(10) Elderly rights,	(10) Women's Groups,	(10) Elderly rights,	(10) Women's groups,
(11) Political,	(11) Peace movements,	(11) Political,	(11) Peace movements,
(12) Patient/Disabled,	(12) Health,	(12) Patient/Disabled,	(12) Health,
(13) Other interests	(13) Other interests	(13) Other interests,	(13) Other interests,
		(14) Trade Unions,	(14) Trade Unions,
		(15) Religious	(15) Religious

Informal Social Networks	
3–4. Meeting friends & colleagues	5–6. Importance family & friends
Meeting Friends/Colleagues every week (Single Item)	Family/Friends very important (Single Item)
Social Trust	
7. Discussing politics	8. Individual generalized trust
Frequently talking about politics (Single Item)	Most people can be trusted (Single Item)
9. Trust in institutions	
Trust Government Trust Parliament Trust Political Parties Trust City Council (Sum Scale)	Trust Education System Trust Press Trust Parliament Trust Social Security System Trust Health Care System Trust Justice System (Sum Scale)

Source: Author's elaboration from EVS (1999–2000) and Eurobarometer 223 (2005)/273 (2006).

*Table 2.4   Number of administrative regions, regions reported in the EVS,
            Eurobarometer and LIS datasets, regions considered for the
            study*

Countries	Administrative	EVS-Eurobarometer	LIS	This Study
Austria	9	9	3	4
Belgium	3	3	3	3
Denmark	16	16	32	4
Finland	19	19	20	4
France	22	8	22	8
Germany	16	16	16	16
Greece	13	13	4	4
Ireland	8	4	8	4
Italy	20	20	20	7
Luxembourg	1	1	1	1
The Netherlands	12	12	1	4
Portugal	5	5	1	4
Spain	17	17	7	7
Sweden	21	8	21	3
UK	12	12	10	12
Total	194	163	169	85

Source: Author's elaboration.

There are three levels of NUTs: level 1 includes sub-national administrative areas with a population between three and seven million inhabitants, level 2 between 800,000 and three million, and level 3 between 150,000 and 80,000 people.[21] In reality, these are only broad indications, because regions like North Rhine-Westphalia (included in NUT 1) have more than 7 million inhabitants (in this specific case 18 million).

The regions considered in this work are mostly NUT 1. However, where NUT 1 includes the entire nation, the second tier NUT 2 has been used. The first level of statistical unit has been applied to: Austria, Belgium, Germany, Italy,[22] Spain, France, Greece, Luxembourg, the Netherlands, Sweden and the United Kingdom; the second to: Finland,[23] Denmark[24] and Portugal;[25] and finally in Ireland a mix of NUT 1 and NUT 2 has been adopted.[26] This choice allows the provision of a uniform definition of regional units: the larger units that are considered in the NUT classification.

In order to account for the potential artificiality of these regions and the constraints proposed by the three datasets, a test is performed comparing the social capital scores obtained with the regional units defined by the measurement and the scores obtained with the smallest territorial units available on the EVS (1999–2000) and Eurobarometer (2005; 2006) datasets (163 regions). There is practically no difference in the regional divergence; the results of this test are discussed in more detail in the next section about the limitations of the measurement.

Under these two constraints, the existence of historical regions[27] and the importance of the largest metropolitan areas is taken into account. The historical regions considered separately are: the Flemish and the Walloon parts of Belgium; the North West, North East, Centre, South and Islands in Italy; Northern Ireland, Wales and Scotland in the United Kingdom; Provence and Nord Pas de Calais in France. In addition to the historical regions, the metropolitan areas are considered as separate units of analysis. These regions are: London (Greater London), Paris (Ile de France), Madrid (Comunidad de Madrid), Rome (Lazio), Milan (Lombardia), Wien, Athens (Attiki), Lisbon (Lisbon and Vale do Tejo), Dublin, Stockholm, Copenhagen and Berlin (for the complete list of regions see Table 2.3).

2.2.4 The Limitations of the Measurement

There are many difficulties in the construction of a regional social capital index, some of which have been overcome, or partially overcome with additional indicators or through the use of other datasets. Some of these difficulties, instead, are intrinsic limitations of the concept explored and the methodology used. These limitations have to be carefully considered because all results and subsequent theoretical conclusions are limited by these assumptions.

There are four main limitations to the methodology proposed. The first two limitations, the failure to satisfy the conditions of exchangeability and identification and the use of standardized questionnaires that may not be interpreted in the same way in different geographical areas, are not solvable and therefore constitute intrinsic limits of the measurement. The other two limitations, the small number of observations for each region and the artificiality of the units of analysis, are partially overcome.

The dimensions used to capture the social capital concept, as we have already mentioned, are only a proxy. Durlauf (2002: 463–5) drastically rejected all measurements operated through survey data because they do not satisfy the conditions of exchangeability and identification. All the models presented in the first part of this chapter and the new index suffer from a failure to satisfy these conditions. All quantitative studies in social science have this problem to some extent, but social capital studies seem to be particularly liable, and this is explained by the vague and controversial nature of the concept. In order to overcome this problem Durlauf proposed the use of experimental psychology methodologies (Sherif et al. 1988). The experiments may allow to control for all variables in the study thereby limiting the problems posed by observational data, however this would imply a shift from the study of attitudes through quantitative questionnaires to the test of people's behaviour through experiments.

In this work we want to account for the interaction between individual choices and the influence exerted by regional structures. In this exploration the impact of certain macro-variables on social capital and the importance of historical and institutional evolutions are considered simultaneously. An experimental approach would not account for this interesting reality. However, Durlauf's criticisms are taken into account, in the attempt to avoid confusion between the input and output variables (see Paxton's critique to Putnam's measurement exposed in the previous section).

The other intrinsic limitation is the use of a standardized questionnaire across European regions. The same questions may be perceived in different ways by Southern Italians, Flemish or Scottish. However, this is a limitation that affects all cross-national studies against which there is nothing that can be done other than forewarn the reader.

The other two limitations, the fact that questionnaires are representative at the national rather than regional level and the artificiality of some regional units, are shortcomings we have partially overcome. The first problem of national representation, previously mentioned in this section, is managed by measuring the same indicator with two different datasets and checking that there are no big differences between the values gathered by both alternative measurements.

The second problem, the artificiality of some of the regional units of analysis, is mitigated by the comparison of measurements between the 85 regions used in the study and the smallest possible level of regional sampling in the European Values Study (1999–2000) and the Eurobarometer 223 (2005)/273 (2006) (see Table 2.5).

The regional divergence in the two subsets of regions has been calculated in order to show that the difference in social capital endowment between the regions considered in the study and in the smallest possible territorial level of analysis, is negligible. The index of convergence has been built starting from social capital values for each region and the national average. The sum of the absolute differences between the regional value and the national average has been divided by the number of regions in every state. The value obtained has been divided, again, by the national average.

The divergence index shows which countries have larger differences among regions.[28] For the purpose of this chapter on methodology, the divergence index is a proof of the fact that using a larger number of regions

*Table 2.5   Difference between the divergence of the regions reported in the
study and the divergence of the original regions reported in the
EVS and Eurobarometer datasets*

Country	Divergence Study's Regions	Divergence Original Regions (EVS-Eurobarometer)	Difference
Austria	0.21	0.19	− 0.02
Belgium	0.28	Same	0
Germany	0.26	Same	0
Denmark	0.10	0.07	+ 0.03
Spain	0.09	Same	0
Finland	0.10	0.13	− 0.03
France	0.08	Same	0
United Kingdom	0.11	Same	0
Greece	0.11	Same	0
Italy	0.22	0.39*	− 0.17
Luxembourg	0	Same	0
Netherlands	0.04	0.06	+ 0.02
Portugal	0.17	Same	0
Sweden	0.06	0.06	0
Ireland	0.04	Same	0

Note: * Only a few regions are included in this indicator: Campania, Emilia Romagna,
Lazio, Lombardia, Puglia, Sicilia, Toscana, Piemonte and Veneto.

Source: Author's elaboration after EVS (1999–2000) and Eurobarometer 223 (2005) /273
(2006).

(163 being the biggest sample obtainable with the existing datasets) would
not have changed our perception of the regional differences and would
have only made our conclusions weaker.[29]

2.3   SUMMARY

In this chapter the definition of social capital and the three dimensions
used to define and measure it, have been discussed in the light of the previous literature. Putnam's definition has been adopted for the purposes of
comparison, however the social norms dimension has been excluded from
the social capital index to avoid confusion between output and input variables. Furthermore, differently from Putnam and in agreement with most
of the literature, output data have been substituted with survey data.

In the last part of the chapter, the technical details of the new measurements have been illustrated, in order to clarify the component parts of each social capital dimension, the selection of comparable regional units and the limitations proposed by this type of measurement. The next chapter completes the first part of the study, which is dedicated to the methodological and conceptual tools used, emphasizing the importance of the regional approach in investigating the determinants of social capital.

NOTES

1. The social capital index is constituted by four items: number of associations, newspaper readership, electoral turnout, and the presence of preference vote.
2. According to Putnam (1995; 2000) the decline of social capital in the United States is mainly explained by four factors: men's working time has decreased, women's working time has increased, commuting time has risen with urbanization, and the appearance of television and electronic leisure.
3. Firstly, volunteer activity, measured as involvement in unpaid work in the last 12 months. Secondly, membership in political associations measured without considering religious affiliation. Thirdly, the minutes spent daily in the following activities: participating as a member of a party, or of a union; voluntary activity as an elected official of an organization; volunteer work for civic purposes; participation as a member of a religious club; union-management; participating in other organizations (family, parent, military, and so on); other forms of membership. Fourthly, the number of evenings spent with relatives, neighbours and friends in social events as a way of measuring social activity.
4. Due to the increase of wage inequality and immigration.
5. The countries analysed in the study were: the United States, the United Kingdom, Germany, Italy and Mexico.
6. Like Paxton he measured social capital through associationism and level of trust. Hall considered people as members of an association only if they had some kind of face to face contact involvement. He looks also at collective actions rather than simply self-help.
7. 'We leave the ideological debate aside and concentrate on empirical questions about the crowding out hypothesis, which in its most general form says: for every welfare state, if social obligations become increasingly public, then its institutional arrangements to an increasing extent crowd out private obligations or make them at least no longer necessary. As a result, voluntary, familial, communal and other interpersonal ties tend to weaken, people will lose their moral sense of collective and communal duties and responsibilities, and they will end up having less trust in their fellow citizens and in the institutions they are surrounded by' (Van Oorschot and Arts 2005: 6).
8. The 14 types of voluntary organizations are: welfare service for elderly, handicapped or deprived people; religious or church organizations; education, arts; music or cultural activities; trade unions; political parties or groups; local community-action on issues like poverty, employment, housing, racial equality; third world development or human rights; conservation, the environment, ecology, animal rights; professional associations; youth work; sports or recreation; women's groups; peace movement; health; other groups.
9. Trade Unions and religious organizations are not included because in Sweden and Denmark the membership of these types of organizations is compulsory for people to be eligible for many social benefits. The same logic is applied to this study.
10. The level of interest in politics and the frequency of discussions about politics with friends (Van Oorschot and Arts 2005: 11).

11. Social norms are measured by the answers to the question: 'Please tell me for each of the following statements whether you think it can always be justified, never be justified, or something in between . . . claiming state benefits you are not entitled to . . . cheating on tax if you have the chance . . . lying in your own interest . . .' This measure refers to particular attitudinal behavioural characteristics of people themselves (Van Oorschot and Art 2005).

12. An update of the research was presented one year later with the article 'Social capital in Europe: measurement and social and regional distribution of a multifaceted phenomenon' (Van Oorschot et al. 2006).

13. Before them only Schneider et al. (2000) proposed a regional analysis but at a different level of analysis (NUT 2).

14. The authors justify this choice in the article with the use of economic indicators of the same year.

15. See http://www.europeanvaluesstudy.eu/evs/about-evs/.

16. There is a standard section that measures the opinion of European citizens of European institutions and a section of special reports that covers various issues. One of these special reports was dedicated to social capital (Eurobarometer 223, 2005). This special issue has been integrated by the Special Eurobarometer 273 (European social reality) for the questions concerning trust in institutions (absent in the Special Eurobarometer 223).

17. In reality we consider only 81 regions because three of the German Länder (Bremen, Hamburg and Saarland) and the North West of England region have a small number of observations (less than 100).

18. Because only meetings outside work are considered.

19. Membership and participation are positively correlated with the willingness to discuss politics and the general trust in other individuals. Therefore both types of formal networks have a positive impact on social trust.

20. LIS dataset is used in Chapter 5 to calculate the Gini coefficients at the regional level.

21. As shown on the European Commission website: http://ec.europa.eu/eurostat/ramon/nuts/basicnuts_regions_en.html.

22. With the addition of two big regions: Lombardia (because it includes Milan) and Lazio (because it includes Rome).

23. With the exclusion of Aland, because the population is too small (only 27,000 people).

24. With the variant of the fusion of Central and North Jutland in one region.

25. With the variant of the fusion of Alentejo and Algarve in one region.

26. Because it was the only level provided by Eurobarometer, on the other hand, EVS does not provide the values for Irish regions. The classification, however, does not propose particular problems because the country is quite homogenous.

27. The administrative regions do not necessarily overlap with the historical ones. In Germany, for example, administrative regions tend to differ from historic regions.

28. The divergence index will be used and discussed in Chapters 5 and 6.

29. Because of the smaller number of observations for each region. The only exception to this conclusion is Italy. This exception is explainable by the fact that the convergence index calculated for the smallest possible level of analysis, takes into account only the largest regions (Table 2.3), because they were the only ones to have more than 100 observations. EU-Silc (2006) could have been a valid alternative to EVS (1999–2000) and Eurobarometer (2005) because of the larger number of observations for each region. However, EU-Silc only provides variables to measure social participation and not the other two social capital dimensions.

3.   Why we need a regional analysis

Social capital has been measured at the comparative regional level by Beugelsdijk and Van Schaik (2005a and b). However, their contribution (see previous chapter) does not illustrate why a comparative regional analysis is useful in discussing the determinants of social capital. For this reason, the objective of this chapter is to explain through historical, institutional and empirical arguments why a comparative regional analysis can complement the cross-national approach.

Etymologically the word *region*, differently from *state* and *nation*, directly refers to a 'ruled territory'. During the Middle Ages, regions were the main political and administrative entity. The creation of the modern states, in countries like Belgium, Italy, the United Kingdom, Spain and Germany did not erase the rich historical heritage that helps to explain why social capital largely diverges among regions of the same country (see Chapter 4).

At the institutional level the progressive devolution of competences from the central governments to the regions is clearly shown by the Regional Authority Index (RAI; Hooghe et al. 2008a and b). One of the most controversial elements of this development is the definition of the impact of the European integration process. Despite the increasing cooperation between the European Union and the regions there is no consensus in the literature about the effect of this process on regional autonomy.

The historical and institutional elements of discussion are complemented by an empirical test at the individual level. A multiple regression model is elaborated to test whether people that feel closer to their region, rather than their local community or nation, tend to have higher social capital scores.

3.1   THE HISTORICAL IMPORTANCE OF EUROPEAN REGIONS

This section discusses from an historical perspective the centrality of regions in Western Europe. Firstly, we refer to the etymological meaning of the word region, emphasizing its original political and administrative connotations. Secondly, the Belgian, British, Italian, Spanish and German cases are described to exemplify how a comparative regional analysis can help to capture the complex reality of fragmented nation states.

The origin of the word region, if compared to nation and state, indicates the political and administrative relevance of this unit of analysis. The word region derives from the Latin *regio* and means a boundary line or territory to rule. *Regio*, with the same root of words like queen, king or royal, was in the past naturally associated to a supreme power of decision-making. The word nation derives from the Latin *natio*, and literally means a set of people, a species, a race but also the action of being born. After the French revolution, the concepts of nation and state melted, and people living in a country become part of the same 'imagined community' (Anderson 1983); the idea of nation gained a strong legitimacy and was often related to the concept of state building (Renan 1882).

The word state literally means 'standing' in Latin and it refers to a condition, or a long term status. The concept was associated in Ancient Rome with the condition of the Republic and this original sense is currently used in the public debate, as for example, the speech on the state of the nation delivered annually by the American president. During the Middle Ages the word state was used to define the legal standing of a person and in particular the condition of the king. In modern times the word became closely associated with the legal order of the entire society.

The centrality of regions in any comparative analysis has to be put into context with the meanings attributed in European societies to both nation and state. Among these terms, as we have seen above, region is the only one that, in the original sense, refers to administrative and political power. Regions (under the form of dukedom and city-state) were the fundamental administrative units of power in the Middle Ages and they are regaining importance today (see next section). European history offers grounds to foster research in a regional direction: Belgium, the United Kingdom, Italy, Spain and Germany[1] include within their borders differentiated realities, which have been characterized by regional administrations much older and more powerful than the national ones.

In Belgium the coexistence in one state of three different communities with two main languages is an historical product of several attempts by external powers to dominate the area. After the end of the Holy Roman Empire, between the eleventh and twelfth centuries, the provinces of Belgium were almost the same as the present ones.[2] In the Middle Ages, cities like Bruges, Antwerp, Brussels and Liège enjoyed their autonomy and their economic development. The pre-existence of these realities and the cultural division between Flemish and Walloons influenced and weakened the unification process of the country under one flag.

The United Kingdom contains four historically autonomous regions, or more correctly constitutes four distinguished nations. The relation between the central power housed in England, and Scotland, Wales and Northern Ireland has been problematic in many respects and is currently a contested issue. Scotland fought many times for independence, and even under English control enjoyed special relationships with the European continent. The Welsh retained their language and culture for a lengthy time despite a very heavy English domination after the thirteenth century. Northern Ireland, after the pacification process, remains a society divided between Catholic and Protestant with a strong legacy of civil conflict.

Italy is a country of fragmentation, an amalgam of regional states and powerful cities which reduced the ability of the Italians to act together, as Machiavelli (Machiavelli and Inglese 1995) noted in the sixteenth century. For this reason, its history fascinated many scholars interested in social participation and social capital (Banfield 1958; Almond and Verba 1963; Putnam 1993). The immense socio-economic differences between the North and the South (the so-called *Questione Meridionale*) have been the object of many analyses and it remains a domain largely contested in the literature. In this context, the analysis of participation and generalized trust has often been scaled down to the regional or sub-regional level (Trigilia 1992; Cartocci 2007).

Prior to unification, Spain had been divided, like Italy, into kingdoms and principalities. During the *reconquista* the two most powerful kingdoms, Castilla and Aragona, conceived the idea of unity through family ties. The unification process did not destroy the ancient cultural and linguistic differences existent in the country. The autonomous regions kept their identity within the national framework. Indeed Catalans and Basques were conscious of political identities which predated the creation of the Unitarian state in 1492. Again, analysing this country as a national mono-bloc would be misleading.

Also Germany has a rich history of principalities and city-states since the constitution of the Holy Roman Empire, and the struggle between the empire and the powerful princes shaped the cultural and political life of the country. The emergence of a new religious community (the Protestants) provoked wars and disputes for centuries and is still a contested issue in the country. The furore of these divisions has cast a shadow traceable even today at a geographical level.[3]

The historical description helps us to understand the evolution of subnational entities and their importance in our analysis, but the historical outlook has to be complemented with an accurate understanding of the institutional developments of regions. This logic is also applied to the in-depth case studies in Chapters 7 and 8, where historical and institutional analyses complement each other to shed light on the Walloon and Southern Italian cases.

3.2 THE REDEFINITION OF REGIONAL AUTONOMY IN EUROPE

A new literature on the opportunity of rescaling the level of analysis has emerged in the last years in opposition to the national paradigm. This new regionalism highlights the necessity to develop a new spatial political economy showing how the breakdown of the nation-state is conferring new importance to the sub-national level of analysis (Brenner 2004; 2009). In this context, the academic debate concentrates on the analysis of institutional changes activated by progressive European integration.

The launch of the European Structural Fund in 1988 has been interpreted as the will of the Commission to undermine the power of the state and open a direct dialogue with the regions themselves. In reality, the scope of this policy was not to bypass the nation state but to re-equilibrate the economic divergence between European regions. In the European Parliament Resolution on Regional Policy (1988), the first two points emphasize that regional disparities, after narrowing down in the first phase of community integration, were increasing again (to reach a level close to the one measured in 1970). The absence of a concrete regional policy to counterbalance the opening of the market on a larger scale and Spanish, Portuguese and Greek accession were leading to a serious widening of economic disparities.[4] This debate on regional disparity influenced the structure and development of new policies, and the European Commission launched the Regional Structural Funds to enhance the development of poorer regions; the implementation of this policy has increased attention to the competence of regions.

Despite this increasing concern for European regions, there is no consensus in the literature about the effect of the European Union on regional empowerment. Scholars have evaluated the effect of European integration on regional autonomy in different ways, arguing that (Bache and Jones 2000; Bourne 2003): (1) the integration process is disempowering regions, (2) the integration process has a neutral effect, (3) the integration process has different effects according to the pre-existent situation and legislative activity of the regions, and (4) the integration process is empowering regions.

The first group includes mainly legal scholars who argue that the process of European integration is reducing the autonomy of regions because the state monopolizes the formal representation in the European context (Bullain 1998; Borzel 2002); Anderson (1990), from a different perspective, draws the same conclusions. He analysed the evolution of the European Regional Development Fund in Germany and Great Britain, discussing with scepticism the possibility that a strengthening of regions could in the future undermine the power of the nation-state as the fundamental gatekeeper for the development of European policies.

The second group includes mainly international relations scholars, who suggest that the process of European integration has a neutral effect on the autonomy of regions. The European integration process is only a free agreement between different states; the states remain the gatekeepers of decision-making in the continent. According to Moravcsik (1993), regions can only be directly empowered by the state through the devolution of power, for this reason the European legislation cannot have a direct role.[5]

A third group includes the theories that explore the question, whether European integration plays a role in the empowerment of regions, with a bottom-up approach (Smyrl 1997). According to Smyrl, regions vary systematically and the variation on the impact of European Policy can only be explained by looking at the structural differences at a sub-national level (Smyrl 1997: 288). His study on the impact of European Community regional policy on Italian and French regions proposed mixed results. On the one hand, those that had already tried to increase their power and the efficiency of their policy enjoyed the benefits of European policy and increased their autonomy; on the other, the most static regions did not experience these effects.

The fourth group includes comparative regionalists and multi-level governance scholars (Bourne 2003). They put forward three arguments to support the idea that the European integration process is empowering regions. Firstly, the new attention which was given to regions by the Commission after 1988 is offering them a new powerful ally in claiming autonomy (from a financial and administrative point of view). Secondly, the Commission is legitimizing regional actors through the development of intensive partnerships to implement regional policies[6] (Kohler-Koch 1996). The development of this joint-venture is enabling the executive power, particularly at sub-national level, to penetrate society more deeply (Kohler-Koch 1996: 375). These networks are more and more independent from the central power of the state; their existence and development is tangible proof that a slow progressive transformation of the system of governance is happening. Thirdly, the enlargement of European competences has largely coincided[7] with the increasing competence of regions.[8] Therefore, even if the decision-making power to allocate structural funds and to conduct negotiations remains in the hands of national governments, the new opportunities opened from European institutions seem to contribute to the acceleration of the devolution process. Despite this lack of consensus on the role of the European integration process to empower regions, Hooghe et al. (2008a and b) showed that the autonomy of regions is increasing everywhere, as illustrated by the variation of the Regional Authority Index (RAI)[9] (Table 3.1, columns 1 and 2). According to the RAI, countries can be divided into high (Austria, Belgium, Germany, Italy and Spain), medium (United Kingdom, France and the Netherlands) and low (Denmark, Finland, Greece, Ireland, Portugal and Sweden) decision making power attributed to the regions (Table 3.2).

In the first group there are federal and regional states, which confer a large autonomy to their regions. After the end of the allied occupation, Austria created nine länder. They have extensive legislative power in many areas: housing policy, poverty, land reform, labour law and public schools. The share of power between the federal state and the land is stable over time (Table 3.1).

Belgium undertook a radical reform in 1993 when the country turned into a fully-fledged federal state with three autonomous regions and communities. The first article of the Belgian Constitution was changed to read as follow: 'Belgium is a Federal State which consists of Communities and Regions.' This was considered the best response to the perpetual tension between Walloons and the Flemish. In the regions, the directly elected assemblies decide territorial interests and have a large constitutional and fiscal autonomy; they can also sign international treaties on issues within their competence.

After the end of the allied occupation in 1949, Germany was divided into eleven länder. Extensive exclusive competencies are attributed to the länder: cultural policies, education, universities, media and television, and police; the länder are also responsible for the implementation of the majority of federal laws. After reunification with East Germany another five länder have been added to the original eleven. Germany, like Austria has had a stable RAI over the last 50 years (Table 3.1).

Italy is a regional state undergoing great evolution in recent years, as shown by the increase of the RAI (Table 3.1). After World War II the new Italian Constitution recognized the existence of 20 regions, but they became a politically elected institution only in the early 1970s (with the exception of five autonomous regions established in 1948). The competencies of the regions progressively increased and in 1997 they obtained residual administrative powers. Then, with the substantial reform of the constitution in 2001, regions obtained extensive concurrent competencies with the central government: European Union relations, education, health, food, sport, civil protection, town planning, ports and airports, cultural and environmental resources, transport and energy. The devolution of

Table 3.1 Percentage of people who declare that they feel part of regions as geographical group, by nations and by selected regions and RAI Index

Nations	Last RAI (2006) [1]	Oldest RAI (1950–1980s) [2]	Difference RAI % [3]	Belonging to Regions % [4]	Regions (Highest level of belonging to regions)	Belonging to Regions % [5]
Austria	18.0	17.0	5.6	31.0	GR Kriti (rest)	50.0
Germany West	29.3	28.3	3.4	29.3	DE Rheinland-Pfalz	43.4
Germany East	–		–	26.8	DK Bornholms amt	40.0
Denmark	10.2	4.1	59.8	22.2	DK Ringkøbing amt	39.3
Belgium	29.0	14.0	51.7	20.5	DE Saarland	37.5
Spain	22.1	10	54.8	16.5	AT Vienna	37.0
Ireland	6.0	0	100.0	15.7	IT Sardegna	36.8
Portugal	3.7	2.5	32.4	14.7	DE Mecklenburg-Vorpommern	35.5
United Kingdom	9.6	9.4	2.1	13.6	DE Brandenburg	35.0
France	16.0	6.0	62.5	12.6	AT Oberoesterreich	34.6
Finland	7.1	1.1	84.5	12.2	Regions (Lowest level of belonging to regions)	
Italy	22.7	8.4	63.0	10.6	SE Götaland	6.0
Greece	10.0	1.0	90.0	10.3	ES Murcia	5.9
Luxembourg	0	0	0	10.3	NL Flevoland	5.9
Sweden	10.0	13.5	−35.0	9.2	GR Dodekanisos	5.9
The Netherlands	14.5	13.5	6.9	7.3	UK London	4.7
					FI Lappi	4.5
					NL Noord-Holland	4.4
					FI Uusimaa	4.0
					NL Gelderland	3.4
					IT Campania	2.7

Source: Author's elaboration from EVS (1999–2000) and Hooghe et al. (2008a and b).

Table 3.2 Institutional frameworks of European regions

Country	No.	Name	Power of Regions	Year Constitution	Competencies
Austria	9	Länder	High	1955	Extensive legislative powers: housing, health policy, poverty, land reform, labour law, public schools.
Belgium	3	Regions	High	1993 (reformed)	Institutions typical of modern federations: directly elected assemblies, a senate representing territorial interests, fiscal federalism, constitutional autonomy, international treaties on issue of their competence (more in Chapter 9).
DK	16	Counties	Low	1950 (modified in 1970)	Administrative powers in welfare provisions, hospitals, secondary education, nature protection, economic development, spatial planning and regional support.
Finland	19	Regions	Low	1993	Regional planning, economic development and education.
France	22	Regions	Medium	1955	Few powers (mostly concentrated in departments) before 2003. After 2003 regional competences increased substantially with the establishment of the principle of sub-national devolution. Competencies: vocational training, secondary schools and school transport, regional and town planning, the environment, cultural policy.
Germany	16	Länder	High	1949	Extensive competencies: culture, education, universities, television, local government, police.
Greece	13	Regions	Low	1986	Implement programs funded by EU.
Ireland	8	Regions	Low	1987	Implement programs funded by EU.

Table 3.2 (continued)

Country	No.	Name	Power of Regions	Year Constitution	Competencies
Italy	20	Regions	High	1970	Consolidation of regional power (reform 2001). Extension of concurrent competencies. Problem in the share of power. Evolution toward a federation (more in Chapter 9)
Luxembourg	1			–	–
The Netherlands	12	Provinces	Medium	1851	Debate on the creation of regions. Shared authority with the central government for transport, infrastructure, investment policy, regional planning, urban development, housing, culture and leisure, environmental planning.
Portugal	5	Regions	Low	1979	Responsible for regional development on behalf of the central government.
Spain	17	Comunidades Autonomas	High	1978	Extensive powers: city and regional planning, health, housing, public works, regional railways and roads, ports and airports, agriculture, fishing, environmental protection, culture, tourism, social welfare, economic development within national objectives, regional political institutions.
Sweden	8	Regions	Low	–	Main powers for the 21 counties. Eight regions have been created recently for statistical purposes.
United Kingdom	11	Regions	Medium	1964	Extensive powers: Scotland, Northern Ireland and Wales. The other regions have limited competencies: attracting investments, infrastructure, improving skills, coordinating economic development and regeneration public policies.

Source: Author's elaboration after Hooghe et al. (2008a, b).

competencies and the future institutional architecture of the state are currently under discussion (see Chapter 8).

In Spain, since the promulgation of the constitution in 1978, a long debate on the extension of regional autonomies led to an increase of the competencies of communities and regions, under the powerful influence of regions like Cataluña. Communities and regions enjoyed a degree of autonomy which had never been allowed under Franco's dictatorship. Thanks to the ideological rejection of centralism, local authorities have been able to expand their powers beyond the competencies officially recognized in the constitution. In less than 30 years, Spain turned from being one of the most centralized states in the world, to the scholarly example of a regional state. The *Comunidades Autonomas* have extensive exclusive powers: city and regional planning, health, housing, public works, regional railways and roads, ports and airports, agriculture, fishing, environmental protection, culture, tourism, social welfare, and economic development.

In the second group there are three countries that have very different characteristics: the United Kingdom, France and the Netherlands (Table 3.2). The United Kingdom has a particular organization dictated more by historical events than by a precise political plan. There are three regions with special powers: Northern Ireland, Scotland and Wales. It is hard to define the relationship of these three regional entities with the central government; the United Kingdom is neither a pure regional state nor a federation.

Scotland and Wales have an autonomous executive which is accountable to a directly elected legislature. Scotland has larger autonomy to write primary law and a different education and legal system. After 2007 Wales moved in a similar direction. In Northern Ireland the powers of the local parliament are similar to the Scottish one, but a long history dating from the establishment of the Home Rule in 1922 created a different type of relationship with the central government.[10] The other regions have limited competencies: attracting investments, infrastructures, improving skills, coordinating economic development and public policies of regeneration. This limited power of the other regions explains the low RAI of the country. However, if Scotland, Wales and Northern Ireland are included, the United Kingdom cannot be considered a state with weak regional autonomies.

In France, 22 planning regions, *Circoscription d'Action Régionale*, were set up in 1955 to follow a top-down economic strategy. At the outset, they were a pure administrative category; only in 1972 did they become, effectively, regions with a limited budget. The Defferre reforms, of 1983, directly established elected assemblies and then a new reform in 2003 articulated the revolutionary principle of sub-national devolution. The competencies of the regions are: vocational training, secondary schools and public transport, regional and town planning and the environment and cultural policies. There is a clear pattern to reinforce the competencies and the decision-making power of the regions (as confirmed by the RAI index increase, Table 3.1) even if France remains a centralized state.

In the Netherlands there is an open debate about the possibility of creating four administrative regions. At the moment the second tier of power is constituted by 12 provinces that share with the central government responsibilities for: transport, infrastructures investment policy, and regional planning, urban development, housing, culture and leisure, and environmental planning.

In the third group (Table 3.2), Denmark, Finland, Greece, Ireland, Portugal and Sweden have regions instituted to deal with European Union requirements, or as in the Scandinavian countries, to improve the collection of statistics. In Denmark regions do not exist, and 16 counties[11] constitute the second tier of power; they manage welfare provisions, hospitals, secondary education, nature protection, economic development, spatial planning and regional support. In Finland 19 regions[12] were constituted in 1993, and they have residual competencies in regional planning, economic development and education. In Greece and Ireland regions have been created to deal with European Union funds, in 1986 and 1987 respectively. In Portugal five regions were formed after the end of the dictatorship in 1974 with residual competencies to deal with EU funds and more in general power to direct regional development according to central government strategies. In Sweden, as in Denmark, there are 21 counties with similar powers, but eight statistical regions have been created recently. Also in the third group of countries, with the exception of Sweden (Table 3.1), regional power has increased dramatically since the 1980s. This demonstrates that also for these countries a regional analysis has a value not only in a future perspective.

Public opinion data show that the amount people feel as if they belong to their region is directly proportional to the amount of autonomy owned by the region itself (Table 3.1). The rank of 15 countries analysed, classified by the percentage of people that affirmed to belonging to regions as a geographical group, is similar to the RAI ranking (Table 3.1).

In Austria and Germany where the power of regions and the RAI has remained constant over a long period of time, people tend to identify themselves a lot more with their region than in the rest of Europe. In Belgium and Spain, where regional autonomy has grown consistently in recent years, the percentage of people who identify themselves with regions is also high (Table 3.1, column 4). Denmark constitutes a peculiar exception. This exception can be explained by the importance that people attribute to counties.[13] If we look at the top ten regional scores (Table 3.1, column 5), two Danish counties occupy the third and fourth positions, with values around 40 per cent. The medium-high score of Portugal can be explained by the high level of identification in the Southern regions (Algarve and Alentejo). The medium score of the United Kingdom is explained by the particular status of the country. In fact the regions with larger powers, Scotland and Wales, score higher than the rest of the country.[14] The other exceptions are Italy and the Netherlands. In Italy the low score of regional belonging can be explained by the tendency of Italians to identify themselves more with their town or local community. Regional identities are strongest in some areas with a particular geographical position, such as Sardinia (Table 3.1, column 5). In the Netherlands the absence of an official regional tier of power can explain the low identification of the population within this institution.

3.3 REGIONAL IDENTIFICATION, NETWORKS AND TRUST: AN EMPIRICAL MODEL

After observing that in countries where regions have a stronger autonomy people generally tend to feel closer to their regions, we tested empirically whether people who feel closer to their region, rather than local community or nations, have also got higher social capital scores. The independent explanatory variable is the sense of geographical belonging, while the dependent variables are the nine items used to measure social capital and its components. The model is completed with a series of control variables often used in social capital literature (Van Oorschot and Arts 2005).

Geographical belonging is measured through the question: 'which of these geographical groups would you say you belong to first of all?' Geographical belonging in regions is measured against geographical belonging in all of the country and locality or town. Social capital is measured according to the definition proposed in the previous chapter. The nine indicators are: membership and participation, to define the formal social networks dimension; meeting with friends and colleagues, importance of family and friends, to define the informal social networks dimension; and discussing politics, generalized and institutional trust, to define the social trust dimension.

Membership and participation are measured through the question: 'please look carefully at the following list of voluntary organizations and activity and say which, if any, do you belong to/you are currently doing unpaid work for?'[15] The variable is dichotomized; the value one is

attributed to people who are members/participate in at least one organization and the value zero to people who are not members/do not participate
in any association.

The frequency of meetings with colleagues is measured through the
question 'I'm going to ask how often you do certain things. Spend time
with colleagues from work or professions outside the work place: every
week, once or twice a month, a few times a year, not at all.' The value one
is attributed for the answer meeting colleagues every week, the value zero
is attributed for all the other answers. The frequency of meetings with
friends is measured according to the same logic.

The indicator of the importance in life of friends is measured through
the question 'how important in your life are friends and acquaintances:
very important, quite important, not important, and not important at all'.
The value one is attributed for the answers 'friends are very important',
the value zero is attributed for all the other answers. The importance of
family indicator is measured according to the same logic as importance in
life of friends.

The frequency of political discussion with friends is measured through
the question 'when you get together with your friends, would you say you
discuss political matters frequently, occasionally or never?' The value
one has been attributed to the answers frequently, the value zero for all
the others. Generalized trust is measured through the question 'generally
speaking, would you say that most people can be trusted or that you can't
be too careful in dealing with people?' The value one has been attributed
for the answer 'most people can be trusted' and zero for the answer 'can't
be too careful'. The average level of institutional trust is measured by
looking at the confidence in six different institutions: the education system,
the press, the parliament, the social security system, the health care system,
the justice system. The value one has been attributed if the interviewee
was confident in more than three institutions. The value zero has been
attributed to all the other cases.

We completed the model with nine control variables. These predictors have been widely used in the literature: income, education, gender,
age, religious affiliation, trust, membership, participation and political
actions.[16] Income is measured by ranking people in a scale from zero to
ten. Zero indicates the lowest segment and ten the highest one.[17] The relationship between income and social capital is central in the literature. The
main objective of these analyses has been the investigation of the relationship between social capital and the generation of wealth at individual and
aggregate (national) level.

Education is measured through the question: 'what is the highest level
you have reached in your education?' There are eight categories, one

indicates 'inadequate and incomplete elementary education', and eight indicates the highest level 'higher education upper level certificate'.[18] The relationship between social capital and education attainments and the fascinating link between the generation of human and social capital (Coleman 1988) has been widely discussed in the last decades.[19]

Age is measured by calculating the age from the question: 'can you tell me your year of birth'. Gender is measured through the question 'sex of respondents'.[20] Religious affiliation variable is measured through the question 'which religious group do you belong to?' In the study only Roman Catholic, Protestants and Orthodox are considered. The relationship between religious categories has always been central in sociological analysis. Max Weber's protestant ethic and more recent works have suggested the importance of the religion and religious affiliation in the creation of social capital (Smidt 2003).

To measure the involvement in political action we considered three forms of involvement: signing a petition, joining in boycotts and attending lawful demonstrations. These three variables were measured through the question 'I'm going to read out some different actions that people can take, and I'd like you to tell me, for each one, whether you have actually done any of these things, whether you might do or would never do these actions, under any circumstances.' They are considered in the model because they demonstrate the willingness of individuals to join in lawful collective action. Finally membership, participation and generalized trust are also alternatively used as predictors.[21]

3.4   RESULTS

Before discussing the correlation between the sense of geographical belonging and social capital, we have to consider the results for the control variables (Tables 3.3 and 3.4). Income tends to be positively correlated with social capital, but for education the interaction is more complex. Higher levels of education are positively correlated with the formal social networks dimension, but negatively correlated with the informal social networks dimension. This empirical test confirms a recurrent theme in the social capital literature. People who are highly educated tend to have a more formal participation in society, while less educated people tend to invest their time and attention in the construction of informal ties mainly relating to friends and family. The result of the social trust dimension is less clear. People who are more educated tend to be more interested in politics, and they have more interpersonal trust. On the other hand, people who are less educated tend to have a higher level of trust in institutions.

Table 3.3   Logistic regression models explaining formal and informal social networks from education, age, gender, religion, lawful political actions, geographical belonging, generalized trust

	Memb.	Part.	Meeting Coll.	Meeting Friends	Import. Family	Import. Friends	M (SD)
Income (higher bracket omitted)							4.76 (2.553)
Lowest segment	−0.654*** (0.093)	−0.471*** (0.94)	0.038 (0.118)	0.347*** (0.086)	−1.117*** (0.132)	−0.011 (0.085)	
Education (higher education – upper-level tertiary certificate omitted)							4.51 (2.133)
Inadequately completed elementary education (lower segment)	−0.899*** (0.085)	−1.019*** (0.097)	0.006 (0.135)	0.655*** (0.078)	0.208* (0.112)	0.358*** (0.077)	
Higher education – lower-level tertiary certificate (segment seven)	0.205*** (0.076)	0.111*** (0.070)	0.053 (0.088)	0.394*** (0.069)	0.209** (0.104)	0.366*** (0.067)	
Gender (male/female)							1.54 (0.498)
Gender (female omitted)	0.166*** (0.032)	0.193*** (0.034)	0.508*** (0.044)	0.215*** (0.031)	−0.509*** (0.44)	−0.062** (0.030)	
Age	0.002*** (0.001)	0.005*** (0.001)	−0.38*** (0.002)	−0.31*** (0.001)	0.001 (0.001)	−0.010*** (0.001)	44.966 (17.181)
Religion (other religions omitted)							2.81 (2.732)
Roman Catholic	−0.747*** (0.125)	−0.608*** (0.126)	−0.187 (0.167)	0.051 (0.119)	0.288* (0.159)	−0.152 (0.116)	

56

	(1)	(2)	(3)	(4)	(5)	(6)
Church of England (Protestant)	0.336***	−0.355***	−0.192	0.161	0.165	0.212*
	(0.129)	(0.128)	(0.171)	(0.122)	(0.163)	(0.119)
Orthodox	−1.221***	−1.005***	0.214	−0.079	−0.173	−0.409***
	(0.129)	(0.131)	(0.172)	(0.122)	(0.162)	(0.120)
Lawful political actions						
Petition (would never do omitted)						1.83
						(0.815)
Petition (have done)	0.621***	0.732***	0.107	0.409***	0.333***	0.257***
	(0.048)	(0.054)	(0.070)	(0.046)	(0.067)	(0.046)
Boycotts (would never do omitted)						2.47
						(0.661)
Boycotts (have done)	0.155**	−0.141***	0.038	0.177***	−0.163*	0.109*
	(0.067)	(0.064)	(0.083)	(0.062)	(0.092)	(0.60)
Demonstration (would never do omitted)						2.15
						(0.769)
Demonstration (have done)	0.417***	0.433***	0.126*	0.124**	0.015	−0.28
	(0.051)	(0.053)	(0.069)	(0.048)	(0.070)	(0.048)
Geographical belonging (world omitted)						2.05
						(1.220)
Locality or town	−0.279***	−0.217***	−0.28	−0.89	0.115	0.134**
	(0.072)	(0.075)	(0.091)	(0.069)	(0.095)	(0.067)
Region	−0.143*	0.186**	−0.078	−0.118	0.074	−0.134*
	0.081	(0.084)	(0.104)	(0.077)	(0.107)	(0.075)

Table 3.3 (continued)

	Memb.	Part.	Meeting Coll.	Meeting Friends	Import. Family	Import. Friends	M (SD)
Geographical belonging (world omitted)							
Nation	−0.237***	−0.202***	−0.09	−0.080	0.186*	−0.146**	
	(0.074)	(0.077)	(0.094)	(0.071)	(0.098)	(0.069)	
Trust (most people can be trusted omitted)	−0.402***	−0.233***	−0.107**	−0.271***	−0.15	−0.337***	0.296
	(0.035)	(0.036)	(0.48)	(0.034)	(0.049)	(0.033)	(0.456)
Constant	1.224***	−0.262	−0.91	1.019***	2.076***	0.354**	
	(0.170)	(0.170)	(0.221)	(0.160)	(0.227)	(0.157)	
−2 log likelihood	23,619.940	21,396.287	13,862.417	25,869.246	14,630.678	26,195.987	
Nagelkerke R square	0.263	0.144	0.121	0.117	0.061	0.084	
Unweighted number of observations	20,252	19,762	16,086	20,075	20,159	20,155	

Notes:
Standard errors are in parenthesis.
Memb.: membership; Part.: participation; Coll.: colleagues; Import.: importance.
***p<0.01; **p<0.05; *p<0.10.

Source: Author's elaboration from EVS 1999–2000.

Table 3.4 Logistic regression models explaining social trust from education, age, gender, religion, lawful political actions, geographical belonging, membership and participation in associations

	Politics	Trust	Institutions	M (SD)
Income (higher bracket omitted)				4.76 (2.553)
Lowest segment	−0.111 (0.107)	−0.516*** (0.091)	−0.072 (0.087)	
Sixth segment	−0.180** (0.099)		−0.147* (0.080)	
Education (higher education – upper-level tertiary certificate omitted)				4.51 (2.133)
Inadequately completed elementary education (lower segment)	−1.496*** (0.113)	−0.410*** (0.087)	0.622*** (0.081)	
Higher education – lower-level tertiary certificate (segment seven)	−0.440*** (0.077)	0.180** (0.070)	0.226*** (0.069)	
Gender (male/female)				1.54 (0.498)
Gender (female omitted)	0.408*** (0.040)	0.022 (0.033)	−0.017 (0.031)	
Age	0.023*** (0.001)	0.006*** (0.01)	0.002** (0.01)	44.966 (17.181)

Table 3.4 (continued)

	Politics	Trust	Institutions	M (SD)
Religion (other religions omitted)				
Roman Catholic	0.321*	−0.261**	−0.147	2.81
	(0.173)	(0.127)	(0.123)	(2.732)
Church of England (Protestant)	0.189	0.510***	0.388***	
	(0.176)	(0.129)	(0.125)	
Orthodox	0.535***	−0.469***	−0.595***	
	(0.177)	(0.132)	(0.127)	
Lawful political actions				
Petition (would never do omitted)				1.83
				(0.815)
Petition (have done)	0.273***	0.222***	−0.098**	
	(0.064)	(0.052)	(0.048)	
Boycotts (would never do omitted)				2.47
				(0.661)
Boycotts (have done)	0.393***	0.492***	−0.042	
	(0.071)	(0.063)	(0.062)	
Demonstration (would never do omitted)				2.15
				(0.769)
Demonstration (have done)	0.613***	0.159***	−0.123**	
	(0.061)	(0.052)	(0.050)	

Geographical belonging (world omitted)

Locality or town	0.000	−0.177**	0.162**	2.05
	(0.086)	(0.073)	(0.071)	(1.220)
Region	0.114	−0.165**	0.180**	
	(0.096)	(0.082)	(0.079)	
Nation	0.073	−0.260	0.182**	
	(0.088)	(0.076)	(0.073)	
Membership (membership omitted)	−0.059	−0.328***	−0.231***	0.476
	(0.051)	(0.042)	(0.040)	(0.499)
Participation (participation omitted)	−0.180*	−0.079***	0.027	0.258
	(0.050)	(0.042)	(0.514)	(0.437)
Constant	−1.579***	−0.803***	−0.256***	
	(0.019)	(0.015)	(0.015)	
-2 log likelihood	17,174.371	22,272.276	24,211.331	
Nagelkerke R square	0.106	0.147	0.063	
Unweighted number of observations	20,225	19,762	18,316	

Notes:
Standard errors are in parenthesis.
***p<0.01; **p<0.05; *p<0.10.

Source: Author's elaboration from EVS 1999–2000.

61

This can be explained by the greater scepticism of highly educated people in respect to the institutions of their country. A final remark on education is how having a first level degree is more positively correlated with all the dependent variables of the model than having a post-graduate degree. This means that above a certain level of education people tend to have less social capital.

Men tend to be part of formal social networks more than women. They also tend to meet more friends and colleagues, while women tend to attribute more importance to family. In terms of social trust, men tend to discuss politics more but there is no significant evidence for the other components of this dimension. A greater age is positively correlated with formal social networks and social trust dimensions but negatively with informal social networks dimension.

Religious affiliation has a strong impact on social capital. Being Roman Catholic is negatively correlated with formal social networks and social trust dimensions, and positively with the only significant component of informal social networks dimension, the importance of family. Being Protestant is positively correlated with the formal social networks dimension and with importance in life of friends, the only significant variable for informal networks. Also a positive correlation with generalized trust exists. Being Orthodox is negatively correlated with the two social networks dimensions. Mixed evidence for social trust exists because there is a negative correlation with generalized trust but a positive correlation with discussing politics. These results seem to confirm the classical Weberian hypothesis of the protestant ethic.

Signing petitions and participating in demonstrations are positively correlated with formal and informal social networks dimensions. Mixed evidence exists for boycotts. Lawful political actions are also positively correlated with discussing politics and generalized trust but they are negatively correlated with trust in institutions. This shows that those who are politically active tend to trust people more than institutions.

After discussing the control variables, we can analyse the central question of our model to see if our original hypothesis is confirmed. The model shows that people who feel they are part of regions as a geographical group tend to have higher membership and participation.[22] On the other hand, the correlation between geographical belonging and informal social networks dimension is not significant. In terms of social trust, people who feel they are part of a region as a geographical group appear to have more generalized trust than those who feel they belong to the local community or the nation. Trust in institutions, instead, tends to increase the further we go up in the tier of administrative power. However, the difference between the three layers is small and practically irrelevant between regions and nations. To sum up, people who identify themselves with regions tend to participate more in formal social networks and tend to have a higher generalized trust. The differences are not as large as for income or education, but they are significant and allow one to draw some conclusions.

The higher membership, participation and generalized trust of people who identify themselves with regions can be explained by the intermediate character of regions, which constitute a secondary geographical identity between the nation and the local community. Durkheim (1893) emphasised how an efficient intermediate tier of decision making is necessary in modern societies to avoid the alienation of individuals from society. On the basis of our empirical model we argue that regions are the most suited institutional tier to support a renewal of social engagement and civic spirit. This is because nations are too big and impersonal to provide a high sense of identification and local authorities are too small to allow the individuals to pursue macro-political objectives.

People who identify themselves with regions are more ready to have an active role in society because they understand that this is the most suitable tier of administrative power to pursue their objectives, and might become the most important from an administrative and political point of view in the near future. The huge process of devolution from the central states to the regions seems to clearly point in this direction.

3.5 SUMMARY

The regional paradigm is assuming more importance in the literature in parallel to the new political agenda of European countries. This new agenda is driven by a continuous devolution of power from the central states to the regions. The institutional devolution of competencies throughout the regions has been discussed in this chapter starting from the RAI elaborated by Hooghe et al. (2008a and b). In this context historical and institutional reasons have been pinpointed to illustrate the need to shift from the national to the regional level of analysis when discussing social capital in Europe.

The chapter concludes by matching the historical and institutional evidence with an empirical model by testing the hypothesis that, individuals who identify themselves more with regions as a geographical group, rather than local communities or nations, tend to have more social capital. In the next chapters, regions will be grouped according to the scores of the three dimensions that constitute the social capital index.

NOTES

1. These five nations contain the majority of the regions analysed (44).
2. The County of Flanders, which included the actual provinces of East and West Flanders but also the French Nord, the region of Lille; the marquisate of Namur; the duchy of Brabant, which included the actual provinces of Flemish and Walloon Brabant, Antwerp, Brussels and also the Dutch region Nord Brabant; the County of Hainaut; Luxembourg; the bishopric of Liège, which included the actual provinces of Liège and Limburg.
3. However, the actual länder are only an approximation of German historical regions.
4. The consequence was that more than 20% of the community population was living in backward regions. The question whether regions (in terms of income per capita and economic development) were converging or diverging was already attracting the attention of economists and decision makers (Magrini 2004). Williamson (1965) used, for the first time, a comparative approach to explain the persistence of cleavages among regions in many countries after their process of modernization, the so-called North–South problem. He argued that the first stages of development are characterized by an increasing North–South dualism and the majority of economic activity tends to be concentrated in a few nodes of growth. Subsequently, the economies of scale and the expansion of the economic activities generate an increase of the regional inequalities. Then, after some development, the wealthier regions enter a mature stage of development; the congestion costs due to an excessive concentration generate a spatial diffusion of the technology. In this way the process of convergence takes place (Williamson 1965: 44). Williamson's study left open the question of whether or not this process of convergence was similar for all poor countries and regions. Twenty-five years later, Barro and Sala-i-Martin (1992) suggested the validity of this general neoclassical theory of progressive convergence. However, despite these contributions the idea of progressive convergence remained contested in the literature (Boldrin et al. 2001; Ezcurra and Rapun 2006; Fingleton 1999; Magrini 1999; Petrakos et al. 2005).
5. Moravcsik re-affirms the validity of the inter-governmental approach (Haas 1975) against the functional argument (supported by the theories of the scholars discussed in the fourth group).
6. The importance of the state is not directly challenged by the Commission and the regions but the increasing importance of European policies is contributing to the creation of new partnerships between public and private actors.
7. According to Keating (2008), this overlap did not mean an increasing representation of regions inside European institutions.
8. The development of European integration re-opened the old discussion about the relationship between nations and states. The emergence of a new central power has been seen with hope by the stateless nations. The idea of a Europe of regions was very appealing for the vindication of regional parties during the 1980s and produced strong support for the European Union integration process. The integration process was seen as a way to reduce the power of the state and allow more freedom to autonomous regions. In reality, European Union institutions never challenged the role of the member states, generating a strong disappointment among the regional parties. For this reason, regional parties changed their attitude and took in the 1990s anti-European positions (Hepburn 2008).
9. The RAI is composed of two indicators: the *Self Rule* and the *Shared Rule*. The *Self Rule* is defined as 'the authority exercised by a regional government or its representatives over those who live in the region'. In order to measure that dimension the 'Institutional Depth', the 'Policy Scope', the 'Fiscal Autonomy' and the 'Representation' are considered (Hooghe et al. 2008b: 258). The *Shared Rule* is defined as 'the authority exercised by a regional government or its representatives in the country as a whole'. In order to measure this dimension the 'Law Making Power', the 'Executive Control', the 'Fiscal

Control', and 'the Constitutional Reform Power' are considered (Hooghe et al. 2008b: 259).

10. This relationship remains a contested issue, even after the agreement of 1998.
11. The Faroe Islands and Greenland have particular agreements with the central government.
12. Aland Island has an autonomous statute with a directly elected assembly.
13. Probably they perceive the question as inherent to the counties, because this is the second tier of power in the country.
14. Northern Ireland is excluded from the sample.
15. The associations included are: welfare, cultural, political, local community action, development/human rights, environment, professional, youth work, recreational, women's groups, peace movements, health and other interests.
16. Lawful political actions and participation in boycotts and demonstrations.
17. Interviewees answered the following question: 'here is a scale of incomes and we would like to know in what group your household is, counting all wages, salaries, pensions and other incomes that you receive. Just give the letter of the group your household falls into, after taxes and other deductions.'
18. The complete scale is: (1) inadequately completed elementary education; (2) completed (compulsory) elementary education; (3) elementary (compulsory) education and basic vocational qualification; (4) secondary, intermediate vocational qualification; (5) secondary, intermediate general qualification; (6) full secondary, maturity level certificate; (7) higher education – lower-level tertiary certificate and (8) higher education – upper-level tertiary certificate.
19. For a complete review see Dika and Singh (2002).
20. The value one is attributed to males and the value two to females.
21. Membership and participation to predict discussing politics, generalized trust and trust in institutions; generalized trust to predict membership, participation, meeting colleagues/friends, importance of family/friends.
22. The difference with national identification is much more consistent for membership rather than for participation.

PART 2

The Socio-economic Analysis

4.   Social capital in European regions

The previous chapters have explored the theoretical debate on the definition of social capital (Chapter 1), the main methodologies used for the measurement (Chapter 2) and the reasons for investigating the main determinants of social capital by a comparative regional analysis (Chapter 3). This chapter introduces the second part of the book: the investigation of the socio-economic determinants of social capital, illustrating the variation of social capital scores across 85 regions. Unlike Chapter 3, social capital is measured at the aggregate rather than the individual level, in order to connect the regional scores to the macro-social predictors, that is, income inequality, economic development, labour market participation, national divergence and density. We bridge the gap between the use of individual data, the aggregate measurement and the historical analysis by referring to the conceptual frameworks elaborated by social network theorists before the appearance of the social capital concept.

More specifically, on the one hand, the aggregate measurement of social capital and the investigation of its macro-social determinants are inspired by the American school's tradition (Chapters 4, 5 and 6), which focused on quantitative methods and pursued a synchronic perspective adhering to a structuralist paradigm. On the other, the in-depth historic-institutional analysis is inspired by the Manchester school (Chapters 7 and 8), which moved from a diachronic perspective, rejected structuralism and interpreted social change as a process rooted in history.

After considering the theoretical implications proposed by the aggregate measurement, nations and regions are divided into seven categories (that is, Synergic, Nordic, Network Based, Informally Jointed, Trust Based, Formally Jointed and Disjointed) based on the three dimensions of social capital and their connection with traditional sociological theory (see Tönnies 1955; Durkheim 1893). The cross-national classification introduces the cross-regional classification in order to test whether: (1) the measurement is consistent with the previous literature and (2) there is a large discrepancy between the national and the regional categorizations.

4.1   SYNCHRONIC AND DIACHRONIC PERSPECTIVES

Social capital theorists have not been the first to measure and discuss the complex relation between individuals, society and the creation of social networks. The Manchester school and the American social network theorists initiated this debate from radically different perspectives.

The Manchester school rose after World War II with a major research project coordinated by Max Gluckman (Werbner 1984) and proposed seminal contributions on the analysis of social networks during a period of three decades. After his seminal contribution, other original works on African and Western countries were proposed. In particular, Barnes (1954a and b) and Bott (1957) rejected the dominant structural and functionalist paradigms, analysing the process that enabled the creation of relations between individuals and social networks rather than the forms of social action.[1] Barnes (1954b) was the first to apply a precise concept of network, defining social structure in terms of social interactions and the presence of people or groups in social networks.[2]

The American social network theorists (Berkowitz 1982; Burt 1992; Freeman 1976; Granovetter 1973; Laumann 1973; Wellman and Leighton 1979; for a review see Knox et al. 2006) approached similar issues to the Manchester school but then they returned to structuralism, recalling Radcliffe-Brown's seminal contribution. According to Radcliffe-Brown (1940: 4), the actual structure of social relationships changes every day through births, deaths, divorces, marriages, and new friendships, but the general structure remains stable over time. In this vein, they focused on the understanding of the general structure rather than the value of individual interactions.

The Manchester school scholars contextualized individual behaviours in a social reality as viewed from a diachronic perspective and interpreted social change as a process of differentiation and evolution rooted in history. American social network theorists described the relation between the units of the system. The morphology and the structure of these units were contextualized in a synchronic situational perspective; historical complexity was rejected and substituted by general models to explain the systemic interrelations (Piselli 1997).

The Manchester school scholars described individuals under the influence of external factors, but at the same time capable of manipulating them in their favour. American social network theorists emphasized the impact of networks on individual behaviours but they considered social actors as completely dependent on social structure. The different theoretical starting points impacted largely on the methodological approach. The

Manchester school scholars collected data through participant observation, and combined situational analysis with in-depth interviews of a limited number of individuals. The American social network theorists used quantitative methodology with large-scale surveys; they interviewed large samples of people, investigating the composition and contents of networks and developed sophisticated models (Piselli 1997).

Both schools have influenced this work. The national and regional measurements presented in this chapter follow Granovetter and the American school's tradition with the aggregate measurement of social capital through quantitative surveys, bridging the gap between the use of observational data as a measure of social capital and its macro social determinants. The diachronic perspective proposed in the historical in-depth discussion of the deviant cases follows the Manchester school's tradition (Chapters 7 and 8).

4.2 CATEGORIZING NATIONS AND REGIONS

Categorization is an essential device in social science. Categories support abstract reasoning, help to propose alternative visions of the world and to a larger extent, enhance scientific research. Emanating from philosophy, the use of categories was adopted by social science (Ferragina and Seeleib-Kaiser 2011). In the comparative research field, Esping-Andersen's categories/worlds of welfare capitalism (1990) have been hotly debated. His theory generated a germane debate and enhanced comparative research in public and social policy. In this work the comparison between the national and the regional categorization absolves two functions: (1) to verify whether the results gathered with the new measurement are consistent with the previous literature and (2) to detect where regional classification diverges from the national one.

Nations and regions are categorized according to their scores in the three social capital dimensions. As already described in Chapter 2, social capital is an umbrella concept, which reinstates the importance of informal social networks, formal social networks and social trust for the correct functioning of societies and institutions (see Putnam 1993). These three dimensions are connected to traditional sociological theory. The informal social network dimension, by measuring the intensity of family and friendship ties, refers to Tönnies' *Gemeinschaft* and Durkheim's idea of *Mechanic* solidarity. The formal social networks dimension, by measuring the intensity of associative membership and participation, refers to Tönnies' *Gesellschaft* and Durkheim's idea of formal solidarity. These two types of networks were distinguished by the founding fathers of sociology to highlight how the modernization of society was generating the disappearance of community-based forms of solidarity and creating the shift to more formal and less binding ties. They put a negative emphasis on this change (see Chapter 1) fearing the excessive 'bureaucratization' of a society based on formal rather than informal solidarity. The social trust dimension, by measuring the attitude of people in the public sphere with regard to political interest, trust in the others and trust in institutions, refers to the idea that the correct functioning of a modern society is based on the existence of a conducive environment in which citizens have a high level of confidence in others and in their institutions (Barber 1983).

In our measurement we assumed, following Putnam's definition, that positive scores in all dimensions indicate high levels of social capital. In this vein and according to the different combinations of the scores in these three social capital dimensions, nations and regions are classified in seven categories:

1. We define as *Synergic* the areas in which all three dimensions' scores are above the average. In these areas citizens tend to be well connected in formal and informal networks and display high levels of trust in their country/regional fellow men and institutions.
2. We define as *Nordic* the areas in which formal social networks and social trust scores are above the average but informal social networks are below. In these areas citizens tend to prefer formal interactions and display high levels of social trust. These areas seem to have followed the evolution predicted by the founding fathers of sociology; modernization has brought a stronger emphasis on associative participation and membership reducing community based forms of solidarity.
3. We define as *Network Based* the areas in which formal and informal social networks scores are above the average but social trust is below. In these areas citizens are well connected but they tend not to trust each other or their institutions.
4. We define as *Informally Jointed* the areas in which only informal social networks scores are above the average. In these areas the modernization process has not broken the community based links among citizens and has not brought about a strong development of formal networks and generalized trust.
5. We define as *Trust Based* the areas in which only social trust scores are above the average. In these areas formal and informal networks are underdeveloped but citizens seem to trust each other and their institutions.

6. We define as *Formally Jointed* the areas in which only formal social networks are above the average. In these areas during the process of modernization formal networks have progressively replaced the community based forms of solidarity, however the level of generalized trust remains low.

7. We define as *Disjointed* the areas in which all dimensions score below the average. In these areas formal and informal networks are underdeveloped and there is a lack of generalized trust.

4.2.1 The National Classification

Nations are divided in five categories (Table 4.1; there are no Trust Based and Formally Jointed countries): (1) Synergic countries (Sweden, Luxembourg, and the Netherlands); (2) Nordic countries (Denmark, Finland, Austria, and Belgium); (3) Network Based countries (Ireland); (4) Informally Jointed countries (United Kingdom, Greece, Spain, and Portugal); (5) Disjointed countries (France, Germany, and Italy).

Sweden is the ideal-typical Synergic country with scores considerably above the European average in each dimension and the highest social capital score. Luxembourg is similar to Sweden but presents lower scores. The Netherlands is a hybrid between the Synergic and the Nordic model because of the lower density of informal social networks.

Rothstein (2001: 208) theorized the existence of a Swedish model, characterized by close collaboration between the state and voluntary sector in the elaboration and implementation of new public policies. In the Swedish case, voluntarism and informal social networks do not seem to be reduced by the generosity of the welfare state system; the cooperation between the different components of the welfare mix is rooted in the institutional and social development of the country. The theoretical argument proposed by Rothstein[3] (2001), is confirmed by the empirical data: Sweden has scores largely above the European average for all social capital dimensions, the highest density of formal social networks in Europe, a high density of informal social networks and a high level of social trust (Table 4.1).[4] Luxembourg occupies the fifth position in the final social capital indicator, ranking consistently at similar positions in all three social capital dimensions: the fifth position for the formal social networks and social trust dimensions, and the sixth position for the informal social networks dimension. The Netherlands occupies the third position in the social capital ranking, with high scores for the formal social networks and social trust dimensions and a level of informal social networks in line with the European average.

Denmark is very close to the Netherlands and the Synergic group.

Table 4.1 *National categories*

Ranking	Regions	SC	FSN	ISN	ST	Type	Notes
1	Sweden	1.25	1.73	0.88	1.16	Synergic	Pure
5	Luxembourg	0.34	0.37	0.27	0.37	Synergic	Pure/Low
3	The Netherlands	0.73	1.39	0.00	0.81	Synergic	Close to 2
2	Denmark	0.87	0.94	-0.04	1.70	Nordic	Close to 1
4	Finland	0.44	0.80	-0.18	0.72	Nordic	Pure
9	Austria	-0.15	0.20	-0.78	0.13	Nordic	Pure/Low
10	Belgium	-0.23	0.18	-0.95	0.08	Nordic	Close to 6
6	Ireland	0.32	0.12	1.29	-0.44	Network Based	Pure
7	United Kingdom	-0.07	-0.14	0.75	-0.82	Informally Jointed	Pure
8	Greece	-0.14	-0.56	0.85	-0.71	Informally Jointed	Pure
13	Spain	-0.65	-1.49	0.05	-0.49	Informally Jointed	Close to 7
14	Portugal	-0.78	-1.72	0.37	-0.98	Informally Jointed	Pure
11	France	-0.42	-0.39	-0.42	-0.45	Disjointed	Pure/Low
12	Germany	-0.54	-0.51	-1.12	-0.01	Disjointed	Close to 5
15	Italy	-0.99	-0.92	-0.96	-1.07	Disjointed	Pure

Groups	Legend		Nations No.
PPP (1)	1	Synergic	3
PMP (2)	2	Nordic	4
PPM (3)	3	Network Based	1
MPM (4)	4	Informally Jointed	4
MMP (5)	5	Trust Based	0
PMM (6)	6	Formally Jointed	0
MMM (7)	7	Disjointed	3

Notes:
SC: Social capital score.
FSN: Formal social networks score.
ISN: Informal social networks score.
ST: Social trust score.

Source: Author's elaboration, after EVS (1999–2000) and Eurobarometer (2005, 2006).

Finland is the quintessential example of a Nordic country, while Austria and Belgium are low intensity Nordic countries. Denmark has the second highest social capital score out of the 15 countries analysed and occupies the third and first position respectively for formal social networks and social trust dimensions. The main difference with Sweden and the Synergic countries is the lower density of informal networks.[5] Finland has a similar profile to Denmark, however social capital and the other three dimension scores are noticeably lower. Austria, unlike the two Scandinavian countries, has a medium-high score for formal social networks and social trust dimensions, and ranks in the fourth quartile for the informal social networks dimension. Belgium has a profile almost identical to Austria.

The Network Based group includes only Ireland. In this country there is a high density of formal and informal networks in a context characterized by low social trust. Ireland has the highest level of informal social networks in Europe and ranks only in eighth and ninth position for formal social networks and social trust dimensions.

The Informally Jointed group includes three Mediterranean nations, Greece, Spain and Portugal, and the United Kingdom. The United Kingdom and Greece have the highest social capital score in the group. Spain and Portugal occupy the 13th and 14th positions respectively on the social capital ranking. The United Kingdom ranks in seventh position thanks to a high density of informal social networks and a high degree of participation in voluntary work (Almond and Verba 1963; Hall 1999). On the other hand, social trust is extremely low thereby reducing the social capital score significantly.

The measurement of social capital in Greece is problematic because the EVS dataset (1999–2000) collected 76 per cent of its interviews in the area of Athens, thus distorting the regional distribution. The comparison between the results gathered from the EVS (1999–2000) and the Eurobarometer (2005; 2006), where the frequency of the regional observations is correctly balanced, shows that with EVS dataset (1999–2000) the formal social networks dimension is overestimated while the other two dimensions have similar values.[6] Despite the higher value detected for this anomaly, the formal social networks dimension score remains below the European average as well as for social trust. Only the informal social networks dimension is largely above the average, confirming that in the Mediterranean area informal social networks are prevalent over formal ties (Van Oorschot and Arts 2005). Spain and Portugal are similar to Greece, but display a lower level of social capital. Spain has low scores for formal social networks and social trust dimensions, and ranks just above the European average for the informal social networks dimension.

Portugal has an even lower score than Spain for formal social networks but a higher density of informal social networks.

The Disjointed group includes France, Germany and Italy in that they share negative scores in the three social capital dimensions. France has the highest ranking in the group and occupies the third quartile in each dimension; Germany has a very low score for formal and informal social networks dimensions but a social trust level close to the European average. Italy occupies the last quartile in each dimension. France ranks in 11th position in the social capital distribution, with similar scores in all dimensions: 11th position for formal and informal social networks and 10th position for social trust. Germany ranks one position below but with a different distribution of the scores in the three dimensions: a low score for formal and informal social networks and a score close to the European average for social trust. Italy occupies the last position. It ranks consistently below the European average in each dimension and is the only Mediterranean country not to score above the European average for the informal social networks dimension.

The cross-national measurement of social capital largely confirms the previous literature (Van Oorschot and Art 2005; Van Oorschot et al. 2006): Scandinavian countries and the Netherlands have the highest level of social capital in Western Europe, Mediterranean countries the lowest, and Anglo-Saxon and continental countries assume middle-range values.

4.2.2 The Regional Classification

As discussed in Chapters 2 and 3, Beugelsdijk and Van Schaik (2005a and b) proposed the first comparative regional index. However, their work was tarnished by methodological shortcomings (see Chapter 2) and did not provide any justification to shift from the cross-national to the cross-regional level of analysis (see Chapter 3). Furthermore in a contradictory way, they confirmed Putnam's theory but in their measurement, the South of Italy and Sicily resulted in having higher social capital scores than the North West of Italy and Lombardia (Table 4.2). These issues caused a proposal for a new regional measurement of social capital[7] before investigating its macro-determinants. Following the same categorization established for the national measurement we classify European regions and we test in which areas there is a big discrepancy between the national and the regional scores.

The Synergic model is prevalent in Scandinavia. Regions that are part of this group are ranked in the first 24 positions of the final social capital ranking (Table 4.3[8]). The synergic integration of the three dimensions of social capital ensures the correct functioning of public policy and provides

Table 4.2 Comparing social capital measurements

Pos.	Authors	Score	Pos1.	Pos2.	Difference	B & VS	Score
1	NL East Netherlands	1.00	1	1	0	NL East Netherlands	100
2	NL North Netherlands	0.96	2	3	-1	NL West Netherlands	90.71
3	NL West Netherlands	0.91	3	17	-14	GB E. Mids	63.79
4	NL South Netherlands	0.84	4	8	-4	BE Vlaams Gewest	61.20
5	GB North East	0.25	5	2	3	NL North Netherlands	60.04
6	GB Eastern	0.23	6	16	-10	GB South East	55.32
7	DE Rheinland-Pfalz	0.23	7	40	-33	DE Baden-Württemberg	52.02
8	BE Vlaams Gewest	0.21	8	14	-6	GB South West	51.74
9	BE Brussels	0.13	9	7	2	DE Rheinland-Pfalz	49.01
10	GB Scotland	0.12	10	33	-23	ES Noreste	48.74
11	DE Niedersachsen	0.12	11	4	7	NL South Netherlands	46.64
12	GB North West	0.05	12	9	3	BE Brussels	44.76
13	GB Yorks & Humbs	0.02	13	11	2	DE Niedersachsen	43.49
14	GB South West	-0.01	14	22	-8	DE Hessen	42.04
15	GB Wales	-0.02	15	6	9	GB Eastern	41.91
16	GB South East	-0.05	16	20	-4	IT Nord Est	41.75
17	GB E. Mids	-0.07	17	18	-1	DE Nordrhein-Westfalen	41.47
18	DE Nordrhein-Westfalen	-0.11	18	31	-13	DE Berlin	41.46
19	FR Ile de France	-0.12	19	37	-18	DE Bayern	40.15
20	IT Nord Est	-0.13	20	13	7	GB Yorks & Humbs	38.72
21	FR Ouest	-0.16	21	5	16	GB North East	37.92
22	DE Hessen	-0.16	22	10	12	GB Scotland	37.60
23	FR Méditerranée	-0.19	23	27	-4	FR Centre Est	37.25
24	GB W. Mids	-0.25	24	44	-20	IT Sud	36.49
25	FR Sud ouest	-0.27	25	35	-10	BE Region Wallone	36.09

Pos	Region	B & VS	Pos2	Pos1	Difference	Region	Score
26	FR Est	-0.27	26	19	7	FR Ile de France	35.56
27	FR Centre Est	-0.30	27	46	-19	IT Isole	34.22
28	ES Comunidad Madrid	-0.31	28	21	7	FR Ouest	33.51
29	FR Bassin Parisien	-0.34	29	30	-1	FR Nord	33.22
30	FR Nord	-0.36	30	15	15	GB Wales	33.18
31	DE Berlin	-0.37	31	42	-11	IT Nord-Ovest	27.40
32	ES Sur	-0.38	32	39	-7	IT Centro	26.95
33	ES Noreste	-0.42	33	25	8	FR Sud ouest	26.61
34	ES Centro	-0.44	34	24	10	GB W. Mids	26.58
35	BE Region Wallone	-0.45	35	43	-8	ES Canarias	23.71
36	ES Noroeste	-0.48	36	26	10	FR Est	21.83
37	DE Bayern	-0.49	37	41	-4	IT Lombardia	21.11
38	ES Este	-0.55	38	29	9	FR Bassin Parisien	17.26
39	IT Centro	-0.57	39	34	5	ES Centro	16.46
40	DE Baden-Württemberg	-0.63	40	23	17	FR Méditerranée	16.36
41	IT Lombardia	-0.69	41	45	-4	IT Lazio	15.72
42	IT Nord-Ovest	-0.79	42	28	14	ES Comunidad Madrid	14.80
43	ES Canarias	-0.81	43	38	5	ES Este	14.50
44	IT Sud	-0.91	44	32	12	ES Sur	12.70
45	IT Lazio	-1.04	45	36	9	ES Noroeste	10.92
46	IT Isole	-1.07	46	12	34	GB North West	6.56

Notes:
B & VS: Beugelsdijk and Van Schaik Social Capital score.
Pos.:   position.
Pos1.:   author's ranking.
Pos2.:   Beugelsdijk and Van Schaik's ranking.
Difference: difference between author's and Beugelsdijk and Van Schaik's ranking.

Source: Author's elaboration and Beugelsdijk and Van Schaik (2005: 1059).

Table 4.3 Regional categories

Ranking	Regions	SC	For.	Inf.	ST	Type	Notes
1	SE Gotaland	1.39	2.08	0.79	1.30	Synergic	Pure
2	SE Svealand and Stockholm	1.28	1.76	0.58	1.50	Synergic	Pure
3	SE Norrland	1.27	2.20	0.51	1.11	Synergic	Pure
4	DK Hovenstansomradet	1.15	1.22	0.01	2.21	Synergic	Close to 2
5	DK Jylland	1.03	1.25	0.02	1.82	Synergic	Close to 2
6	NL East Netherlands	1.00	1.84	0.10	1.05	Synergic	Close to 2
8	DK Fyn (Syddanmark)	0.91	1.20	0.04	1.51	Synergic	Close to 2
10	NL South Netherlands	0.84	1.52	0.26	0.74	Synergic	Close to 2
13	FI West Finland (Lansi)	0.77	0.97	0.29	1.03	Synergic	Pure
19	LX Luxembourg	0.44	0.60	0.20	0.53	Synergic	Pure/Low
24	DE Rheinland-Pfalz	0.23	0.29	0.09	0.30	Synergic	Pure/Low
7	NL North Netherlands	0.96	2.09	-0.13	0.93	Nordic	Pure
9	NL West Netherlands	0.91	1.50	-0.01	1.24	Nordic	Pure
11	DK Sjaelland	0.81	0.99	-0.22	1.67	Nordic	Pure
12	FI North Finland (Pohjois)	0.80	1.35	-0.03	1.09	Nordic	Pure
15	FI South Finland (Etela)	0.61	0.96	-0.17	1.02	Nordic	Pure
20	AT West-Osterrich	0.38	0.81	-0.13	0.46	Nordic	Pure/Low
21	FI East Finland (Ita)	0.38	1.10	-0.67	0.70	Nordic	Pure
25	BE Vlaams Gewest	0.21	0.91	-0.74	0.45	Nordic	Pure
27	BE Brussels	0.13	0.23	-0.11	0.28	Nordic	Pure/Low
29	DE Niedersachsen	0.12	0.43	-0.50	0.42	Nordic	Pure
31	AT Ost-Osterrich	0.05	0.46	-0.74	0.42	Nordic	Pure
42	AT Sud-Osterrich	-0.11	0.29	-0.75	0.13	Nordic	Pure/Low
46	DE Hessen	-0.16	0.08	-1.04	0.47	Nordic	Close to 5
47	AT Wien	-0.17	0.07	-0.83	0.26	Nordic	Close to 5
14	IE Munster	0.61	0.68	1.56	-0.41	Network Based	Pure

16	IE Dublin	0.56	0.57	1.31	-0.21	Network Based	Pure
17	IE Rest of Leinster	0.55	0.65	1.11	-0.12	Network Based	Pure
18	IE Connaught/Ulster	0.48	0.23	1.57	-0.38	Network Based	Pure
23	UK Eastern	0.23	0.54	0.65	-0.49	Network Based	Pure
26	UK Northern Ireland	0.18	0.14	0.71	-0.32	Network Based	Close to 4
28	UK Scotland	0.12	0.01	0.64	-0.28	Network Based	Close to 4
36	UK South West	-0.01	0.05	0.54	-0.61	Network Based	Close to 4
37	UK Wales	-0.02	0.02	0.66	-0.74	Network Based	Close to 4
38	UK South East	-0.05	0.01	0.41	-0.57	Network Based	Close to 4
30	GR Voreia Ellada	0.10	-1.33	1.71	-0.08	Informally Jointed	Pure
32	UK North West	0.05	-0.22	1.01	-0.65	Informally Jointed	Pure
34	UK Yorks & Humbs	0.02	-0.42	0.91	-0.43	Informally Jointed	Pure
35	GR Kentriki Ellada	0.00	-0.80	1.08	-0.27	Informally Jointed	Pure
39	UK E. Mids	-0.07	-0.29	0.69	-0.62	Informally Jointed	Pure
40	GR Nisia aigaiou, Kriti	-0.07	-0.59	1.68	-1.31	Informally Jointed	Pure
48	GR Attiki	-0.17	-1.15	1.02	-0.38	Informally Jointed	Pure
49	FR Méditerranée	-0.19	-0.18	0.08	-0.48	Informally Jointed	Close to 7
51	UK W. Mids	-0.25	-0.27	0.39	-0.86	Informally Jointed	Pure
55	PT Lisboa and Vale do Tejo	-0.31	-1.42	1.18	-0.69	Informally Jointed	Pure
61	ES Sur	-0.38	-0.95	0.19	-0.39	Informally Jointed	Pure/Low
62	ES Noreste	-0.42	-0.80	0.03	-0.48	Informally Jointed	Close to 7
63	ES Centro	-0.44	-1.66	0.49	-0.14	Informally Jointed	Pure/Low
65	ES Noroeste	-0.48	-1.33	0.38	-0.49	Informally Jointed	Pure
71	PT Alentejo and Algarve	-0.63	-1.79	0.78	-0.89	Informally Jointed	Pure
33	DE Sachsen	0.02	-0.21	-0.28	0.55	Trust Based	Pure
41	DE Nordrhein-Westfalen	-0.11	-0.09	-0.39	0.16	Trust Based	Pure
43	FR Ile de France	-0.12	-0.18	-0.35	0.17	Trust Based	Pure
56	ES Comunidad Madrid	-0.31	-1.00	-0.22	0.28	Trust Based	Pure
57	DE Sachsen-Anhalt	-0.31	-0.19	-1.26	0.51	Trust Based	Pure

Table 4.3 (continued)

Ranking	Regions	SC	For.	Inf.	ST	Type	Notes
60	DE Berlin	-0.37	-0.42	-1.14	0.44	Trust Based	Pure
74	DE Brandenburg	-0.76	-1.23	-1.21	0.17	Trust Based	Pure
44	IT Nord Est	-0.13	0.37	-0.24	-0.52	Formally Jointed	Pure
59	FR Nord	-0.36	0.34	-0.87	-0.53	Formally Jointed	Pure
45	FR Ouest	-0.16	-0.13	-0.11	-0.22	Disjointed	Pure/High
50	UK London	-0.19	-0.05	-0.13	-0.40	Disjointed	Close to 6
52	FR Sud ouest	-0.27	-0.43	-0.11	-0.28	Disjointed	Close to 4
53	FR Est	-0.27	-0.04	-0.38	-0.41	Disjointed	Close to 6
54	FR Centre Est	-0.30	-0.08	-0.43	-0.40	Disjointed	Close to 6
58	FR Bassin Parisien	-0.34	-0.16	-0.47	-0.40	Disjointed	Close to 6
64	BE Region Wallone	-0.45	-0.26	-0.90	-0.19	Disjointed	Pure/High
66	DE Bayern	-0.49	-0.14	-1.13	-0.19	Disjointed	Pure/High
67	ES Este	-0.55	-1.49	-0.02	-0.14	Disjointed	Close to 4
68	IT Centro	-0.57	-0.32	-0.93	-0.47	Disjointed	Pure
69	DE Thüringen	-0.58	-0.37	-1.18	-0.18	Disjointed	Close to 5
70	DE Baden-Württemberg	-0.63	-0.60	-0.99	-0.29	Disjointed	Pure/High
72	IT Lombardia	-0.69	-0.75	-0.34	-0.98	Disjointed	Pure
73	PT North	-0.74	-1.43	-0.14	-0.65	Disjointed	Close to 4
75	PT Center	-0.76	-1.39	-0.03	-0.86	Disjointed	Close to 4
76	IT Nord-Ovest	-0.79	-0.67	-0.70	-0.99	Disjointed	Pure
77	DE Mecklenburg-Vorpommern	-0.80	-0.76	-1.57	-0.08	Disjointed	Close to 5
78	ES Canarias	-0.81	-1.33	-0.76	-0.35	Disjointed	Pure
79	IT Sud	-0.91	-1.07	-0.73	-0.93	Disjointed	Pure
80	IT Lazio	-1.04	-1.32	-1.03	-0.76	Disjointed	Pure
81	IT Isole	-1.07	-0.95	-1.07	-1.20	Disjointed	Pure

Groups	Legend		Regions N.
PPP (1)	1	Synergic	11
PMP (2)	2	Nordic	14
PPM (3)	3	Network Based	10
MPM (4)	4	Informally Jointed	15
MMP (5)	5	Trust Based	7
PMM (6)	6	Formally Jointed	2
MMM (7)	7	Disjointed	21

Notes:
SC: Social capital score.
For.: Formal social networks score.
Inf.: Informal social networks score.
ST: Social trust score.

Source: Author's elaboration, after EVS (1999–2000) and Eurobarometer (2005, 2006).

an ideal framework for citizens to participate and contribute in the development of civic and social life. The group is not completely homogeneous. It is possible to recognize three different sub-categories: the pure synergic, the hybrid and the low score synergic regions. There are five pure synergic regions: Gotaland, Svealand, Norrland, West Finland and South Netherlands. These regions have high scores in every dimension. There are four hybrid synergic regions, two Danish (Hovenstansmoradet and Jylland) and two Dutch (East and South Netherlands), in which the informal social networks dimension is very close to the average. In the third sub-group there are the low score synergic regions. These are the only non-North European regions to be included in this cluster (Luxembourg and Rheinland-Pfalz).

The Nordic cluster includes Dutch, Belgian, Finnish, Danish, German and Austrian regions. The difference with the Synergic group is in the below-average score for the informal social networks dimension. In these regions the robust presence of formal associations and generous welfare provisions seems to be accompanied by 'weak strong ties' (Fukuyama 1995; Etzioni 1995). This group is less homogeneous than the Synergic cluster. The region with the highest social capital score in this group, the North Netherlands, occupies the seventh position in the final ranking, while the last region included, Wien, occupies the 47th position. Three different sub-categories are also recognizable in this group: the pure Nordic, the hybrid and the low score Nordic regions.

The large majority of the regions in this cluster can be considered purely Nordic (9 out of 13). West Netherlands, Sjaelland, North, South and East Finland have similar scores in each dimension: they rank in the first quartile for formal social networks and social trust dimensions and in the third quartile for the formal social networks dimension. Flanders also belongs to this sub-category but with a lower score for informal social networks and social trust dimensions. To complete this sub-group, Niedersachsen and Ost-Osterreich share similar characteristics and can be considered pure Nordic with low intensity. There are only two hybrid Nordic regions: Hessen and Wien. These two regions have low scores for the formal networks dimension and they are similar to the regions in the Trust Based cluster (discussed below). Finally, in the third sub-group, the low score Nordic group includes West Osterreich, South Osterreich and Brussels.

The Network Based group includes all Irish and six British regions. These regions share a geographical proximity and a similar residual social security system. The residual nature of the welfare state constitutes an incentive to build safety nets and reduce the general and institutional trust. The network based group is quite homogeneous: there are only 24 positions between the first region of the group (Munster), which ranked in

14th position, and the last one (the South East of England) which occupies the 38th position. In this case there are only two sub-groups: the pure Network Based and the hybrid Network Based regions.

The pure Network Based regions are: Munster, Dublin, Rest of Leinster, Connaught/Ulster and Eastern England. The four Irish regions share similar characteristics, and rank in the first quartile of social capital distribution, in the first quartile for informal social networks, in the third for social trust, Munster and Rest of Leinster in the first quartile for formal social networks and Dublin and Connaught/Ulster in the second. The high scores for the informal social networks dimension are in line with the Catholic tradition. The analysis confirms also the popular stereotype of Irish people attached to their family and their friends but with little willingness to trust unknown people and institutions.

The remaining five British regions are hybrid Network Based regions. This sub-group includes: Northern Ireland, Scotland, South West, Wales and South East. All British regions which have a particular national character and a strong administrative autonomy (Wales, Scotland and Northern Ireland) are part of this sub-group. These regions are similar to the Informally Jointed regions (discussed above), that includes the other four British regions (with the exception of London). Scotland, Wales and to a lesser extent Northern Ireland are in the middle, between Irish and English regional characteristics. The long history of conflicts and control from the central English authority affected the factors previously highlighted, that is, geographical proximity and the residual nature of the welfare system, shaping a group of regions in which informal social networks are very important and a lower level of trust exists compared to other Northern European regions.

The Informally Jointed group includes Mediterranean and British regions. The presence of eleven Mediterranean (Greek, Spanish, Portuguese and French) regions calls to mind the amoral familism hypothesis formulated by Banfield (1958). According to him, informal social networks (in particular the relation with the immediate family) are so strong that they destroy all forms of formal associations and trust in institutions (for an empirical test of the amoral familism hypothesis see Ferragina 2011).

Social capital scores are predominantly below the European average. Only three regions have positive values: Voreia Ellada, North West of England and Yorkshire and Humberside. This group is highly heterogeneous, including regions between the 30th and 71st positions in the social capital ranking. There are three sub-groups: pure Informally Jointed, hybrid and low score Informally Jointed regions.

The large majority belongs to the first sub-group (11 regions): Voreia Ellada, North West of England, Yorkshire and Humberside, Kentriki

Ellada, E. Mids, Nisia Aigaou/Kriti, Attiki, W. Mids, Lisboa and Vale do Tejo, Noroeste and Alentejo/Algarve. Greek regions share similar characteristics: they occupy the last part of the second and the first part of the third quartile[9] in the final social capital index; they have low values for membership and participation in associations; they are ranked in the first ten positions for the informal social networks dimension;[10] and they are in the third quartile for social trust.[11] The remaining regions in this sub-group (four British regions, Lisboa and Vale do Tejo, Noroeste and Alentejo/Algarve) are similar to Greek regions. However, they have a weaker density of formal and informal social networks. There are only two hybrid Informally Jointed regions: Méditerranée and the Noreste of Spain. These two regions have similar formal networks and social trust dimension scores, but have a lower density of informal networks. For these reasons they are similar to the Disjointed group (described below). The last sub-group, the low score Informally Jointed regions, includes two Spanish regions. These regions have lower scores than the rest of the group in all three dimensions.

There are only seven Trust Based regions: five German regions (Sachsen, Nordrhein-Westfalen, Sachsen-Anhalt, Berlin, and Brandeburg) and two big cities (Paris and Madrid). With the exception of Sachsen (second quartile) and Brandeburg (last quartile) they occupy the third quartile of social capital distribution, constituting a homogeneous group.

Four out of five German länder in this category were part of East Germany: Sachsen, Sachsen-anhalt, Berlin and Brandeburg. If we consider the other two eastern länder (Thuringen and Mecklenburg-Vorpommern), which are part of the Disjointed cluster but with scores very close to the Network Based regions, it is possible to draw some conclusions. Where the state is too oppressive, according to Tocqueville's comparative studies of the United States and France, formal and informal social networks are progressively destroyed. In a state where relationships were mainly vertical and the state never supported the development of synergies with horizontal networks, the result has been the progressive destruction of associationism. Social cohesion went unrealized under the communist period, and the excessive emphasis on collective values and lack of choice and opportunity to cultivate weak private ties had a baleful effect on social networks (Völker and Flap 2001).

The analysis of the eastern German ties during the communist period reveals that networks were small and dense. There were only strong ties with people who somebody could really trust. All weak ties were dangerous; nobody would talk of politics in front of somebody unknown (everybody feared the presence of spies). Thus, weak ties were a potential liability (Völker and Flap 2001). After the end of the regime, the situation did not change suddenly, because people were disorientated, unable to see the utility of weak ties and suspicious of associations.[12] In addition, the utility and density of strong ties decreased after communism; there was no longer a need for a strong separate private sphere. The only feeling of cohesion in society was supported by the presence of the state: the idea that institutions would have provided a job and a house. This explains the presence of a high level of social trust in a disjointed context where formal and informal networks are weak.

This group is completed by the presence of two big urban areas: Ile de France and Comunidad de Madrid, which present similar characteristics to the German länder, but have also some peculiarity. In particular, Ile de France has a score close to zero for formal social networks, carrying some characteristics of the Nordic model; on the other hand, Comunidad de Madrid has a lower level of formal networks but more informal ties, carrying some characteristics of the Informally Jointed regions.

Only two regions are part of the Formally Jointed group: North East of Italy and Nord of France. Here, social cohesion is based on the existence of formal ties. The North East peculiarities have been described by Bagnasco (1977) with the concept of *Terza Italia*.[13] Bagnasco's work opened a germane debate, demonstrating that it was too simplistic to describe Italy as a dual country (consisting of an industrialized North West and a poor and agricultural South). There was also a third Italy in which the high density of weak ties between small companies operating in the same industry dealt with a growing demand for Italian handcraft products. In a system of free market, where the state was unable to provide adequate support, the existence of these ties helped small companies to shoulder big risks and expand their market share.

The Nord of France has similar scores for formal social networks and social trust dimensions but a lower level of informal social networks. The history of this region is remarkably different from the North East of Italy. The heritage of the nineteenth century was marked by a great industrial agglomeration, which slowed down the integration of this region with the rest of Europe. The main city of the area, Lille, has a difficult challenge to face, namely to reverse the decline of an industrial area and to transform the region into a service-provider connected to Paris and Brussels (Giblin-Delvallet 2004). The presence of good participation in associations shows that the importance of weak ties is growing; however the situation remains negative for the other social capital dimensions.

The Disjointed group includes Italian, French, German, Portuguese, Spanish, Belgian and British regions. This is the most heterogeneous category, including 21 regions below the European average. This category can be divided in five sub-groups with distinctive characteristics: the purely disjointed, the high score purely disjointed and three types of hybrid regions. The purely disjointed sub-group includes eight regions: six Italian and two Spanish. As already discussed in the previous section, Italy is a disjointed society. The regional analysis shows that the low social capital score is not only a Southern problem.

The second sub-group includes four high scoring purely disjointed regions: Ouest of France, the Region Wallone, Bayern and Baden-Württemberg. The Ouest of France's social capital score is close to the European average (45th position). The Region Wallone has a low score for informal social networks[14] but has the highest scores, in this category, for formal social networks and social trust dimensions.[15] Bayern and Baden-Württemberg are similar to the Region Wallone, but with lower scores for informal and formal social networks.[16]

The other three sub-groups are hybrid regions: the hybrid with the Formally Jointed, the hybrid with the Trust Based and the hybrid with the Informally Jointed.

(1) Greater London and three French regions (Est, Center Est and Bassin Parisien) share similar characteristics with the Formally Jointed regions. They have a comparable endowment of formal social networks, identical values of social trust, but lower scores for informal networks dimension. (2) Two German länder, Thuringen and Mecklenburg-Vorpommern are very similar to the Trust Based regions but with a lower level of social trust. (3) The third sub-group includes only 'Mediterranean/Southern' regions (Sud Ouest of France, Este of Spain and finally the North and the Centre of Portugal). They have values close to the European average for informal networks, weaker formal ties and lower social trust.

To conclude, only in four cases are all regions classified in the same cluster as their country, namely Austria, Greece, Ireland and Sweden (Table 4.4). The homogeneity of Greece, Ireland, and Sweden is not surprising. In these countries regions have only a marginal role and they have been created to respond to European regulations. The Austrian case is very different. This nation has länder with much autonomy, however the regions analysed have similar scores in the three social capital dimensions. This can be explained by the homogeneity of the Austrian population.[17]

In the other cases many regions belong to different groups (Table 4.4). In Denmark and the Netherlands the discrepancy can be explained by the fact that both nations are on the edge of the Synergic and the Nordic models, therefore their regions are equally divided into these two groups.[18] In Belgium the characteristics of Wallonia clearly diverge from those of Brussels and Flanders. This cleavage will be discussed in detail in the third

Table 4.4   Comparing national and regional classifications

Nation	Category	Region	Category	Same/ Different Classification
		Similar		
Austria	Nordic	AT Ost-Osterrich	Nordic	Same
		AT Sud-Osterrich	Nordic	Same
		AT West Oster.	Nordic	Same
		AT Wien	Nordic	Same
Greece	Informally Jointed	GR Voreia Ellada	Informally Jointed	Same
		GR Kentriki Ell.	Informally Jointed	Same
		GR Attiki	Informally Jointed	Same
		GR Nisia aigaiou	Informally Jointed	Same
Ireland	Network Based	IE Connaught	Network Based	Same
		IE Dublin	Network Based	Same
		IE Munster	Network Based	Same
		IE R. of Leinster	Network Based	Same
Sweden	Synergic	SE Gotaland	Synergic	Same
		SE Svealand	Synergic	Same
		SE Norrland	Synergic	Same
		Dissimilar		
Belgium	Nordic	BE Brussels	Nordic	Same
		BE Vlaams Gew.	Nordic	Same
		BE Wallonia	Disjointed	Different
Denmark	Nordic	DK Hovenstanso.	Synergic	Different
		DK Sjaelland	Nordic	Same
		DK Fyn	Synergic	Different
		DK Jylland	Synergic	Different
Finland	Nordic	FI East Finland	Nordic	Same
		FI South Finland	Nordic	Same
		FI West Finland	Synergic	Different
		FI North Finland	Nordic	Same
France	Disjointed	FR BassinParisi	Disjointed	Same
		FR Centre Est	Disjointed	Same
		FR Est	Disjointed	Same
		FR Ile de France	Trust Based	Different
		FR Méditerranée	Informally Jointed	Different
		FR Nord	Formally Jointed	Different
		FR Ouest	Disjointed	Same
		FR Sud ouest	Disjointed	Same
Germany	Disjointed	DE Baden-Wü.	Disjointed	Same
		DE Bayern	Disjointed	Same
		DE Berlin	Trust Based	Different
		DE Brandenburg	Trust Based	Different

Table 4.4   (continued)

Nation	Category	Region	Category	Same/ Different Classification
		Dissimilar		
Germany	Disjointed	DE Bremen	Non classified	–
		DE Hamburg	Non classified	–
		DE Hessen	Nordic	Different
		DE Mecklenburg	Disjointed	Same
		DE Niedersach.	Nordic	Different
		DE Nordrhein-W.	Trust Based	Different
		DE Rheinland-Pf.	Synergic	Different
		DE Saarland	Non classified	–
		DE Sachsen	Trust Based	Different
		DE Sachsen-Anh.	Trust Based	Different
		DE Schleswig-H.	Non classified	–
		DE Thüringen	Disjointed	Same
Italy	Disjointed	IT Nord-Ovest	Disjointed	Same
		IT Lombardia	Formally Jointed	Different
		IT Nord Est	Disjointed	Same
		IT Centro	Disjointed	Same
		IT Lazio	Disjointed	Same
		IT Sud	Disjointed	Same
		IT Isole	Disjointed	Same
Netherlands	Synergic	NL North Neth.	Nordic	Different
		NL East Neth.	Synergic	Same
		NL West Neth.	Nordic	Different
		NL South Neth.	Synergic	Same
Portugal	Informally Jointed	PT North	Disjointed	Different
		PT Center	Disjointed	Different
		PT Lisboa	Informally Jointed	Same
		PT Alentejo	Informally Jointed	Same
Spain	Informally Jointed	ES Noroeste	Informally Jointed	Same
		ES Noreste	Informally Jointed	Same
		ES Madrid	Trust Based	Different
		ES Centro	Informally Jointed	Same
		ES Este	Disjointed	Different
		ES Sur	Informally Jointed	Same
		ES Canarias	Disjointed	Different
United Kingd.	Informally Jointed	UK E.Mids	Informally Jointed	Same
		UK Eastern	Network Based	Different
		UK London	Disjointed	Different
		UK North East	Non classified	–
		UK North West	Informally Jointed	Same
		UK Scotland	Network Based	Different
		UK South East	Network Based	Different

Table 4.4   (continued)

Nation	Category	Region	Category	Same/ Different Classification
		Dissimilar		
United Kingd.	Informally Jointed	UK South West	Network Based	Different
		UK W. Mids	Informally Jointed	Same
		UK Wales	Network Based	Different
		UK Yorks & Hu.	Informally Jointed	Same
		UK Northern Ir.	Network Based	Different

Source: Author's elaboration

part of the book, because Wallonia is one of our two divergent cases. Similarly to Belgium and Italy, only the North East deviates from the national pattern. This finding seems to contradict Putnam's theory and will be discussed in more detail in Chapters 7 and 8.[19]

In Madrid, Paris, and Lisbon and other regions with a peculiar historical development (Méditerranée, North of France, Canarias, North and Centre of Portugal) we find different characteristics from the rest of the country. Germany and the United Kingdom are the most diverse nations; eight and seven regions respectively are classified differently from the rest of the country. In Germany the national measurement does not account for the difference between eastern Germany and other länder such as Rheinland-Pfalz and Sachsen. In the United Kingdom, the regional analysis demonstrates how Scotland, Northern Ireland, Wales, and also the North diverge substantially from the national categorization.

4.3   SUMMARY

The theoretical foundations of the aggregate measurement of social capital have been discussed referring to the seminal contribution of the American and Manchester schools. Subsequently the regional measurement has been introduced by the cross-national analysis, to illustrate the consistency of the national scores with the previous literature and identify where the regional classification diverges from the national one. Only four countries, namely Austria, Greece, Ireland and Sweden have a coherent classification at the national and the regional level, in the remaining European countries one or more regions differ from the rest of the country (Germany and the United Kingdom are the most diverse countries). This finding underlines the importance of the cross regional analysis, supporting the historical, institutional and empirical arguments elaborated in the previous chapter.

The next chapter focuses on the theoretical discussion of the potential macro-social determinants of social capital. In this respect, we apply pure deductive logic, discussing the connection between these macro-variables and social capital at the theoretical level before embarking on the empirical analysis (Sartori 1970).

NOTES

1. They used network analysis to shed light on social stratification, social class, social mobility, and genesis of conflicts, and to reconstruct the relationship between family and external environments.
2. 'I find it convenient to talk of a social field of this kind as a network. The image I have is of a set of points some of which are joined by lines. The points of the image are people, or sometimes groups, and the lines indicate which people interact to each other' (Barnes 1954b: 43).
3. The Swedish case speaks against the theoretical argument that an extensive welfare state crowds out social capital (Putnam 1995; Etzioni 1995; Fukuyama 2000; Uslaner 2000–2001). In particular informal social networks are not reduced by a high involvement of the state in social care, as suggested by Van Oorschot and Art (2005). Tamilina (2008) argued that this discussion has been misinterpreted for the use of welfare expenditure indicators to measure welfare generosity. This simplistic choice has reduced the possibility to consider the mixed effect of different welfare programmes on social capital, and it has not allowed targeting particular segments of the population. Her results demonstrate that different welfare programs have different impacts on assorted segments of the population. However, the issue remains controversial because Tamilina's social capital measurement includes only social trust dimension.
4. All data discussed in this section refer to Table 4.1.
5. Denmark ranks in ninth position for this dimension.
6. Due to this concentration of observations in Athens, the regional measurement for Greece has been performed using only the Eurobarometer dataset (2005; 2006).
7. The comparison between Beugelsdijk and Van Schaik's and our measurement is not straightforward because of some methodological difference: the use of a larger number of regions; the inclusion of larger number of variables to capture more accurately social capital; the creation of a different scale for the ranking; the equal weight attributed to each item in the new measurement rather than the use of factor analysis. These differences allow us to compare only 46 regions, that is, German, French, British, Spanish, Belgian and Dutch regions (Table 4.2). The new indicator identifies a lower social capital in the German regions and higher scores in French, British and Spanish regions. The other comparable regions, that is, Belgium and Dutch regions have similar rankings in both measurements.
8. All data discussed in this section refer to Table 4.3.
9. With the exception of Nisia Aigaiou/Kriti.
10. Voreia Ellada and Nisia Aigaiou/Kriti have the highest values in Europe.
11. With the exception of Nisia Aigaiou/Kriti which is in the fourth quartile.
12. 'Former German Democratic Republic citizens nowadays suspect and eschew all organized life since all state sponsored associations have collapsed' (Völker and Flap 2001: 424).
13. *The Third Italy*.
14. Very similar score to the Nord of France (neighbour region).

15. The difference between this area and the rest of the country is the object of an in-depth analysis in the rest of the work (Chapters 7 and 8).
16. Also in this case the geographical proximity between the two länder seems to play an important role.
17. With reference to culture (mainly language) and religion (Catholicism).
18. A similar situation is detected also in Finland with a region that belongs to the Synergic rather than the Nordic group.
19. It will be shown that although Northern and Central regions have more social capital than Southern regions, this difference is quite small if analysed from a European perspective.

5. The determinants of social capital

After measuring social capital across European regions, this chapter illustrates the theoretical arguments that support the choice of income inequality, labour market participation, national divergence, and economic development[1] as explanatory variables of social capital variation over other predictors (Table 5.1).

Previous theoretical (see Tocqueville 1961; Gorz 1992; Putnam 1993) and quantitative work (Knack and Keefer 1997; Costa and Kahn 2003; O'Connel 2003) indicates that these predictors constitute an adequate deductive framework and should explain a lot about social capital variation.

Income inequality was considered by Tocqueville to be the main explanation for the high level of social participation and trust in the United States (Tocqueville 1961: 8). Furthermore, at the empirical level, many scholars (Knack and Keefer 1997; O'Connel 2003; Paxton 1999; Costa and Kahn 2003) showed the existence of a negative correlation between income inequality and social capital.

Labour market participation captures the existence of a potential relationship between work involvement and willingness to participate in voluntary associations, to network with family and friends and to trust others and institutions (Gorz 1992). Also the correlation between social capital and labour market participation has been investigated at the empirical level. However, much attention has been devoted to the analysis of the impact that social capital has on the access to the labour market (De Graaf and Flap 1988; Granovetter 1973; Fernandez et al. 2000; Munshi 2003), rather than exploring the potential effect that a variation of labour market activity may have on social capital.

Regional fragmentation, which we define as the existence of a large social capital variation among the regions of the same country, might also impact on social capital. As illustrated in Chapter 3, this work attempts to shed light on the analysis of social capital variation by taking into account a regional perspective to complement the seminal works developed at the cross-national level (Knack and Keefer 1997; Van Oorschot and Arts 2005). In this vein, the national divergence index verifies whether in more homogeneous countries regions display higher social capital scores.

Table 5.1 Independent variables (regional cases)

	Gini Coefficient (2000)	GDP Per Capita Euro (2005)	Density (2005)	Activity Rates% (2005)	National Divergence %
1 AT Ost-Osterrich	0.27	22,599.77	80.12	58.4	0.21
2 AT Sud-Osterrich	0.25	24,788.72	67.88	57.3	0.21
3 AT West-Osterrich	0.26	29,136.30	86.01	61.8	0.21
4 AT Wien	M	39,773.80	3,949.16	58.1	0.21
5 BE Brussels	0.28	53,875.90	6,251.85	53.9	0.28
6 BE VlaamsGewest	0.28	26,903.19	448.27	54.4	0.28
7 BE RegionWallone	0.28	19,577.17	202.14	51.1	0.28
8 DE Baden-Württemberg	0.25	28,841.55	300.41	61.4	0.26
9 DE Bayern	0.28	30,390.25	176.90	61.3	0.26
10 DE Berlin	0.33	22,074.90	3,815.49	60.1	0.26
11 DE Brandenburg	0.24	17,800.60	86.72	61	0.26
12 DE Bremen	0.33	35,183.90	1,642.82	54.9	M
13 DE Hamburg	0.31	45,271.30	2,331.87	59.9	M
14 DE Hessen	0.30	31,250.83	288.33	58.9	0.26
15 DE Mecklenburg-Vorpommern	0.24	17,546.90	73.39	61.4	0.26
16 DE Niedersachsen	0.28	22,701.28	167.76	56.9	0.26
17 DE Nordrhein-Westfalen	0.28	25,597.57	529.44	56.1	0.26
18 DE Rheinland-Pfalz	0.25	23,243.28	204.36	58.1	0.26
19 DE Saarland	0.25	24,698.20	407.28	53.9	M
20 DE Sachsen	0.23	18,866.21	232.40	58.9	0.26
21 DE Sachsen-Anhalt	0.23	18,441.00	120.11	59.3	0.26
22 DE Schleswig-Holstein	0.29	22,983.20	179.61	59.2	M
23 DE Thüringen	0.22	18,010.10	139.34	61.4	0.26
24 DK Hovenstansomradet (Copenhagen area)	0.24	36,073.10	638.50	65.6*	0.10

Table 5.1 (continued)

	Gini Coefficient (2000)	GDP Per Capita Euro (2005)	Density (2005)	Activity Rates% (2005)	National Divergence %
25 DK Sjaelland, Lolland-Falster, Bornhom (excl. Hovenstadomradet)	0.21	21,265.20	111.89	65.6*	0.10
26 DK Fyn (Syddanmark)	0.21	25,767.50	97.43	65.6*	0.10
27 DK Jylland	0.21	26,299.22	85.44	65.6*	0.10
28 ES Noroeste	0.34	19,662.60	95.13	51.6	0.09
29 ES Noreste	0.31	27,521.85	60.18	56.8	0.09
30 ES Comunidad Madrid	0.33	29,997.20	732.40	61.6	0.09
31 ES Centro	0.34	19,340.05	25.16	52.2	0.09
32 ES Este	0.34	24,946.03	205.63	59.7	0.09
33 ES Sur	0.35	18,284.96	92.86	54	0.09
34 ES Canarias	0.35	20,982.20	259.30	58.5	0.09
35 FI East Finland (Ita)	0.25	19,114.00	13.65	54.5	0.10
36 FI South Finland (Etela)	0.23	29,823.10	82.08	63.8	0.10
37 FI West Finland (Lansi)	0.24	22,819.80	18.00	58.8	0.10
38 FI North Finland (Pohjois)	0.22	22,209.30	4.25	59.4	0.10
39 FR BassinParisien	0.26	21,911.28	72.79	56.6	0.08
40 FR Centre Est	0.26	23,710.95	104.92	58.2	0.08
41 FR Est	0.23	21,563.49	110.18	57.6	0.08
42 FR Ile de France	0.29	38,666.10	952.78	61.4	0.08
43 FR Méditerranée	0.29	21,925.11	123.77	50.8	0.08
44 FR Nord	0.28	19,847.40	325.24	55.9	0.08
45 FR Ouest	0.25	22,194.51	96.29	55.4	0.08
46 FR Sud Ouest	0.26	22,271.73	63.31	54.7	0.08

47	UK E. Mids	0.32	24,431.37	276.93	62.8	0.11
48	UK Eastern	0.34	25,450.94	290.84	64.1	0.11
49	UK London	0.39	40,615.07	4,706.32	63	0.11
50	UK North East	0.32	21,597.58	296.13	57.7	M
51	UK North West	0.33	23,335.01	482.74	60.6	0.11
52	UK Scotland	0.34	24,915.44	65.34	62.4	0.11
53	UK South East	0.35	29,123.26	428.19	65	0.11
54	UK South West	0.32	25,012.97	212.13	62.5	0.11
55	UK W. Mids	0.33	23,742.08	411.32	61.1	0.11
56	UK Wales	0.32	20,642.53	142.28	57.7	0.11
57	UK Yorks & Humbs	0.33	23,041.11	327.97	60.9	0.11
58	UK Northern Ireland	0.32	21,726.30	121.84	58.8	0.11
59	GR Voreia Ellada (NorthernGreece)	0.33	16,700.80	62.72	53.2	0.11
60	GR Kentriki Ellada (Central Greece)	0.34	17,431.56	45.64	51.9	0.11
61	GR Attiki	0.30	29,360.70	1,054.94	51.2	0.11
62	GR Nisia aigaiou, Kriti	0.30	18,492.69	63.55	55.2	0.11
63	IT Nord-Ovest	0.29	25,315.84	178.41	49.07	0.22
64	IT Lombardia	0.30	30,566.90	398.57	54.20	0.22
65	IT Nord Est	0.30	27,647.79	172.22	54.31	0.22
66	IT Centro	0.28	26,229.14	161.80	51.18	0.22
67	IT Lazio	0.28	28,660.30	313.77	50.40	0.22
68	IT Sud	0.34	15,584.13	192.22	43.00	0.22
69	IT Isole	0.37	15,807.05	134.03	43.60	0.22
70	LX Luxembourg	0.26	59,201.00	182.75	M	M
71	NL North Netherlands	0.23*	27,917.28	204.07	62.9	0.04
72	NL East Netherlands	0.23*	24,633.91	356.43	65.3	0.04
73	NL West Netherlands	0.23*	32,292.85	881.14	65.7	0.04
74	NL South Netherlands	0.23*	28,435.61	501.61	64	0.04
75	PT North	M	13,399.40	175.75	63.1	0.17

97

Table 5.1 (continued)

	Gini Coefficient (2000)	GDP Per Capita Euro (2005)	Density (2005)	Activity Rates% (2005)	National Divergence %
76 PT Center	M	14,287.30	84.55	66	0.17
77 PT Lisboa and Vale do Tejo	M	23,816.10	949.47	60.3	0.17
78 PT Alentejo	M	16,432.92	29.85	56.9	0.17
79 SE Gotaland (including Malmö and Goteborg)	0.24	25,430.54	50.81	72	0.06
80 SE Svealand and Stockholm	0.26	31,932.37	75.90	70.4	0.06
81 SE Norrland	0.21	24,760.69	5.91	67	0.06
82 IE Connaught/Ulster	M	M	M	62.0*	0.04
83 IE Dublin	0.31	M	M	62.0*	0.04
84 IE Munster	M	M	M	62.0*	0.04
85 IE Rest of Leinster	M	M	M	62.0*	0.04
Average	0.28	24,770.08	426.17	58.55	0.15
Standard deviation	0.05	6202.54	998.22	5.57	0.08

Notes:
M (Missing)
*National value assumed.

Source: Author's elaboration from LIS, EVS (1999–2000); Eurobarometer (2005–2006); Eurostat Regional Statistics (2005).

The relation between economic development and social capital, and also the role of social capital to enhance economic growth and prosperity have doubtlessly been themes that attracted major attention in the literature (see Helliwell and Putnam 1995; Grootaert and Van Bastelar 2002 a and b; Knack 2002; OECD 2001). Two comparative studies of European regions tested whether: (1) economic growth and social capital are positively correlated, and (2) economic development is more important than cultural factors to explain social capital variation (Beugelsdijk and Van Schaik 2005b; Schneider et al. 2000). The results proposed by these studies to discuss Putnam's original hypothesis (1993) are divergent and contradictory. As illustrated in the introduction (Chapter 1), this work does not attempt to address this question, but considers macro social variables and historical and institutional developments as complementary explanations of social capital variation. The chapter concludes with a discussion of the omitted variable problem and illustrates the choice to select few predictors in the empirical model.

5.1 INCOME INEQUALITY AND SOCIAL CAPITAL

The reflection on the relation between income inequality and social capital is articulated in four steps, discussing: (1) the evolution of the idea of inequality in European countries, (2) the public debate on the connection between income inequality and social capital, (3) the determinants of income inequality and its recent increase in Western countries, and (4) the construction of the indicator used to measure income inequality at the regional level.

The principle of equality[2] assumes different forms, that is, equality of treatment, equality of opportunities and equality of conditions (Brown 1991). The creation of modern welfare state systems fostered the application of this theoretical principle in its various forms[3] through the taxation of income, the development of redistributive mechanisms and the provision of public services.

In the 1970s, though, the economic landscape changed, and with it the willingness to redistribute wealth. The construction of a more egalitarian society was progressively seen as an obstacle to growth. There was new tension between the idea of the equality of conditions and the creation of efficient markets being regulated more lightly by the state. The advent of Margaret Thatcher was a decisive turning point; between 1978 and 1990 the Gini coefficient in the United Kingdom increased by 10 points (Atkinson 2003). The idea that competition and growth were irreconcilable with higher welfare expenditure and greater redistribution of wealth became dominant in many European countries.

Social-democratic parties progressively accepted market principles and the idea that competition was necessary to reduce the costs of public administration. In this convergence of ideas, they re-elaborated their long-standing socialist tradition by proposing a new way to look at equality. *The Third Way* by Anthony Giddens (1998) is the intellectual manifesto of this new vision, and the election of Tony Blair is the political expression. In Blair's mind, *The Third Way* was an attempt to simultaneously defend the social-democratic tradition of labour party, the communitarian values progressively eroded by modernization and the necessity of financial capitalism. He merged the principle of equality of opportunity with the social capital concept assuming that this fusion could keep universalism and traditional values together (Rose 2000: 1397).

The redistribution of wealth was not a primary objective anymore; the main goal for New Labour was to foster the principle of equal opportunity, preserving social capital existent in communities and families. The support of these networks was considered essential to reduce public expenditure for social services, helping the state to concentrate its spending power so as to guarantee equal opportunities. The results and the social implications of this shift are contested and the application of the principle of equality of opportunity does not seem more accomplished after Blair's mandates (Bevir 2005: 103–105).

The importance of income equality in the creation of social capital, intended as a reduction of inequality of conditions, remained absent from the political agenda.[4] However, at a moment when inequalities appear to be increasing almost universally in Western Europe (Atkinson 2003) and the virtuous path of growth seems irreversibly interrupted, it seems important to rethink the causal nexus between equality of conditions and the creation of social capital. If the negative correlation between income inequality[5] and social capital (observed by Knack and Keefer 1997; Costa and Kahn 2003; O'Connell 2003) is confirmed by the empirical model, the discussion on the causes of inequality and the role played by public institutions in this respect would assume a pivotal relevance in understanding of social capital variation at the regional level.

Kuznets (1955) initiated the debate on the causes of income inequalities, affirming that the progressive concentration of savings in the hands of the upper income segment of the population and the large movement from rural to urban areas was conducive to further disparity. In the following decades, data became available so that this hypothesis could be tested empirically. Alderson and Nielsen (2002) systematically reviewed[6] and tested the main arguments proposed in the attempt to explain income inequality. They divided the causes into three groups testing the impact of every component and its relative intensity: 1) globalization-related, 2) Kuznet's arguments and institutional factors, and 3) institutional factors.[7] They provided a longitudinal explanation of the causes of inequality, suggesting the percentage of labour force employed in agricultural activities as main factor (confirming Kuznets), followed by globalization related causes.

Atkinson[8] (1999) focused on the institutional contribution to the reduction of inequality and strongly criticized the idea that the parallel rise of inequalities in the US and unemployment in Europe was solely dependent upon a shift of the demand from unskilled to skilled workers and fostered by de-industrialization and globalization (the so called transatlantic consensus). Instead, according to Atkinson, the increase of inequalities in countries like the United States and the United Kingdom was not dependent upon a growing separation between skilled and unskilled workers, because the median worker proportionally loses more income than the unskilled worker relative to high earners (Atkinson 1999: 2). The comparison of different trends of inequalities in the last decades in the United Kingdom, Finland and Canada would suggest that in reality when redistributive policies have been conducted, the increase of inequalities generated from the market is significantly reduced (Atkinson 1999: 13). Atkinson concludes that the rise in inequality is not an inevitable phenomenon resulting from globalization, but is strictly correlated to policy-making choices and the societal attitudes towards redistribution: 'A society which shifts away from redistributive pay norms is likely to shift away from fiscal redistribution. But this is not inevitable, and can be influenced, just as the pay distribution can be influenced, by public policy. National governments are not, on this approach faced with absolute constraints. There is scope for political leadership' (Atkinson 1999: 22). We will come back to this argument in the conclusion (Chapter 9).

The level of income inequality in European regions is measured with the Gini coefficient,[9] the most widely used indicator of inequality in social science.[10] The Gini coefficient used in the empirical model is based on disposable personal income[11] calculated including (see Atkinson et al. 1995: 23; Mahler 2002: 119): private sources of income, that is, wages and salaries; gross self-employment income; realized property income, including interests, rents and property income received on a regular basis; occupational pensions, regular inter-household cash transfers; court-ordered payments, that is, alimony and child support; and income from public benefits programmes, that is, sick pay, disability pay, retirement benefits, child or family allowances, unemployment compensations, maternity pay, war benefits, and means-tested public assistance. The possibility to reliably measure income inequality and relative poverty indices at the regional level with LIS[12] (2000) have been demonstrated by Mahler (2002) and others (Jesuit 2008; Jesuit et al. 2002).

5.2   LABOUR MARKET PARTICIPATION AND SOCIAL CAPITAL

The complex interaction between social capital and the labour market has been discussed in the literature and much evidence has been provided to support the claim that the correct use of social networks is fundamental to find jobs (De Graaf and Flap 1988; Granovetter 1973; Fernandez et al. 2000; Munshi 2003). After these seminal contributions, many authors discussed more specific aspects of the relationship between social capital and the labour market: considering the potential use of social capital to integrate women and disadvantaged groups in the labour market (Brook 2005; Schneider 2005); analysing the effects of social networks on employment and inequality (Calvo-Armengol and Jackson 2004); discussing the relationship between networks of kinships and the labour force participation as represented by employment and hours worked (Aguilera 2002); and showing how certain types of social capital can mitigate the precariousness of the labour market (Sabatini 2008).

In this literature, social capital is often considered an independent variable that can potentially have a positive impact on reducing the costs of transaction by matching supply and demand of labour. This reasoning is reversed in the empirical model, in testing whether or not there is a higher density of social capital in regions where people are more involved in the labour market. The general trend of activity rates in Europe is positive, showing a constant increase in the last ten years.[13] In this environment, the structural reforms that took place in the last years may directly impact on social capital.

Broadly speaking, all measures undertaken to enable social protection systems to become more active and responsive to citizens' needs can be considered under the umbrella of activation policy (Barbier and Ludwig-Mayerhofer 2004). The development of activation policies has been advocated mainly for two reasons: to correct the inefficiencies and address the lack of results that occurred with the distribution of benefits without a reciprocal requirement of active involvement by the recipients, and to foster a new model of social citizenship that should enable members of society and institutions to be more proactive.[14]

Many scholars have discussed the implementation of this policy, focusing on the scope of the programmes and on the potential convergence of

European and American social security models (Gilbert and Van Voorhis 2001; Gilbert 2004; Esping-Andersen et al. 2002; Goul Andersen et al. 2002). Effectively, after the introduction in Denmark and the United States, activation policies were extended to the majority of European countries.

The similarity between the Danish and the American reforms,[15] in the absence of empirical evidence, generated a controversial debate about the transformation of the traditional Scandinavian model. The debate developed between those who believed that activation policy would generate a decline of social citizenship (Torfing 1999) and those who believed that activation policies are in continuity with previous labour market policies designed to foster an active society (Halvorsen and Jensen 2004; Andersen and Svarer 2007). From our perspective, the continuity proposed by the Danish reform is clear and constitutes an interesting case to explore the relation between labour market and social capital.

The idea of consolidating an active society has always been the bottom line in Denmark and other Scandinavian countries (Halvorsen and Jensen 2004: 463). Cultural and religious backgrounds, that is, the protestant ethic together with the constant engagement of the state as 'fellow player' (Halvorsen and Jensen 2004: 464), fostered the importance of being active in the labour market. To achieve individual freedom and maintain generous universal benefits, everybody had to contribute to the system by working and paying taxes.

Policy makers emphasized this ethic, conceiving of labour market policy as an instrument to include all citizens and the weaker groups in society. In particular, women and the elderly have been strongly encouraged to stay in the labour market with specific programmes aimed at balancing family care and work and to postpone retirement. The result is that Denmark has the highest activity rate among European countries: 78.1 per cent in 2008 (Eurostat 2009).

If the word 'activation' is a new term, the idea to create a system of 'flexicurity' is not new in Denmark and other Scandinavian countries (Andersen and Svarer 2007). Flexicurity is a system of labour regulations that entitles, on the one hand, companies to be flexible to hire and dismiss easily, and on the other hand entitles citizens to generous compensations and opportunities for training when this occurs. This two-leg system was already in place during the 1970s, and the activation labour market policy during the 1990s is more a third pillar of this strategy rather than a revolution of the social security system.

Another line of continuity is the emphasis on the local level of implementation. In fact, in the last 30 years, Danish policy makers have tried to develop labour market policy delegating many functions to local

authorities. Long-term unemployed, for example, were hired for municipal jobs for some periods of time, in order to get access to unemployment
benefits and at the same time foster their inclusion in local communities
(Halvorsen and Jensen 2004: 468).

This point relates back to the relationship between labour market participation and social capital. If long-term unemployed are progressively
reintegrated starting from small jobs in local communities, individuals
may have the opportunity to create new social contacts and re-activate
themselves. The central issue, in this regard, is whether activation policy
can really enhance this involvement and increase social capital in particular areas. Gorz (1997) and others (see Van Parijs [1992] for a review)
strongly criticized this perspective. According to them, the conditionality
of the benefits would reduce the spontaneous creation of social capital.[16]

In the context of increased flexibility of labour market demand,
they revived (following previous contributions, namely Russell 1918;
Winstanley 1649; Paine [1796] 1974; Fourier 1836; for a review see Van
Parijs 1992: 9–11) the opposite of activation; the proposition of a universal benefit to enhance equality and match economic efficiency with the
strengthening of social networks and trust in society.

Gorz (1988; 1997) discussed the complex relation between new ways of
looking at the labour market and the possible impact that would impinge
on communities and social capital. He argued that humanity should fight
against the well-established idea that paid work is the main source of
rights. In this perspective, trying to integrate people who are unemployed
or excluded with workfare or activation programs is useless and most
of the time counterproductive, because these programs stigmatize the
unemployed. The unemployed become convinced that the main cause of
their lack of professional success is their attitude and their personality.
Therefore they accept the most menial tasks only to fulfil the obligations
of these programs (Gorz 1999: 81). Gorz advocates, instead, a new political commitment, a universal and non-selective new set of rights for all citizens, so that everybody in society will become able to perform his preferred
activities, without being obliged to accept jobs at any cost just to survive.
In this new framework, a society of flexible time, in which people could
develop many activities at the same time, would progressively substitute
the present 'work-based society', on the basis of 'competitive cooperation'
with others to pursue excellence and improve collective well-being:

> For multi-activity to develop, society will have to organize itself to achieve it
> through a range of specific policies. Social time and space will have to be organ-
> ized to indicate the general expectation that everybody will engage in a range
> of different activities and modes of membership of the society. To indicate
> that the norm is for everyone to belong – or at least to be able to belong – to

a self-providing co-operative, a service exchange network, a scientific research and experiment group, an orchestra or a choir, a drama, dance or painting workshop, a sports club, a yoga or judo group, etc.; and that the aim within the sports or arts 'societies' is not to select, eliminate or rank individuals, but to encourage each member to refresh and surpass him/herself ever anew in competitive cooperation with the others, this pursuit of excellence by each being a goal common to all. This is how the 'cultural-based' society (for which the Western prototype was Athenian society) is distinguished from the work-based society. (Gorz 1999: 78.)

However Gorz's proposal appears too generic and would require the complete dismantling of capitalism. A more pragmatic version of this argument was proposed by a French governmental commission. The *Report Boissonnat* suggested introducing a social basic income, for its potential ability to enhance greater flexibility, without completely reversing the idea that people should work in some way in order to deserve social assistance. The compromise between the need for more social inclusion and freedom for citizens and the needs of companies to run their businesses have to be considered in synergy by the state.

In this sense, Gorz's ideas are modified to fit into a capitalistic system; the establishment of activity contracts could allow people to maintain employment in companies, even when there is a contraction of economic activity and the need for fewer employees (similarly to the Danish flexicurity). The surplus employees, for a certain period of time, could serve the community or other companies: 'When a group of companies has no need of all its employees, it would be able to lend its temporary surplus of labour to "other public or private bodies: local communities, schools, various associations" or put them on "social utility leave (e.g. family leave)" or on training leave' (Commissariat Général du Plan 1995: 30–31). A positive correlation[17] between labour market participation and social capital would constitute an additional justification to reflect on the potential impact of activation policy and the realization of a 'multi-activity society' from a social capital perspective (in this regard see also Chapter 9).

5.3 THE OTHER PREDICTORS AND THE PROBLEM OF THE OMITTED VARIABLES

This section analyses the potential impact of national divergence and economic development on social capital,[18] and investigates the potential omission of some predictors from our empirical model. The national divergence[19] index has already been introduced (Chapter 2) together with the need to conduct a regional analysis (Chapters 3 and 4) and will test whether, in more homogeneous countries, regional scores of social capital are higher. By introducing this variable we hypothesize that the existence of large social capital disparities among regions within the same country will probably affect the social capital score of each region.

The impact of economic modernity on social capital has already been analysed at the cross-national (Knack and Keefer 1997) and the cross-regional level of analysis (Putnam 1993; Beugelsdijk and Van Schaik 2005b; Schneider et al. 2000). Putnam considered economic modernity, measured through the GDP per capita (Putnam 1993: 83–5), the most important socio-economic predictor of social capital variation among Italian regions. However, even though he recognized a strong correlation between this variable and social capital, he suggested that the region's historical development was more important in predicting social capital variation. Beugelsdijk and Van Schaik (2005b) and Schneider et al. (2000) continued this debate, the first confirming Putnam's hypothesis and the second refuting it. The empirical model does not aim to revisit this controversial issue,[20] but simply to test the effect of economic development (measured through the GDP per capita [Eurostat 2005]) on social capital alongside the other socio-economic predictors selected for the empirical analysis.

Many studies have proposed alternative predictors of social capital to those selected in this study, focusing on the individual[21] and aggregate[22] levels of analysis (Table 5.2). On the one hand, the impact of the most commonly used predictors at the individual level, that is, income, education attainment, gender, age, religious confession, has been already tested in Chapter 3, confirming the results of previous literature (Brehm and Rahn 1997; Van Oorschot and Arts 2005); on the other, as previously discussed, the use of aggregate socio-economic predictors is limited to income inequality, labour market participation, national divergence and economic development.[23]

The choice of a restricted number of predictors reflects: (1) the use of a specific theoretical framework (Sartori 1970) based on Tocqueville's (Tocqueville 1961 [1960]), Gorz's (1992) and Putnam's (1993) arguments and the shift from the cross-national to the cross-regional level of analysis (Chapter 3); (2) the presence of a limited number of cases (85 regions); (3) the fact that the regional unit of analysis does not allow us to test the effect of many predictors used at the cross-national level;[24] and (4) the fact that the inclusion of many predictors does not always reduce the risk of omitting relevant variables (Clarke 2005) and might contribute instead to wash out the effect of the variables selected at the theoretical level (Breiman 1992). This last point requires some additional consideration.

Table 5.2   The determinants of social capital

Predictors	Authors
Macro level	
Welfare effort	Van Oorschot and Arts 2005
Social security expenditure	Scheepers et al. 2002
Welfare regime	Van Oorschot and Arts 2005
% of protestants	Van Oorschot and Arts 2005
Income inequality	Van Oorschot and Arts 2005;
	Costa and Kahn 2003;
	Knack and Keefer 1997;
	O'Connel 2003;
	Kawachi et al. 1997;
	Uslaner 2000–2001
Economic development	Knack and Keefer 1997;
	Inghlehart 1999;
	Paxton 2002
	Van Oorschot and Arts 2005
Racial fragmentation	Costa and Kahn 2003
Fraction black	Costa and Kahn 2003
Birth place fragmentation	Costa and Kahn 2003
Fraction foreign born	Costa and Kahn 2003
Labour force growth	Knack and Keefer 1997
Black market premium	Knack and Keefer 1997
Property rights	Knack and Keefer 1997
Currency depreciation	Knack and Keefer 1997
Institutional investor credit rating	Knack and Keefer 1997
Transparency	O'Connel 2003
R & D expenditure	O'Connel 2003
Work satisfaction	O'Connel 2003
Social satisfaction	O'Connel 2003
Urbanization	Scheepers et al. 2002
Corruption	La Porta et al. 1999;
	Putnam 1993
Unemployment level	Hall 1999
Individual level	
Income	Brehm and Rahn 1997;
	Hall 1999;
	Knack and Keefer 1997;
	Putnam 2000
Education	Brehm and Rahn 1997;
	Fukuyama 2000;
	Knack and Keefer 1997

Table 5.2 (continued)

Predictors	Authors
Individual level	
Gender	Brehm and Rahn 1997; Lin 2000
Age	Brehm and Rahn 1997
Religion	Brehm and Rahn 1997; Inghlehart 1999; La Porta et al. 1997; Uslaner 2006
Religiousness	Van Oorschot and Arts 2005
Partisanship	Brehm and Rahn 1997; Van Oorschot and Arts 2005
Region of origin	Brehm and Rahn 1997
Size of the city	Brehm and Rahn 1997
Marital status	Brehm and Rahn 1997
Life satisfaction	Brehm and Rahn 1997
Ethnic origin	Brehm and Rahn 1997
Economic expectations	Brehm and Rahn 1997
Employment status	Hall 1999; Van Oorschot and Arts 2005
Civil society activity	Brehm and Rahn 1997; Paxton 2002
Sociability	Paxton 1999; Rothstein and Uslaner 2006

Source: Author's elaboration

Clarke (2005: 341) emphasized how influential methodological textbooks and basic econometric theory (King et al. 1994) supported the use of an excessive number of predictors in political science. Leading journals in the field, namely the *American Political Science Review*, the *American Journal of Political Science*, the *Journal of Conflict and Resolution*, the *Journal of Politics*, and the *Journal of Political Analysis*, published articles that display often more than 10 predictors, and in some cases more than 20 (Clarke 2005).

However, the standard conditions defined by econometric theory rarely apply in practice and often including many predictors carries only undesirable consequences. 'The mathematics of regression analysis simply does not support the logic of control variables previously laid out. Including more variables in a regression, even relevant ones, does not necessarily make the regression results more accurate' (Clarke 2005:

348). Therefore, the addition of other variables can make the equation inefficient, washing up important effects without effectively reducing the omitted variables problem (this problem has been often debated in econometric literature, for example Akaike 1973; Clarke 2001; 2003; 2005; Cox 1961; Hendry and Richard 1982; Mallows 1973; Schwartz 1978; Sims 1980; Stein 1955; Vuong 1989; for a good review Miller 1984). Following Breiman's (1992) suggestion we focus on the effect of four predictors, reducing their number even further in the next chapter by using stepwise models, to accurately discuss the effects of these variables and propose a parsimonious model based on a deductive approach (Sartori 1970).

5.4 SUMMARY

Economic equality, labour market participation, national divergence and economic development have been selected to explain the variation of social capital across European regions, following much theoretical literature and earlier empirical work. Economic equality refers directly to Tocqueville's explanation of the high level of social participation in the United States; labour market participation captures Gorz's idea that in a more active society social participation should also be higher; national divergence tests whether, in more homogeneous countries, regional social capital scores are higher; and economic development recalls Putnam's work and the ensuing debate. In the final part of the chapter, the necessity to follow a deductive framework based on few predictors has been suggested by discussing the 'phantom menace' of potential omitted variables (Clarke 2005). After the theoretical reflection on the predictors, the next chapter will test their effect on social capital variation across European regions and will open the debate on the importance of historic-institutional evolutions through the selection of two deviant cases.

NOTES

1. In addition to the four predictors, population density completes the lot of variables to control for the potential effect of the size and population of each region.
2. The attitudes toward equality changed dramatically over the course of history. Through the epochs of Greece, Rome and the Middle Ages, society was based on a natural order established by divine power and the only forms of help were organized around informal networks. The idea of equality of treatment was, nevertheless, somehow considered. The Greeks developed the principles of law of nature and law of reason, which are the cornerstones of modern declarations of rights. Humanists proposed a new world vision attributing to man a new spatial position not encapsulated in the vertical space defined

by the church, but along an horizontal space determined by his acts (see Pico della Mirandola 1994). The existence of this paradigm heavily contributed to the advent of political liberalism and successively of socialism.

3. Redistribution has been undertaken with a different intensity in Europe (Esping-Andersen 1990; Ferragina 2009a; Ferrera 1993; 1997 for a detailed analysis).

4. On the other hand, in the academic debate the importance of the equality of conditions to enhance social capital development has been debated and considered (Costa-Kahn 2003; O'Connel 2003; Paxton 1999).

5. In this literature, the term equality is considered as equality of conditions, strictly referred to the personal disposable income owned by citizens.

6. Gustafson and Johansson (1999) proposed another interesting empirical model. In their research for smoking guns to explain the variation of income inequalities over the time, they emphasized the importance of: the economic sector composition, the size of public and social security spending and the age structure of the population.

7. Three phenomena are directly connected to globalization: (1) the rise of foreign direct investments; (2) the increase of North–South trade; and (3) the increase of migration flows. The rise of foreign direct investments is contributing to accelerate the de-industrialization of countries (see Anderson and Nielsen 2002). Progressive de-industrialization is reducing the opportunity for bargaining of home country's workers. The result is the irreversible change in the balance between capital and labour factors of production and the reduction of the need for low-skilled workers. Similar arguments have been proposed in relation to the increasing trade between the North and the South. The delocalization of the activities in the South reduces the average wage in the North, increasing the disparities between skilled and unskilled workers. Finally, growing migration flows should also coincide with increasing inequalities. This is explicable by the decrease of the average skills of immigrants and the growing divergence between skilled and unskilled immigrants.

   The second set of explanations includes Kuznets' central argument about the transformation from agricultural to industry-based society, the demographic changes, the impact of higher educational attainment and the role of women in the labour market. Kuznets' argument has been modified to allow empirical testing. The original variable was the movement from rural to urban areas. In the empirical test it became more static, as the percentage of people employed in agriculture. At a demographic level, a growing presence of young people should foster differences of income distribution. This argument was stronger in Western societies in the past decades; it is less relevant today with the rapid ageing of the European population. The educational argument postulates that a growing presence of qualified people should increase the dispersion of income distribution in society. Also a stronger participation of women in the labour market should also increase inequalities with the growing proportion of the female-headed households, which tend to have lower incomes.

   The last set of explanations includes institutional arguments. The progressive de-unionization, the national agreements of wage setting, and the degree of decommodification fostered by different types of social security systems are important factors to explain many cross-national differences in the level of inequalities. The reduction of the bargaining power of the unions combined with a lower regulation of wage-setting generates an increase of inequality. Income inequalities are also stronger in countries that are more commodified (Esping-Andersen 1990).

8. Piketty (1999) published another interesting paper approaching this issue in a similar way analysing the French case.

9. The coefficient is based upon an ideal egalitarian distribution of income represented by a Lorenz curve. The area existent between the income distribution and the Lorenz curve is the Gini coefficient; the larger this area, the larger the inequalities in a given region will be (Gini 1912). The Gini coefficient and its application generated a germane debate (Dalton 1920; Gini 1921; Atkinson 1970; Champernowne 1974; Bourgignon 1979) about the measures of income dispersion.

10. The use of another measurement such as the Atkinson index would not have changed the final results of the regression model presented in Chapter 6. For a technical discussion on the opportunity to use different indicators to grasp alternative aspects of inequalities see Atkinson (1970), Champernowne (1974) and Bourgignon (1979).

11. There is a wide consensus in the literature to use the equivalent disposable income to construct inequality indices (Gustafsson and Johansson 1999).

12. The majority of the scholars interested in income distribution tend to use it (Atkinson et al. 1995: 25–38).

13. In the 15 countries analysed, activity rates went up from 60.7% in 1997 to 67.3% in 2008 (Eurostat 2009). This increase is manly due to the larger participation of women in the labour force. However, the current slowdown of European economies might have a negative impact in the future.

14. Unfortunately, there is not much empirical evidence to help us understand whether the increase in labour market activity rates is positively correlated with these new activation policies (Barbier and Ludwig-Mayerhofer 2004).

15. The social security system is seen as an important instrument to support companies and people, keeping market distortions to a minimum. This paradox is only apparent and partially explained by the need, in a highly competitive context, to provide social protection to workers and flexibility to companies. However, it is important to note that in Denmark, the generosity and extent of benefits is traditionally much larger (Barbier and Ludwig-Mayerhofer 2004).

16. Gorz did not use the term social capital directly, but proposed the idea of a multi-active society, pointing out the importance of recreating social networks and trust at the local level.

17. The data is gathered from Eurostat (Eurostat Regional Statistics 2005) and regions have been adjusted to fit with the ones proposed in the study (see Table 5.1).

18. In addition to the other predictors, the density of each region is used as a control variable. Most of the time comparative studies do not account for the different distribution of population in large and small areas. This variable also captures other important factors that may impact on social capital, for example the distribution of population in cities or rural/loosely populated areas.

19. The index is constructed to avoid the overlap with the dependent variable.

20. We have already (Chapter 1) argued that socio-economic factors and historical evolutions need to be explored recurring to synchronic and diachronic approaches simultaneously.

21. Namely income, education, gender, age, religion, partisanship, region of origin, size of the city of residence, marital status, life satisfaction, ethnic origin, economic expectations, employment status, civil society activity, sociability.

22. Namely welfare effort, social security expenditure, welfare regime type, percentage of protestants, income inequality, economic development, racial fragmentation, fraction of black people, birth place fragmentation, fraction of foreign born, labour force growth, black market premium, property rights, currency depreciation, institutional investor credit rating, transparency, R & D expenditure, work satisfaction, social satisfaction, urbanization, corruption and unemployment level.

23. This does not mean that other important variables like racial fragmentation or welfare state expenditure do not play an important role to explain the variation of social capital.

24. Variables like welfare state expenditure cannot be calculated in every country at the regional level.

6. Explaining social capital variation across Europe

The previous chapters have illustrated: the measurement of social capital (Chapter 2); the historical, institutional and empirical reasons to complement the cross-national with a cross-regional analysis (Chapter 3); the social capital regional ranking and the categorization of European regions according to the density of formal social networks, informal social networks and social trust (Chapter 4); and the theoretical reasons to select income inequality, labour market participation, national divergence and the level of economic development to explain the variation of social capital across Europe (Chapter 5). This chapter is the focal point of the book, because it analyses the effect of the macro social variables on social capital and its dimensions, and selects the South of Italy and Wallonia as deviant cases for the in-depth historic-institutional analysis.

The integration of the synchronic and diachronic analyses allows us to revisit Putnam's hypothesis (1993), tackling simultaneously his lack of focus on the socio-economic conditions of society (Skocpol 1996; Skocpol et al. 2000; Knack and Keefer 1997; Costa and Kahn 2003; O'Connel 2003) and the excessive determinism of the historical analysis (Lupo 1993; Lemann 1996; Tarrow 1996).

The impact of the independent variables on social capital and its dimensions is empirically tested using ordinary least square regressions (OLS) and evaluating their semistandardized coefficients and maximum impact. The analysis is completed by investigating in detail the effect of the level of economic development on social capital, dropping in rotation from the general OLS model the independent variables, that is, labour market participation, economic inequality and national divergence.

The OLS model is used also to detect the deviant cases from the general pattern. The comparison between deviant and regular cases is a convenient methodological device to overcome the selection bias (Skocpol 1979) and draw general conclusions from the in-depth historic-institutional analysis of few cases (Lijphart 1971).

The regression model shows that European regions displaying social capital scores above the average tend to have positive residuals, while regions with social capital scores below the average tend to have negative residuals. This implies that, according to the socio-economic predictors, regions above the average should have lower social capital scores and vice versa. On the contrary, the South of Italy and Wallonia rank at the bottom of the social capital classification of European regions (Table 4.3) and display at the same time high positive residuals. This means that according to the socio-economic predictors these two regions should have lower social capital scores than currently detected. These findings challenge Putnam's cultural and historical explanation of the lack of social capital in the South of Italy because they suggest that the socio-economic context is not conducive to the creation of social networks and trust. In Chapters 7 and 8, Wallonia and the South of Italy will be compared to two regular cases (Flanders and the North East of Italy) to sharpen the findings emerging from the socio-economic model and propose an alternative interpretation of the influence of historical and institutional development on social capital.

6.1 THE GENERAL MODEL

The impact of the socio-economic predictors on social capital and its dimensions is tested using a series of OLS models and five indicators derived from it. First, the effect of each predictor on the dependent variables is evaluated using the model with five independent variables (Table 6.1), their semistandardized coefficients and four maximum impact indicators (Table 6.2). Second, the effect of the level of economic development on social capital is further investigated by proposing four different configurations of the explanatory model, in which one or two variables are dropped in turn (Table 6.3).

The semistandardized coefficient measures the potential effect of an increase of one standard deviation of the Gini coefficient, activity rates and national divergence in variation of social capital standard units.[1] For example, if activity rates in one European region increase by 5.3 per cent (equivalent to a standard deviation) the model predicts that the social capital score should rise by 0.212 standard units. This would represent an improvement of 12/13 positions in the regional ranking (Table 6.2, column 1).

The maximum impact measures the effect of each predictor on social capital, but differently from the semistandardized coefficient, it considers the maximum range of values assumed by the predictors in the dataset.[2] Hence, it indicates which predictor has the maximum impact according to the current level of income inequality, labour market participation, national divergence and economic development in the regions sampled.

Table 6.1   Linear regression model explaining social capital and its components from activity rates density, GDP per capita, Gini coefficient, national divergence

	Social Capital [1]	T. Stand. (% variance explained) [1bis]	Formal Social Network [2]	T. Stand. (% variance explained) [2bis]	Informal Social Network [3]	T. Stand. (% variance explained) [3bis]	Social Trust [4]	T. Stand. (% variance explained) [4bis]	M (SD)
Activity rates	0.040*** (0.010)	3.986 (19.6%)	0.054*** (0.017)	3.278 (14.2%)	0.015 (0.015)	0.994	0.049*** (0.013)	3.691 (17.3%)	58.774 (5.307)
Density	0.000 (0.000)	0.517	2.574E-5 (0.000)	0.245	-2.753E-5 (0.000)	-0.283	9.840E-5 (0.000)	1.164	496.184 (1,046.471)
GDP per capita	0.000 (0.000)	0.850	2.125E-5 (0.000)	1.259	-3.760E-7 (0.000)	-0.024	5.120E-6 (0.000)	0.377	25354.606 (7,840.177)
Gini coefficient	-4.858*** (1.116)	-4.352 (22.6%)	-10.061*** (1.862)	-5.402 (31%)	5.138*** (1.727)	2.975 (12%)	-9.668*** (1.500)	-6.447 (39%)	0.2839 (0.045)
National divergence	-2.775*** (0.637)	-4.357 (22.6%)	-2.364** (1.062)	-2.225 (7.1%)	-5.150*** (0.985)	-5.227 (29.6%)	-0.798 (0.855)	-0.932	0.1419 (0.077)
Constant	-0.776 (0.800)	-0.957	-0.478** (1.334)	-0.359	-1.676 (1.238)	-1.354	-0.148 (1.074)	-0.138	58.774 (5.307)
R square	0.640		0.602		0.442		0.628		
Number of observations	71		71		71		71		

Notes:
Standard errors are in parenthesis.
Stand.: Standardized.
***p<0.01; **p<0.05; *p<0.10.

Source: Author's elaboration from EVS 1999–2000.

Table 6.2 Measure of relative importance of variables statistically significant in models describing social capital and its predictors

Variables	Semistandardized Coefficient [1]	Maximum Impact [2]	Impact 80%–20% [3]	Impact 50%–10% [4]	Impact 90%–50% [5]
Social Capital					
Activity rates	0.212	1.16	0.343	0.306	0.262
Gini coefficient	−0.217	−0.874	−0.534	−0.243	−0.291
National divergence	−0.215	−0.666	−0.389	−0.189	−0.416
Formal Social Network					
Activity rates	0.287	1.566	0.463	0.413	0.353
Gini coefficient	−0.450	−1.810	−1.107	−0.503	−0.604
National divergence	−0.183	−0.567	−0.331	−0.161	−0.355
Informal Social Networks					
Gini coefficient	0.230	0.924	0.565	0.256	0.308
National divergence	−0.398	−1.236	−0.721	−0.350	−0.773

Table 6.2 (continued)

Variables	Semistandardized Coefficient[1]	Maximum Impact[2]	Impact 80%-20%[3]	Impact 50%-10%[4]	Impact 90%-50%[5]
Social Trust					
Activity rates	0.260	1.421	0.420	0.374	0.321
Gini coefficient	-0.433	-1.740	-1.063	-0.483	-0.580

Notes:
[1] Unstandardized regression coefficient multiplied by the sample standard deviation of the independent variable X. It represents the change in Y associated with an increase of one standard deviation in X, in original units of Y.
[2] Unstandardized regression coefficient multiplied by the maximum range (maximum minus minimum) of X across regions. It represents the maximum possible impact of X on Y across regions.
[3] Unstandardized regression coefficient multiplied by the range 80-20% (80% minus 20%) of X in the sample. It represents the possible impact of X on Y across regions ranking between 80% and 20% of Y score distribution.
[4] Unstandardized regression coefficient multiplied by the range 50-10% (50% minus 10%) of X in the sample. It represents the possible impact of X on Y across regions ranking between 50% and 10% of Y distribution.
[5] Unstandardized regression coefficient multiplied by the range 90-50% (90% minus 50%) of X in the sample. It represents the impact of X on Y across regions ranking between 90% and 50% of Y distribution.

Source: Author's elaboration after Alderson and Nielsen (2002).

Table 6.3 Linear regression model explaining social capital from activity rates density, GDP per capita, Gini coefficient, national divergence (Stepwise Model)

	Dropping Activity Rates [1]	T-Standard [2]	Dropping Gini Coefficient [3]	T-Standard [4]	Dropping National Divergence [5]	T-Standard [6]	Dropping Activity Rates and Gini Coefficient [7]	T-Standard [8]	M (SD) [9]
Activity rates			0.047*** (0.010)	4.811	0.056*** (0.010)	5.477			58.774 (5.307)
Density	2.148E-5 (0.000)	0.309	-9,470E-5 (0.000)	-1.456	-2.903E-5 (0.000)	-0.420	0.000** (0.000)	-2.069	496.184 (1,046.471)
GDP per capita	2.026E-5* (0.000)	1.889	2.717E-5** (0.000)	2.588	-1.072E-5 (0.000)	0.940	4.248E-5*** (0.000)	3.644	25,354.606 (7,840.177)
Gini coefficient	-6.671*** (1.129)	-5.910			-3.628*** (1.218)	-2.977			0.2839 (0.045)
National divergence	-3.766*** (0.649)	-5.802	-2.320*** (0.706)	-3.288			-2.997*** (0.730)	-4.106	0.1419 (0.077)
Constant	1.925*** (0.475)	4.049	-3.101*** (0.607)	-5.107	-2.532** (0.778)	-4.022	0.544* (0.306)	-1.777	58.774 (5.307)
R square	**0.552**		**0.508**		**0.535**		**0.331**		
Number of observations	71		71		71		71		

Notes:
Standard errors are in parenthesis.
Standard: standardized.
***p<0.01; **p<0.05; *p<0.10.

Source: Author's elaboration from EVS 1999–2000.

In order to account for the impact of the most extreme cases and analyse the effect of the predictors on regions with different rankings, three alternative maximum impact indicators are proposed (Table 6.2, columns 3, 4 and 5): (1) the maximum impact 80 per cent-20 per cent, which considers the effect of the independent variables excluding the regions at the top and the bottom 20 per cent of the social capital ranking; (2) the maximum impact 50 per cent-10 per cent, which considers the regions with social capital scores below the average (excluding the bottom 10 per cent); and (3) the maximum impact 90 per cent-50 per cent, which considers the regions with social capital scores above the average (excluding the top 10 per cent). As for the semistandardized coefficient, the maximum impact is also measured according to the variation of the dependent variables standard units.

The regression model explains 64 per cent of the variance of social capital across European regions and shows that income inequality, labour market participation and national divergence are significantly correlated to the dependent variable. Income inequality (22.6 per cent of the variance explained), labour market participation (19.6 per cent) and national divergence (22.6 per cent) have a similar impact on social capital. A decrease of income inequality, a decrease of national divergence and an increase of the labour market participation of the order of one standard deviation[3] would potentially generate an increase of social capital of respectively 0.220, 0.215 and 0.212 standard points (Table 6.2, column 1). This increase would be equivalent for a region ranking in the middle of social capital distribution, as for example, South West of England or Wales (see Table 4.3), to a jump of 13/14 positions in the case of income inequality and national divergence and 12/13 positions for labour market participation.

Differently from the general model and the semistandardized coefficient, when the maximum impact is considered, labour market participation displays a stronger effect than national divergence and income inequality (Table 6.2, column 2). This might be explained by the extreme polarization of labour market conditions across European regions,[4] because when the most extreme cases are excluded from the analysis, income inequality and national divergence have again a stronger effect than labour market participation on social capital (Table 6.2, column 3). The intensity of the effect of each predictor varies considerably according to the different ranking of the European regions. If regions have a social capital score above the average, the national divergence becomes the most important predictor followed by the Gini coefficient (Table 6.2, column 5), whilst if regions have a social capital score below the average, labour market participation is the main predictor (followed also in this case by the Gini coefficient).

These findings suggest that a reduction of income inequality and national divergence, and an increase in labour market participation might positively impact on social capital at the aggregate level. More specifically, income inequality seems to be the best explanation of the variation of social capital when the majority of the regions are considered, while national divergence is a better explanation of the variation for the regions ranked above the average in the social capital ranking and labour market participation for those below.

In order to disentangle more accurately the effect of each predictor, the same analysis is extended to the three dimensions of social capital. Income inequality, labour market participation and national divergence explain 60 per cent of the formal social networks variation across European regions (Table 6.1, column 2). The direction of the effect is the same described for social capital; lower income inequality, lower national divergence and higher labour market participation would predict a higher density of formal social participation, however the magnitude of the effects is quite different. The Gini coefficient is by far the most important explanatory variable of the variation of formal social networks (31 per cent of the variance explained) followed by the activity rate (14.2 per cent) and the national divergence (7.1 per cent).

A decrease of income inequality and national divergence and an increase of labour market participation of the order of one standard deviation would potentially generate an increase in formal social networks of respectively 0.450, 0.183 and 0.287 standard points (Table 6.2, column 1). Considering also the four measures of maximum impact, the Gini coefficient remains the most important predictor followed by labour market participation and national divergence[5] (Table 6.2, columns 2, 3, 4 and 5).

The model explains 44 per cent of the variance of informal social networks across European regions and only income inequality and national divergence seem to have a significant effect (Table 6.1, column 3). The direction of this effect partially changes in comparison to the predictive model of formal social networks. An increase of income inequality has a positive impact on informal social networks, while the national divergence is negatively correlated. National divergence is the main predictor explaining 29.6 per cent of the variance followed by the Gini coefficient (12 per cent of the variance explained). An increase of income inequality and a decrease of national divergence of the order of one standard deviation would potentially generate an increase of informal social networks of respectively 0.230 and 0.398 standard points (Table 6.2, column 1). Also when we consider the four measures of maximum impact, the national divergence remains the main predictor followed by the Gini coefficient (Table 6.2, columns 2, 3, 4 and 5).

These findings might suggest that when income inequality increases within a region, people tend to react against the higher incertitude by strengthening their safety nets, that is, the bonding relationships with family and friends. This is a confirmation of the idea put forward by communitarians that redistributive policy tends to destroy reciprocity and strong ties (Fukuyama 1995; Etzioni 1995). The reduction of income inequality proposes a trade off between the positive effects generated on formal social networks and the negative effects generated on informal social networks.

The model explains 62.8 per cent of the variance of social trust (Table 6.1, column 4). The Gini coefficient is the most important predictor (39 per cent of the variance explained) followed by labour market participation (17.3 per cent). The relative variance explained by the predictors on the social trust dimension is similar to that observed on formal social networks, the only difference being that the national divergence index here is not significant. A decrease of income inequality and an increase of national divergence of the order of one standard deviation would potentially generate an increase of social trust of respectively 0.433 and 0.260 standard points (Table 6.2, column 1). Also considering the four measures of maximum impact, income inequality remains the main predictor followed by the labour market participation (Table 6.2, columns 2, 3, 4 and 5). This means that in regions with a higher participation in the labour market and low income inequalities, the institutional/generalized trust and the willingness to discuss political issues are more pronounced.

Contrary to what has been argued in much literature (Beugelsdijk and Van Schaik 2005b; Helliwell and Putnam 1995; Knack and Keefer 1997; Schneider et al. 2000; Zak and Knack 2001), the most surprising finding is that the level of economic development does not seem to have a significant effect on the variation of social capital and its dimensions. For this reason a most accurate investigation of the effect of the level of economic development on social capital is proposed by dropping in rotation all significant predictors: labour market participation, economic inequality, national divergence and finally, labour market participation and economic inequality simultaneously (Table 6.3, columns 1–8).

By dropping labour market participation, the variance explained by the model decreases from 64 per cent to 55 per cent. The Gini coefficient and the national divergence remain the most important predictors of social capital exercising a similarly sized effect (Table 6.3, column 2). In this model, the economic development becomes a significant predictor of social capital, however the strength of its effect is three times weaker than economic inequality and national divergence. By dropping the Gini coefficient, the variance explained by the model decreases substantially (from 64 per cent to 48 per cent). In this new configuration of the model, the strongest effect on social capital is generated by labour market participation, followed by the national divergence and the level of economic development (Table 6.3, column 4).

By dropping the national divergence indicator, the variance explained by the model falls from 64 per cent to 53 per cent, however in this case the economic development is not significant. Finally, if activity rates and Gini coefficient are dropped simultaneously from the model, the level of economic development seems to impact more strongly than in the previous cases on social capital (Table 6.3, column 8). However in this configuration of the model, the variance explained drops from 64 per cent to only 33 per cent. This finding shows the level of economic development has a significant impact on social capital only if economic inequality and labour market participation are not considered.

Summing up, the empirical evidence proposed in this section suggests that income equality, labour market participation and national divergence accurately explain the variance of social capital across European regions. In particular, income inequality is the most important predictor of formal social networks and social trust while national divergence has a major role in predicting the variance of informal social networks.

The effects have the same directionality; an increase of income inequality and national divergence are negatively correlated to social capital and its dimensions, while an increase of labour market participation would have a positive effect. The only remarkable exception is the positive correlation between an increase of income inequality and informal social networks. This confirms the argument proposed by the communitarians which emphasized how redistributive policy might destroy reciprocity and strong ties.

Furthermore, it has been assessed that the level of economic development has a positive impact on social capital only if labour market participation or income inequality are dropped from the model. This might suggest that too much attention has been devoted in the literature to the relation between economic development and social capital, rather than focusing on the effect of other socio-economic predictors, as for example, income inequality and labour market participation.

6.2   THE DEVIANT CASES

The selection of the cases that deviate from the general pattern illustrated by the regression model is a methodological tool to gather general conclusions from the in-depth historic-institutional analysis of few cases (Lijphart 1971). As highlighted by Skocpol (1979) case selection is one of the most problematic aspects of comparative historical analysis;

therefore, the integration between the synchronic and diachronic perspectives is undertaken on the basis of the regression model rather than simply evaluating at the theoretical level commonalities and differences among European regions.

The regression model tends to overestimate social capital for regions ranked above the average and underestimate the scores for regions ranked below. This finding might be explained by the positive reinforcing effect of well functioning institutions (Rothstein 2001), and by the consolidation over time of social networks and generalized trust contexts where the degree of participation is already high. In contrast, where social capital scores are currently below the average, the negative reinforcing effect may be explained by the poor functioning of institutions (Woolcock 1998) and the absence over time of generalized trust (Table 6.4 and Figure 6.1).

Therefore, the regions in which social capital is largely below the average but the residuals (the residual is the difference between the observed value and the value predicted by the model under investigation) are positive, are particularly interesting cases to be analysed because the model indicates that social capital scores should be even lower. It is suggested that in these regions the impact of historic-institutional evolutions on social capital assumes peculiar connotations that can be explored by comparison with the regular cases, and allow us to draw some general conclusion on the mechanisms behind the formation/destruction of social capital, overcoming the mono-dimensional socio-economic explanation provided in the previous section.

The selection of the deviant cases for the in-depth historic-institutional analysis is undertaken in two steps. First, the potential presence of outliers is investigated so as to understand whether the regression model was biased by the presence of extreme observations. Second, the deviant cases are detected, by analysing whether there are cases that do not follow the general pattern of positive residuals coefficients in the presence of social capital scores above the average and vice versa (Table 6.4 and Figure 6.1).

The presence of potential outliers in the four models is investigated using Cook's distance indicator. Cook's distance indicator measures the overall influence of a case on the model thus detecting potential outliers (Field 2005: 727). Cook and Weisberg (1982) established that values greater than 1 are potentially a source of concern. According to this framework, there are no outliers in the model (Table 6.4).

The regression model shows there are 14 regions that do not conform to the general pattern of positive residuals in concomitance of social capital scores above the average and vice versa (Table 6.4 and Figure 6.1). On the one hand, there are two regions that have social capital scores above average and display negative residual coefficients ([123][6] West Netherlands and [62] the South of Finland, see Table 6.4 and Figure 6.1). However,

Table 6.4   Residuals

	Min	Max	Mean	Standard Deviation Variable	No.
Residual Summary					
Expected value	−1.3077	0.9719	−0.0001	0.47211	71
Residual	−0.73039	0.71380	0.00000	0.35394	71
Standard deviation expected value	−2.770	2.059	0.000	1.000	71
Cook's distance	0.000	0.251	0.017	0.034	71

No.	Regions	Standard Deviation Residual	Social Capital
Residual Regional Ranking			
1	BE Vlaams Gewest	1.943	0.21
2	GR Voreia Ellada (Northern Greece)	1.423	0.10
3	GR Kentriki Ellada (Central Greece)	1.408	0.00
4	DE Niedersachsen	1.401	0.12
5	FI West Finland (Lansi)	1.239	0.77
6	DK Hovenstansomradet (Copenhagen area)	1.175	1.15
7	SE Gotaland (including Malmo and Goteborg)	1.138	1.39
8	DE Rheinland-Pfalz	1.131	0.22
9	SE Svealand and Stockholm	1.121	1.28
10	UK North East	1.079	0.25
11	FI North Finland (Pohjois)	1.007	0.80
12	SE Norrland	0.973	1.27
13	FI East Finland (Ita)	0.860	0.38
14	IT Nord Est	0.846	−0.13
15	AT West-Osterrich	0.795	0.38
16	UK Northern Ireland	0.783	0.18
17	DE Nordrhein-Westfalen	0.761	−0.11
18	IT Sud	0.751	−0.91
19	DK Jylland	0.730	1.03
20	BE Region Wallone	0.695	−0.45
21	IT Isole	0.647	−1.07
22	BE Brussels	0.634	0.13
23	NL North Netherlands	0.593	0.96
24	AT Ost-Osterrich	0.549	0.05
25	UK Eastern	0.510	0.23
26	NL East Netherlands	0.507	1.00
27	DE Hessen	0.477	−0.16
28	UK Scotland	0.426	0.12

Table 6.4   (continued)

No.	Regions	Standard Deviation Residual	Social Capital
	Residual Regional Ranking		
29	DK Fyn (Syddanmark)	0.414	0.91
30	UK Wales	0.380	−0.02
31	DE Sachsen	0.336	0.02
32	GR Nisia aigaiou, Kriti	0.306	−0.07
33	UK North West	0.297	0.05
34	DK Sjaelland, Lolland-Falster, Bornholm (excl. Hovenstadomradet)	0.246	0.81
35	UK Yorks & Humbs	0.204	0.02
36	GR Attiki	0.123	−0.17
37	NL South Netherlands	0.109	0.84
38	ES Sur	0.104	−0.38
39	DE Berlin	0.075	−0.37
40	FR Méditerranée	0.009	−0.19
41	NL West Netherlands	−0.007	0.91
42	ES Centro	−0.016	−0.44
43	FI South Finland (Etela)	−0.037	0.61
44	ES Noroeste	−0.074	−0.48
45	AT Sud-Osterrich	−0.083	−0.11
46	UK South West	−0.218	−0.01
47	IT Centro	−0.245	−0.57
48	UK South East	−0.315	−0.05
49	UK E. Mids	−0.406	−0.07
50	IT Nord-Ovest	−0.465	−0.79
51	UK W. Mids	−0.576	−0.25
52	DE Sachsen-Anhalt	−0.586	−0.31
53	UK London	−0.600	−0.19
54	IT Lombardia	−0.755	−0.69
55	DE Bayern	−0.915	−0.49
56	FR Ouest	−0.938	−0.16
57	FR Sud ouest	−1.029	−0.27
58	ES Noreste	−1.049	−0.42
59	FR Nord	−1.105	−0.36
60	ES Comunidad Madrid	−1.120	−0.31
61	ES Este	−1.271	−0.55
62	FR Ile de France	−1.408	−0.12
63	FR Bassin Parisien	−1.416	−0.34
64	IT Lazio	−1.511	−1.04
65	FR Centre Est	−1.525	−0.30

Table 6.4 (continued)

No. Regions	Standard Deviation Residual	Social Capital
Residual Regional Ranking		
66 ES Canarias	−1.629	−0.81
67 DE Thüringen	−1.671	−0.58
68 DE Baden-Württemberg	−1.678	−0.63
69 FR Est	−1.725	−0.27
70 DE Brandenburg	−1.844	−0.76
71 DE Mecklenburg-Vorpommern	−1.989	−0.80

Source: Author's elaboration.

the negative magnitude of their residual coefficient is of a negligible size (−0.007 for West Netherlands and −0.037 for South of Finland). On the other hand, there are 12 regions that have social capital scores below the average and positive residual coefficients. In these regions, social capital scores are higher than the socio-economic model would predict. For this reason, they fulfil the previously exposed conditions and constitute a group of potential candidates for the in-depth historic-institutional analysis.[7]

These 12 regions can be split into three sub-groups according to the proximity of social capital scores to the average and the magnitude of the positive residual coefficient. Only the 'most deviant cases' from the general model, that is, those that display social capital scores largely below the average in concomitance of high positive residuals, are selected for the in-depth historic-institutional analysis. The first sub-group includes regions with a social capital score close to the average (North East of Italy, Nordrhein-Westfalen, Hessen, Wales and Sachsen; Table 6.4); the second includes regions with a low positive residual (Attiki, Berlin and Méditerranée; Table 6.4); and the third includes the regions selected for further analysis, namely Wallonia, the South of Italy and Isole.[8] These regions fulfil the conditions discussed above, having a social capital score largely below the average (Table 4.3), belonging to the disjointed cluster (see Chapter 4) and displaying high positive residual coefficients (Table 6.4 and Figure 6.1).

This finding is particularly interesting if the South of Italy is considered. First, this area occupies the last position in the social capital ranking despite the fact that according to the socio-economic model the social capital score should be at an even lower level. Second, the lack of collective action and social networks in this area has been constantly debated by social scientists since the 1950s (Banfield 1958; Putnam 1993; Ferragina

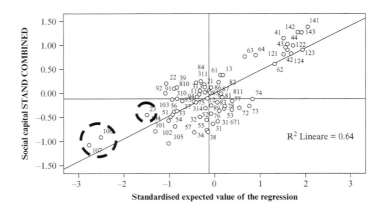

Note:

No.	Region	No.	Region	No.	Region
11	AT Ost-Osterrich	51	ES Noroeste	812	UK Northern Ireland
12	AT Sud-Osterrich	52	ES Noreste	91	GR Voreia Ellada
13	AT West-Osterrich	53	ES Comunidad Madrid	92	GR Kentriki Ellada
14	AT Wien	54	ES Centro	93	GR Attiki
21	BE Brussels	55	ES Este	94	GR Nisia aigaiou, Kriti
22	BE Vlaams Gewest	56	ES Sur	101	IT Nord-Ovest
23	BE Region Wallone	57	ES Canarias	102	IT Lombardia
31	DE Baden-Württemberg	61	FI East Finland (Ita)	103	IT Nord Est
32	DE Bayern	62	FI South Finland (Etela)	104	IT Centro
33	DE Berlin	63	FI West Finland (Lansi)	105	IT Lazio
34	DE Brandenburg	64	FI North Finland	106	IT Sud
35	DE Bremen		(Pohjois)	107	IT Isole
36	DE Hamburg	71	FR Bassin Parisien	111	LX Luxembourg
37	DE Hessen	72	FR Centre Est	121	NL North Netherlands
38	DE Mecklenburg-	73	FR Est	122	NL East Netherlands
	Vorpommern	74	FR Ile de France	123	NL West Netherlands
39	DE Niedersachsen	75	FR Méditerranée	124	NL South Netherlands
310	DE Nordrhein-	76	FR Nord	131	PT North
	Westfalen	77	FR Ouest	132	PT Center
311	DE Rheinland-Pfalz	78	FR Sud ouest	133	PT Lisboa and Vale do
312	DE Saarland	81	GB E. Mids		Tejo
313	DE Sachsen	82	UK Eastern	134	PT Alentejo and Algarve
314	DE Sachsen-Anhalt	83	UK London	141	SE Gotaland
315	DE Schleswig-Holstein	84	UK North East	142	SE Svealand and
316	DE Thüringen	85	UK North West		Stockholm
41	DK Hovenstansomradet	86	UK Scotland	143	SE Norrland
42	DK Sjaelland, Lolland-	87	UK South East	151	IE Connaught/Ulster
	Falster, Bornhom (excl	88	UK South West	152	IE Dublin
	Hovenstadomradet)	89	UK W. Mids	153	IE Munster
43	DK Fyn (Syddanmark)	810	UK Wales	154	IE Rest of Leinster
44	DK Jylland	811	UK Yorks & Humbs		

Source: Author's elaboration.

Figure 6.1 Regression explaining social capital from all dependent variables

2009b; 2010b). Nevertheless, unlike Banfield and Putnam, it is argued that the peculiarity of this area can be more accurately interpreted through a comparative historic-institutional analysis (including the other deviant case and two regular cases belonging to the same nation) rather than simply analysing the case in isolation.

Italy and Belgium present unique similarities: the existence of independent and wealthy cities during the Middle Ages, the long struggle against large powers, and foreign domination for many centuries. The unification of both states during the nineteenth century was achieved under a weak monarchy, and was accompanied by the affirmation of the centralism to counterbalance the presence of strong and defined local powers. This situation has been managed with a top-down approach, based on large public expenditure. The evolution towards a regional and then a federal state in the last three decades has shown a shift as the problems generated by centralism were repaired. In this context social capital scores are connected to a *sui-generis* historic-institutional evolution. In this vein, the comparison between Wallonia and the South of Italy with Flanders and the North East of Italy will be used to: (1) provide an alternative historical interpretation to Putnam's explanation (1993) of the lack of social capital in the South of Italy, and (2) to draw some conclusion on the importance of history and institutional configurations to explain the variance of social capital across European regions, therefore sharpening the results gathered from the socio-economic model.

6.3   SUMMARY

Income inequality, labour market participation and national divergence partially explain the variation of social capital and its dimensions across European regions, while the level of economic development seems to have an impact only if at least one of the other three predictors is excluded from the analysis. These results suggest previous literature (Beugelsdijk and Van Schaik 2005b; Helliwell and Putnam 1995; Schneider et al. 2000) might have excessively overemphasized the nexus between social capital and the level of economic development due to a lack of focus on the importance of other predictors, that is, economic inequality, labour market participation and national divergence.

A decrease of income inequality, a decrease of national divergence and an increase in labour market participation are conducive to the creation of social capital (Table 6.5). The three predictors have similarly sized effects; however income inequality has a stronger impact on regions which are not ranked at the top and bottom 20 per cent of the social capital distribution, labour market participation on regions below the average of the social

Table 6.5   *Ranking effect of the significant predictors on the dependent*
              variables

	Direction Effect	Ranking Intensity	Maximum Impact Ranking	80-20 Impact Ranking	50-10 Impact Ranking	90-50 Impact Ranking
			Social Capital			
Gini coefficient	Negative	1	2	1	2	2
National divergence	Negative	2	3	2	3	1
Activity rates	Positive	3	1	3	1	3
			Formal Social Networks			
Gini coefficient	Negative	1	1	1	1	1
Activity rates	Positive	2	2	2	2	3
National divergence	Negative	3	3	3	3	2
			Informal Social Networks			
National divergence	Negative	1	1	1	1	1
Gini coefficient	Positive	2	2	2	2	2
			Social Trust			
Gini coefficient	Negative	1	1	1	1	1
Activity rates	Positive	2	2	2	2	2

Source: Author's elaboration.

capital distribution, and the national divergence has the strongest impact
on regions above the average (Table 6.5).

The level of income inequality is the most important predictor of the
variation of the density of formal social networks and social trust followed
by labour market participation, while national divergence is the most
important predictor of the variation of informal social networks followed
by the level of income inequality (Table 6.5).

The directionality of the effect of the independent variables is similar
in all dependent variables, with the exception of the positive impact of an
increase of income inequality on the variation of formal social networks.
This finding shows the existence of a sort of trade-off between, on the one
hand, the effect of income inequality on formal social participation and
social trust, and on the other, the effect on informal social networks. A
stronger level of economic redistribution seems to have a positive impact

on formal, one could say 'modern', forms of solidarity (Durkheim 1893), and at the same time a more equal redistribution of income seems to disincentive the creation of informal, one could say 'mechanic', forms of solidarity (Durkheim 1893). From a quantitative point of view the positive effect of a decrease of income inequality seems to be stronger on formal social networks and social trust than the positive effect of an increase of income inequality on the creation of informal social networks. This result has strong implications directly linked to traditional sociological theory (Tönnies 1955; Durkheim 1893; Weber 1946) and the communitarian approach (Fukuyama 1995; Etzioni 1995), which will be discussed in detail in the conclusion (see Chapter 9).

The last contribution in this chapter is the selection of two deviant cases for further historic-institutional analysis of the third part of the book. The case selection has been guided by the results of the socio-economic model and the concomitant presence of poor social capital scores and high positive residuals. It has been argued that this criterion helps to overcome one of the main limits of comparative historical analysis, the non systematic case selection (Skocpol 1979), and helps to sharpen the findings of the socio-economic model by proposing the comparison between two deviant and two regular cases (Lijphart 1971). This evidence is interpreted as an indication of the fact that historical and institutional developments assumed an original connotation in Wallonia and the South of Italy, and for this reason the comparison with two regular cases, located in the same country, might contribute to fostering the debate on the determinants of social capital in European regions.

NOTES

1. Or formal social networks, informal social networks and social trust standard units.
2. From the maximum to the minimum value.
3. Respectively 0.045, 0.077 and 5.3 per cent.
4. The region (Table 5.1) with the highest labour market participation is Gotaland (72%) and those with the lowest are the South of Italy and the Isole (43%; Table 5.1). These regions are also at the top and the bottom of the social capital regional ranking.
5. With the exception of the maximum impact 90%-50%. In this case the national divergence has a stronger impact.
6. The number in parenthesis is the value attributed to regions in Figure 6.1 (see table attached to the figure for a complete list).
7. These regions are: (103) North East of Italy (0.846), (310) Nordrhein-Westfalen (0.761), (106) South of Italy (0.751), (23) region Wallone (0.695), (107) Isole (0.645), (37) Hessen (0.477), (810) Wales (0.380), (94) Nisia Aigaiou, Kriti (0.306), (811) Yorkshire and Humberside (0.204), (93) Attiki (0.123), (33) Berlin (0.075) and (75) Méditerranée (0.009).
8. In the rest of the book the South of Italy and the Isole are analysed as a single case because of their similar historic-institutional evolution.

PART 3

The Divergent Cases

7. Why does social capital 'sleep'?

In the previous chapter we saw how income inequality, labour market participation and national divergence are important socio-economic factors which in turn explain the variation of social capital across the European regions. Furthermore, the regression analysis has revealed that Wallonia and the South of Italy diverge from the general pattern because they display social capital scores largely below the average and positive residuals at the same time. This means that, according to the socio-economic factors, in Wallonia and the South of Italy social capital scores should be lower than currently detected. For this reason, they diverge from the other regions analysed, where according to the socio-economic conditions social capital scores should be higher in regions ranked below the average and lower in regions ranked above (Figure 6.1).

These findings seem to challenge Putnam's[1] (1993) historical explanation of the lack of social capital in the South of Italy (based on the absence of medieval towns in the twelfth and thirteenth centuries) and offer an interesting puzzle that we try to disentangle from a comparative perspective. In this respect, the aim of this chapter is to assess the impact of historical evolution on social capital, starting from the interpretation of what the causal model leaves unexplained. The comparison between regular and deviant cases permits us to refine the findings gathered from the general model through the integration of the synchronic and the diachronic perspectives (on the theoretical value of this research design see Chapter 1 and Lijphart 1971).

The deviant cases (Wallonia and the South of Italy) are compared to two regular cases (Flanders and the North East of Italy) because they display positive residuals in the presence of highly different social capital scores. The concomitance of positive residuals in all areas suggests that the large social capital gap between these regions cannot be solely explained by different historical evolutions (as suggested by Putnam [1993]).

We argue, differently from Putnam, that in the divergent cases the negative effect of low labour market participation and high income inequality overshadows the potential positive impact of the historical evolution. In this respect, Coleman's theory of the 'appropriable social capital' is re-elaborated to explain the relation between socio-economic and historical factors. Coleman (1990) defined 'appropriable social capital' as a particular type of social capital generated at a certain point of time, which is mobilized later to extend its scope from the original one. In order to illustrate this theory, he considered the example of the Korean student revolt during the 1980s. The students used a network, started during childhood by participating in local church activities, to enhance a revolution. Similarly, we suggest that only when a region achieves a certain socio-economic development, does the value of past historical experience become fully appropriable, leading to a larger social capital increase than the one generated by the simple improvement of labour market participation and income redistribution. At this stage, the 'original past of the region' can be rediscovered, and becomes a new source of social trust and social participation. The Flemish case is utilized to illustrate this theory.

Flanders, an underdeveloped region during the nineteenth century, became more connected to the international economy and experienced a sustained growth from the 1880s (Keating et al. 2003). This development impacted positively on the socio-economic conditions of the region. In parallel, the Flemish movement re-invented the glorious past of the fourteenth century County of Flanders, legitimizing their socio-economic achievements. During the 1960s the Flemish economy overtook the Wallonian economy (after a period of steady decline of this area in the twentieth century) and this event helped to reinforce the creation of a new image of Flanders, an image based on the success of the fourteenth century and not on the period of crises of the seventeenth, eighteenth and nineteenth centuries (Keating et al. 2003: 82). We suggest that, at a certain level of development, the revival of past traditions can reinforce the positive effect played by the socio-economic factors on social capital. This in turn acts again to reinforce self-consciousness and pride in local history and increases social capital even more.

Where this virtuous process did not take place, as for example, in Wallonia and the South of Italy, social capital 'sleeps'. On the basis of a comparative historical analysis, we argue that improvement of the labour market conditions and a higher degree of redistribution can support the initiation of a 'virtuous cycle'. Wallonia and the South of Italy are not condemned by their past, on the contrary, their regional history could even be a future asset which might increase social capital levels once socio-economic conditions improve.

In what follows, Vico's doctrine of the *New Science* is used to contextualize the comparative historical analysis (Sections 7.1. and 7.3), to open the discussion on the results gathered from the socio-economic model (Section 7.2). In conclusion, an example of social engagement and self-organization that took place in Sicily during the nineteenth century is examined as an argument against the image of passivity of Southern peasants (Section 7.4) and to support the sleeping social capital theory.

7.1 VICO'S DOCTRINE AND COMPARATIVE HISTORICAL ANALYSIS

The formation of social networks and the variation of social trust can be understood as part of the general historical development of human action (Vico et al. 1968). The creation of social capital is not in fact an absolute reality released from the historical context, and the socio-economic model cannot fully answer the research question proposed in this work. For this reason, the comparative historical analysis has the function of sharpening the findings of the synchronic model (see Chapter 6) and investigating, by diachronic analysis, the role of historical and institutional evolutions.

Vico, in *New Science*, suggested that history is not a mere succession of happenings[2] (Berlin 1978: 487) but a series of cyclical events that can be interpreted through the identification of precise laws.[3] In this chapter we do not aim to identify the laws theorized by Vico, but only to embrace his idea of reading history as in a state of flux. This starting point is used to clarify the relation between the present socio-economic conditions and certain historical evolutions, in order to reinterpret social capital theory. The systematic comparison proposed by the socio-economic model is matched with an exercise of 'disciplined imagination' to reconstruct the original past (Collingwood et al. 1999: XIV) of the deviant cases.

The description of certain events does not always reflect real historical periods but it has a heuristic function. History is a perpetual striving of men to maintain and transform relationships among themselves (Berlin 1978: 488). For this reason, the following of Vico's perspective means to analyse the history of a particular area and its institutional evolution as a perpetual exercise of problem solving (see next chapter).

The dismissal of the idea of history as a perpetual problem solving exercise of human kind (Fukuyama 1992; Putnam 1993) contributed to the generation of deterministic visions. Such determinism has indeed reduced the heuristic potential of history to a pre-established path to modernity, as exemplified by Putnam's theory: only the regions with well-developed medieval towns in the twelfth and thirteenth centuries have a good level of social capital today and as a consequence they have institutions that function well. In order to avoid this determinism, we compare how similar ideas and events took place in different unrelated contexts at the same time: 'Uniform ideas originating among entire peoples unknown to each other must have a common ground of truth' (Vico 1968: 144).

The comparison challenges Putnam's (1993) deterministic historical interpretation, showing that the *comuni* in the twelfth and thirteenth centuries in Belgium and Italy were not a model of democracy and did not create by default stronger horizontal ties, and in this respect they were not different in the North East and the South of Italy. On the basis of this comparison, we promote the *sleeping social capital theory* showing that in response to the imperfect process of national unification, the divergent regions (Wallonia and the South of Italy) reacted differently from those that followed a pattern closer to the other European regions (the control cases, Flanders and the North East of Italy). Socio-economic success fostered pride and recognition of a glorious regional past in Flanders and the North East of Italy. On the other hand, the negative interpretation of the past in Wallonia and the South of Italy (derived from the failure of their socio-economic model) fostered a pessimistic vision, which reduced the interpretation of the history of these regions to a series of mistakes, directly related to the present underdevelopment.

The historical analysis is focused mainly on the nineteenth century, the crucial period of national unification, but the reference to other periods, such as the age of medieval towns in the twelfth and thirteenth centuries, has the heuristic function described by Vico: certain events tell us important details about the evolution of a society, therefore they have a significance which goes beyond their historical time. As we shall see, the comparative historical analysis is introduced by some socio-economic considerations in the four areas analysed.

7.2   CASE SELECTION AND SOCIO-ECONOMIC ANALYSIS

In the South of Italy and Wallonia the relation between socio-economic factors and social capital has been largely mediated by historical and institutional evolution. This relation has been extensively discussed in the literature, attributing to each region's past a negative connotation[4] (Banfield 1958; Putnam 1993; Reid and Musyck 2000). The results of the empirical model (see Chapter 6) suggest a radically different interpretation. However, before embarking on the historical comparison, this section discusses the results of the socio-economic model.

In Italy and Belgium there are five regions in which the residuals of the regression model are positive, therefore the predictors underestimate social capital scores. These regions are divided into two categories:

- the first group follows the general pattern[5] (Flanders, the North East of Italy and Brussels[6]);
- the second group, characterized by low social capital scores, deviates from the general pattern (Wallonia and the South of Italy).

In the comparative historical analysis the first group is used to control the second. The peculiarity of the divergent cases can only be understood in relation to the cases that follow the general model, providing a broader insight into the relation between socio-economic variables and historical evolution and their impact on social capital. These regions share common historical evolutions, a chaotic institutional development (which will be analysed in the next chapter) and positive values of the residuals but have different social capital scores (Table 7.1).

Flanders has the highest positive residual across the European regions (Table 7.1). The high social capital score (24th position) in concomitance with medium-low scores in the socio-economic predictors[7] suggests that historical evolution played a largely positive role in the creation of social capital (see next section). The situation is similar in the North East of Italy (with lower social capital scores [44th position] and residuals [14th position]). The North East is also the only Italian region with a social capital score close to the European average.[8]

The value of the residual is slightly lower in the South of Italy than in the North East (18th position). Also in this case the socio-economic predictors would suggest a lower social capital score, but differently from Flanders and the North East of Italy, the socio-economic conditions are so poor, that the region remains at the bottom of the social capital ranking (79th). The situation is similar in Wallonia, with a higher social capital score (64th position) and a slightly lower value of the residual (20th position).

There are three main differences between Flanders and the North East of Italy on the one hand and Wallonia and the South of Italy on the other:

- In Flanders and the North East of Italy there is a higher participation in the labour market: 3 percentage points difference between Flanders and Wallonia, 11 percentage points between the North East and the South of Italy.
- In the North East there is a lower level of income inequalities than in the South of Italy.[9]
- The residual of the regression model is higher in Flanders and the North East.

The different level of labour market participation is the main determinant[10] of the social capital gap between Flanders and Wallonia on the one

Table 7.1 Dependent and independent variables and values of the residuals

Dependent Variable				Independent Variables									
Regions	Social Capital	P	Regions	GDP% EU	P	Regions	Gini Coeff.	P	Regions	Activity Rates	P	Regions	National Divergence
Vlaams Gewest	0.21	24	Brussels	217	2	Vlaams Gewest	0.28	35	Vlaams Gewest	54.40	67	Nord-Ovest	0.22
Brussels	0.13	27	Lombardia	123	12	Brussels	0.28	36	Nord Est	54.31	68	Lombardia	0.22
Nord Est	−0.13	44	Lazio	116	20	Brussels	0.28	38	Lombardia	54.20	69	Nord Est	0.22
Wallonia	−0.45	64	Nord Est	111	23	Lazio	0.28	39	Brussels	53.90	71	Centro	0.22
Centro	−0.57	68	Vlaams Gewest	108	25	Centro	0.28	40	Centro	51.18	78	Lazio	0.22
Lombardia	−0.69	72	Centro	106	27	Wallonia	0.29	44	Wallonia Wallone	51.10	79	Sud	0.22
Nord-Ovest	−0.79	76	Nord-Ovest	102	32	Nord-Ovest	0.30	48	Lazio	50.40	81	Isole	0.22
Sud	−0.91	79	Wallonia	79	65	Nord Est	0.30	50	Nord-Ovest	49.07	82	Brussels	0.28
Lazio	−1.04	80	Isole	64	78	Lombardia	0.34	67	Isole	43.60	83	Vlaams Gewest	0.28
Isole	−1.07	81	Sud	63	79	Sud	0.37	77	Sud	43.00	84	Wallonia Wallone	0.28

Residuals

Regions	Social Capital	P	Regions	Formal Networks	P	Regions	Informal Networks	P	Regions	Social Trust	P
Vlaams Gewest	1.943	1	Vlaams Gewest	2.093	1	Brussels	1.646	5	Vlaams Gewest	1.26	5
Nord Est	0.846	14	Isole	1.757	2	Nord Est	0.488	19	Sud	0.94	15
Sud	0.751	18	Nord Est	1.393	5	Lombardia	0.329	24	Isole	0.92	16
Wallonia	0.695	20	Sud	1.135	9	Vlaams Gewest	0.146	31	Wallonia	0.44	25
Isole	0.647	21	Wallonia	0.746	16	Wallonia	−0.080	36	Centro	−0.24	40
Brussels	0.634	22	Centro	0.278	28	Nord-Ovest	−0.110	37	Nord Est	−0.30	43
Centro	−0.245	47	Nord-Ovest	0.093	35	Sud	−0.480	48	Brussels	−0.38	48
Nord-Ovest	−0.465	50	Brussels	−0.090	43	Centro	−0.490	49	Lazio	−0.79	56
Lombardia	−0.755	54	Lombardia	−0.530	50	Lazio	−0.640	54	Nord-Ovest	−0.87	58
Lazio	−1.511	64	Lazio	−1.370	65	Isole	−1.400	69	Lombardia	−1.29	65

Notes:
P: Position in the European Ranking (Chapters 4 and 5).
Coeff: coefficient.

Source: Author's elaboration.

139

hand, and the North East and the South of Italy on the other (as shown by the maximum impact measurement in Table 6.2, column 4).

Italy and Belgium both have a dual labour market as emphasized by many economists (for a good account see Estevao [2003] and Reid and Musyck [2000] for Belgium, and Bertola and Garibaldi [2002], Boeri and Garibaldi [2000 and 2005] and Destefanis and Fonseca [2005] for Italy). Labour market participation[11] is only one indicator among many that shows the marked duality between the control and the divergent cases: unemployment is 6–7 percentage points higher in Wallonia and the South of Italy,[12] youth unemployment is 22–23 percentage points higher,[13] and finally, the shadow economy is extremely spread out in the divergent cases.[14]

This persistent difference in the same national context is not explained by traditional economic theory. Over-regulation of the labour market, heavy taxation and social security burdens are similar factors all over the two countries. Therefore, there must be other forces at work. Several explanations of this duality have been advanced: the lack of enforcement of the regulations (Boeri and Garibaldi 2000), the lack of matching jobs and workers[15] (Destefanis and Fonseca 2005), and the presence of certain social norms that impact on the choice of economically efficient behaviours (Akerlof 1980: 750).

From our point of view the poor conditions of the labour market and especially low participation, contribute to the destruction of social capital. This cleavage is even more pronounced in the Italian case and cannot be considered a simple historical consequence: 'the north-south differential in employment rates increased by almost four percentage points in the last decade of the twentieth century because of an increasing gap in labour force participation rates rather than larger differences in the incidence of unemployment across the two macro-regions' (Boeri and Garibaldi 2000: 22). In what follows, the comparative historical analysis of Italian and Belgian regions complements the socio-economic model.

7.3   THE COMPARATIVE HISTORICAL ANALYSIS

This section explores the relation between the socio-economic and historical factors by explaining social capital variation in the Belgian and Italian regions. (1) It challenges Putnam's historical analysis of medieval towns in the twelfth and thirteenth centuries and (2) reflects on a peasant's life in the nineteenth century. It (3) describes the complex construction of a national historical narrative during the Italian and Belgian unification process and (4) analyses the current awakening of pre-existent regional identities. It is argued that, in this context a different self-awareness and pride of regional history has developed in strict relation to the socio-economic success of the regions. This section concludes with the (5) formulation of the *sleeping social capital theory*.

7.3.1 Putnam's Theory of Historical Fallacies: A Brief Re-visitation of Medieval Towns

Medieval towns are not unanimously considered to be symbols of freedom, the creation of horizontal links and embryonic democratic life. In *Making Democracy Work*, Putnam (1993) neglects the division within municipal towns and their dearth of civic participation; the experience of the Northern realities are misinterpreted, the growth of important towns in the South of Italy disregarded, and the positive effects on social networks generated by Frederic the Second's policy, ignored.

The great historian Henry Pirenne, focusing on Belgian towns, gave a detailed account of municipal democracies. These cities, created by the burgers, were only functional to their interests (Pirenne 1963: 156), they were divided microcosms 'with the absence of the feeling of democracy' (Pirenne 1963: 158–9). The medieval towns were not construction sites of future democratic life like the Greek *Poleis*,[16] but places where 'the commonwealth interposed the group of comrades' and the interests of different crafts were the only reason to act[17] (Pirenne 1963: 112–13).

Pirenne's description of municipal towns in Belgium is confirmed by Brezzi in Italy. They were divided and administered by a narrow aristocratic minority (Brezzi 1959: 32). Furthermore, medieval towns were not homogeneously spread out in the Northern part of the country. In his analysis, Putnam refers to Lombard towns, although in the North East there were no large important cities at the time (Brezzi [1959: 78] defined them of minor importance).

In the South of Italy, municipal life was not absent. In many areas the creation of new towns, namely Lecce, Foggia, Catanzaro and Amalfi, between the ninth and the twelfth centuries, was more of a relevant phenomenon than in the North (Various Authors 1981: 11). The Kingdom of Sicily was not only a destroyer of horizontal ties during this period. Innovative policies were developed to foster international commercial networks, such as the 10 years tax exemption for all merchants who decided to live in the South of Italy and the guarantee of a strong tax reduction to those who decided to actively trade within the Kingdom (Yver 1968: 4–5). The development of trading life, domestic exchange being boosted in many ways, and a protected agricultural economy, made the Kingdom of Sicily the most prosperous state in Europe (Yver 1968: 6).

After clarifying the fallacies of Putnam's historical reconstruction of medieval town life, we revisit the peasants' conditions, highlighting the fact that in the nineteenth century the Belgian and Italian agrarian situation was not so different.

7.3.2   Revisiting Peasants' Reality

The historical status of land ownership has been advocated by Banfield (1958) and Putnam (1993) as one of the main reasons for the absence of civic engagement in the South of Italy. They suggested that the domination of absentee landowners from the Middle Ages to World War II destroyed all horizontal ties. The comparison between Italy and Belgium helps to shed a different light on this historical interpretation. The situation of land ownership in the nineteenth century and the consequent migration towards other areas of the country was similar in Flanders, the North East and the South of Italy. The implementation of protectionist policy after unification, and the clientelistic management of agrarian reforms after World War II worsened the conditions of the labour market and contributed to the increase of income inequality, progressively eroding horizontal ties.

Land ownership and the political influence of the aristocracy were similar in Belgium and Italy at the beginning of the nineteenth century (Delfosse 1994: 54). In Italy, the aristocracy was in absolute control of the peasants. The small size of the land cultivated by peasants condemned many families to poverty and migration[18] (Delfosse 1994: 55; Bevilacqua 1993).

In particular, in the South of Italy, the socio-economic conditions at the beginning of the nineteenth century were less problematic than a century later. The Bourbon legislation during the 1830s created an embryonic partnership between land owners, the state and collectivity. The land owners were called on to participate in the realization of land reclamation and other measures to heal the landscape with the support of the Kingdom. This was an attempt to merge private and public interests, reduce the diffusion of malaria and improve the quality of the environment, intended already as a public good (Bevilacqua 1993: 57). The Bourbons were trying to create a large convergence of interests based on the interactions among different components of society. The experience of cooperative behaviour in land reclamation could have contributed to the creation of horizontal ties and social engagement (Bevilacqua 1993: 58). After unification, the liberal government dismissed this policy and blindly supported the harassment of the peasants by the landowners.

Moreover, the situation of the *latifondo*[19] in the nineteenth century differed from Banfield's and Putnam's description. Despite poverty and peasant illiteracy, the *latifondo* was an effective safety net and a network of exchange. A certain level of social security was provided through the guarantee of a job. Another decision of the government, the restriction of free-trade in 1887, signed the end of this unique form of social organization in many areas of the South of Italy: 'it is now well established that the impact of protectionist legislation on Italy's trade in farm products was especially damaging to commodities typically produced in the south, that is, wine, olive oil, liquorice and citrus fruits' (Petrusewicz 1997: 37). Traditional importers of Mediterranean products increased their tariffs; the South of Italy paid for its specialization and the narrowness of Italian markets.

In order to continue its exports, the *latifondo* changed brutally and kinship and job security were curtailed (Petrusewicz 1997: 37). The disappearance of the security net was not substituted by any governmental initiative. *Latifondo* disappeared without heirs at the end of the nineteenth century during a period of economic and social unrest; the capitalist *latifondo* took its place, becoming an infamous protagonist of the Mezzogiorno's history in the first half of the twentieth century (Petrusewicz 1997: 39). Putnam's and Banfield's descriptions refer to this late evolution and not to the original configuration of land control. The long historical evolution does not reveal a systematic destruction of horizontal ties.

The governmental decisions after unification impacted on labour market conditions and contributed to further inequalities, protect the rising industry of the North West and abandoning Southern peasants to their *miseria* (Salvadori 1977: 65). The increasing migration in connection with the agrarian reforms half a century later contributed to the reduction of social engagement and political participation even further. The agrarian reform arrived later[20] (after World War II) and turned into an occasion to impose the hegemony of the Christian Democratic Party on the Southern Italy (Bevilacqua 1993:99). The land was assigned according to clientelistic principles causing corruption and reducing trust in institutions (see next chapter).

7.3.3 Researching a Continuous Historical Narrative: A Hazardous Process of Unification

The use of past legacy to legitimize the creation of a new national state assumed particular connotations in Belgium and Italy. The task undertaken by historians, finding a narrative to justify the existence of the nation, proved to be very problematic.[21] The lack of any continuous historical narrative runs parallel to the chaotic development of their political institutions (see next chapter). Constructing a coherent and homogenous historical narrative was hard due to the similar nature of Italy and Belgium; both states having been, for different reasons, two cultural bridges sitting on two important fractures within the European space.

In fact, both countries have different regional profiles, despite efforts by historians to propose a common national narrative (Tollebeek 1998: 338). The only two unifying elements were the opposition to foreign domination and the Catholic tradition. In this respect the historians read the unification process as something which was determined by the glorious ancestors of the nation, almost a Messianic truth: 'The Belgians needed to write their own history. They needed to tell the quiet tale of their own ancestors, and they needed to do this with an almost religious devotion. National history was a legacy, and just like all legacies, it was an obligation; it had to be accepted and continued' (Tollebeek 1998: 344).

So, Catholicism suddenly became the *Volkgeist* of the nation, following Herder's romantic definition (Tollebeek 1998: 341). The existence of a Catholic genius was evoked also in Italy through the neo-guelfian school, led by Alessandro Manzoni (in the literary world) and Vincenzo Gioberti (in the philosophical and political field), asserting that the Popedom was the only national institution able to pursue the project of independence.

In the background of institutional weakness and lack of social trust there is a problematic reconstruction of national historical narrative. In this context the multiple identities existent in the nation awaken, providing an alternative sense of identification for the population which did not feel completely engaged in the new nation. These multiple identities derive from the cultural and geographical nature of the two countries. Belgium was at the crossroads between the Latin and Germanic world (Linden 1920: 22), and Italy between Northern Europe and the Mediterranean area. Both Belgians and Italians reacted to the lack of national integration in opposite ways: the Flemish and the North Eastern Italians embellished their past with pride, Walloons and Southern Italians progressively downgraded their self-image and regional history. The different socio-economic achievement is a key factor in understanding the different values attributed to regional culture and history.

7.3.4 A Different Self-Image

The coexistence of strong regional cultures and the problematic search for meaningful, national historical narratives contributed in different ways to the shaping of their regional identities. Today, Walloons and Southern Italians each perceive their own history with an inferiority complex fuelled by the superior socio-economic development of Flanders and North

Eastern Italy. According to Van Dam and Nizet (2002: 65), the Walloons naturally select the Flemish as a comparative group, but on the other hand the Flemish hardly use the comparison with the Walloons to define their own characteristics (Van Dam and Nizet 2002: 65). This means that Walloons suffer a sentiment of submission linked to a feeling of inferiority (Van Dam and Nizet 2002: 58).

The Southern Italians consider their past in an even more derogatory way than the Walloons. The current representation of the Mezzogiorno has often been reduced to a kind of non-history: a long account of what could have happened but did not happen, the history of a perpetual inferiority compared with the rest of the country (Bevilacqua 1993: VIII). In the media and in popular culture the South of Italy represents the negative incarnation of a question, an obscure problem, almost a social disease for which it is necessary to express a feeling of moral reprobation (Bevilacqua 1993: IX). Putnam and Banfield's theories have been nourished by this collective image.

In reality, there is a profound difference between the South as portrayed by the media[22] and the one described by the academic studies, between the perpetrated stereotypes and the reality (Bevilacqua 1993: XII). The poor Southern Italian and Walloon socio-economic performances have been interpreted in social capital literature as direct consequences of disastrous historical paths. The past has become like an original sin against which nothing can be done.

However, the lack of pride and self-esteem and the positive/negative image of past events do not constitute a perpetual reality. The Flemish case shows that the nineteenth century image had been successfully removed, taking its secular inferiority complex with it (Quariaux 2006). From this consideration, the analysis moves to the comprehension of the interaction between socio-economic and historical factors to explain social capital endowment.

7.3.5 Sleeping Social Capital

In the last part of the twentieth century the development of Flanders and the North East of Italy has become a success story. However, during the nineteenth century and early twentieth century, these areas were predominantly characterized by agricultural activity and a virtually non-existent industrial sector with massive migration towards the more industrialized parts of the country.[23] The situation changed progressively, thereby generating fast socio-economic development. This development was based on the creation of small and medium sized companies able to exploit the traditional know-how of the area (Keating, Loughlin and Deschouwer 2003: 78).

The economic miracle of the North East of Italy was faster and more celebrated than the parallel *Flemish Renaissance*. During the 1960s and the 1970s this area became famous for its industrial districts. This successful economic model was based on traditional craftsmanship, family company structure, efficient local administrations and the progressive accumulation of capital from migrants. The connection between these elements boosted a period of innovation and growth described by Bagnasco in the *Terza Italia*[24] (1977).

During the same period the Flemish overtook the Walloon economy. The socio-economic success and the echoes of a glorious past, rediscovered by the Flemish movement during the nineteenth century contributed to change Flanders' image. Flanders was no longer identified with the mass of poor peasants obliged to work in the Walloon factories (during the nineteenth century) but with the fourteenth century County of Flanders, despite the fact that the County of Flanders was only a collection of independent and wealthy cities and not a cohesive nation. However, in the atmosphere of successful socio-economic growth in the region, the image was reconstructed to portray a developed nation characterized by a well-established manufacturing sector and substantial trade with the rest of Europe. This idealized image of Flanders in the fourteenth century characterized modern Flanders in a period of decline of the traditional Walloon superiority. The humiliation of the past centuries and the backward rural image which had characterized the area for three centuries were rapidly forgotten.[25] A re-elaborated cultural legacy mixed with its socio-economic success translated into the reinforcement of Flemish self-confidence and pride, contributing to social capital growth.

In the North East of Italy there is also an attempt to reconstruct the glorious origins of the region and to progressively erase the backward and agricultural image of the nineteenth and the first part of the twentieth centuries. The metaphor of the *vento del nord*[26] used by the Lega Nord Party's leaders became especially successful in this area.[27] The image of an industrious and pragmatic population[28] (the Celtics), heirs to the Republic of Venice, has been successfully (in electoral terms) juxtaposed against the laziness of the Southerners (the Mediterraneans). The expression *Roma ladrona*,[29] coined by Umberto Bossi,[30] became part of the Italian jargon.

In Wallonia, the socio-economic growth of the nineteenth and the first half of the twentieth centuries did not generate the same positive effect on social capital as described in Flanders and the North East of Italy. The heavy industrialization was different from the endogenous development driven by small and medium sized companies (Reid and Musyck 2000: 183). The coal-mining and steel industries required a considerable level of capital resources which were not controlled at local level. 'As a result, the Walloon economy was, from an early stage, controlled by investors concerned by their interests on a national and international level rather than directly with the future of the region' (Reid and Musyck 2000: 184). With the end of heavy industrialization and the economic downturn, the capital invested in Wallonia moved away. The absence of endogenous development generated a negative impact on the level of labour market participation, reducing social capital and entrepreneurship.

The case of Southern Italy presents some important similarities with Wallonia, although it emerges from a different set of historical circumstances. The absence of infrastructures (see next chapter), the reversing of a local industrialization process from the Bourbons to the unified Kingdom of Italy (Bevilacqua 1993: 31), and the top-down approach,[31] destroyed the small germs of entrepreneurship in the area. We now bring to the argument the notion that this process had a stronger impact on social capital than the presumed absence of civic tradition in the twelfth and thirteenth centuries (as previously discussed).

During the twentieth century in parts of the South of Italy (Calabria, Sardegna and Basilicata) a process of de-industrialization[32] took place. In this way, agricultural activity became the only economic activity in the Mezzogiorno, consolidating the structural difference with the Northern part of the country (Bevilacqua 1993: 66). The destruction of local industry transformed the South into an area in which people were almost anthropologically devoted to agriculture. Why would a wealthy landowner or a trader have invested their capital into modern and unexplored industrial activities in preference to siphoning off agrarian profits into banks that offered high interest rates? In this context productive investment was profoundly curtailed (Bevilacqua 1993: 72).

From the observation of these four cases we can draw some general conclusions: if endogenous development does not generate an improvement of socio-economic conditions, in particular a higher participation in the labour market and a larger redistribution of wealth, then social networks and social trust are dramatically affected. In this context the positive influence of past historical events to foster social cohesion and civic engagement is disregarded and the culture of the area becomes progressively associated with backwardness, with the destruction of social capital. In Wallonia and the South of Italy the negative effects of low labour market activity rates and the low degree of redistribution on social capital overshadowed the existence of historical examples of civic and social engagement.

Historical and cultural influences are similar to the 'appropriable social capital' defined by Coleman (1990) using the example of the Korean students. The networks formed during childhood through attendance at local churches became functional in another context many years later: the student revolt. The relation between historical evolutions and the socio-economic variables described in the model is similar. Only after reaching a sufficient threshold of labour market activity and income redistribution can the memory of historical events of social engagement become fully appropriable by the population, leading to the development of innovative forms of socio-economic growth. This cycle further increases social capital, when socio-economic development is matched with the revival of historical and cultural traditions. The 'unique past' became a source of pride for the area increasing intra-regional solidarity, boosting social networks and social trust.

The Flemish case (and to a lesser extent the North East) can be used to describe the practical consequences of this process. We have already considered how the socio-economic improvements were matched by the revival of the Flemish tradition. The positive effect on social capital generated by the socio-economic improvement has been multiplied by the reconstruction of the Flemish identity. This pride and self-confidence has in turn, increased the feeling of solidarity and contributed to generate a level of social capital which is hardly explicable by single socio-economic predictors.

In these divergent cases, the value of a cultural and historical legacy is curtailed by the negative impact of socio-economic factors; it is a 'sleeping social capital'. The biased and simplistic interpretations of the negative effect of history on social capital can be overthrown only when the socio-economic conditions reach a sufficient level, enacting the cycle that has been described for Flanders. Wallonia and the Mezzogiorno have to work in two directions, if we are to learn from the Flemish experience: (1) by proposing new policies in the labour market and reducing inequalities, and (2) by starting both the rediscovery and re-invention of their past, by presenting a new collective image that will reinforce social capital when socio-economic conditions improve. Hence, history and culture in these areas are not the cause of the lack of social capital but a potential factor for improvement. As we shall see, an important moment of social engagement, involving the Sicilian peasantry at the end of the nineteenth century, is described. The collective image of Walloons and Southern Italians should take heart from these almost forgotten examples of collective history.

7.4   *I FASCI SICILIANI*: A FORGOTTEN EXAMPLE OF SOCIAL CAPITAL CREATION

In this section the centrality of the *Fasci Siciliani* movement for social capital theory is discussed providing some historical detail forgotten by the national historical narrative. The *Fasci Siciliani* was a spontaneous peasants' movement that took place in Sicily between 1893 and 1894. The description of this movement assumes a symbolic meaning in the light of the sleeping social capital theory, helping to reflect upon:

- the biased vision proposed by the mainstream literature of a Southern Italian culture which generated the passivity of citizens,
- the negative role of governmental intervention that did not allow the further development of innovative forms of social participation,
- the opportunity to reread historical events to preserve an important memory of collective engagement.

The *Fasci Siciliani* lasted for almost one year and were not a simple sporadic peasant revolt; their organization impressed European observers and it was compared by the Belgian Socialist Congress to the spontaneous organization of working class leagues in Wallonia of March 1866: 'In Sicily, the socialist movement is rising: it developed with a rapidity similar to the formation of Belgian working class leagues, after the events of March 1866.'[33]

The advent of this organized movement of revolt, contradicts the image of the so-called passive Southern peasantry, which was never involved in social or political life, described by Putnam (1993) and Banfield (1958). The peasantry reacted many other times to abuse of power[34] but the *Fasci Siciliani* acquired a territorial penetration never before reached by other revolts in the country. Tired of witnessing the state as only tax collector and *carabiniere*,[35] the peasants wanted government action to improve their conditions of work (Nitti 1900: 11).

The *Fasci Siciliani* showed the ability to propose a pacific model of social engagement through the collective occupation of land and the consolidation of a capillary rooted organization. After the spontaneous bottom-up approach, springing from its roots, the movement's aim was agrarian reform to be achieved through the election of representatives in the city councils and the parliament. Thanks to the formulation of a political strategy, the movement provided the first political socialization for the peasants; they were able to understand the most important principle of democracy: citizens and workers have duties but also rights that nobody can take away.

The invasion of the land represented a collective act which involved thousands of peasants[36] and hundreds of communities (Rossi Doria 1999: 94). The *Fasci* had an ad hoc federal organization that allowed widespread penetration in Sicilian rural areas.[37] There was a subscription quota and a structured internal organization which developed relevant forms of solidarity and self-help, such as the distribution of part of the subscriptions to the widows of the peasants killed by the landlords and the army. The rising of collective solidarity and the creation of horizontal ties shed a different light on Southern peasants. They were not all self-interested in their short term gain as Banfield portrayed them.

The government opposed itself strongly against the *Fasci* in support of the unproductive absentee landowner, reinforcing the lack of trust of the peasants toward the institutions. The army repressed their manifestations in bloodshed. Colajanni calculated that during the strikes 92 peasants had been killed and only one soldier, confirming the pacific character of the revolt (Crainz 1999: 53). Such government action was the catalyst of violent reaction; on 20 January 1894 in the small village of Caltavuturo 500 peasants peacefully and symbolically occupied land that belonged to the government. The army killed 13 unarmed people without any reason (Colajanni 1894: 171).

Crispi, the Sicilian prime minister, used false documents in the parliament to invoke cohesive action against the *Fasci*, which according to him were only a conspiracy with the Bourbons and the *briganti*[38] to detach Sicily from the rest of the country; this connection was never proved to be true (Colajanni 1894: 246). The government did not listen to the peasants' proposals and refused to mediate on their behalf with the landlords; the right to strike was not guaranteed and the increase of the daily salary never considered as an option.

The state did not seem to realize that for the first time the peasants were consciously entering into the history of their country (Colajanni 1894: 173). A movement of free expression was stifled with violence, which destroyed the rising of social and civic engagement of the Sicilian peasants (Colajanni 1894: 5). The repression destroyed the potential creation of a dialectic relationship between public power and the population; the peasants did not have the chance to fully experiment a form of political and social organization in way that would have probably increased their collective consciousness (Bevilacqua 1993: 84). Many peasants realized that the social struggle was a useless and dangerous business and turned instead to taking care only of their family and their clientele.

However, the example of the *fasci* remained an important reference for peasants' revolts in various Southern regions for the first part of the twentieth century. The struggles continued in different forms also after World War II and contributed to change the political equilibrium in certain areas of the South, confirming that the peasantry was not completely passive and unable to have a political affiliation different from the clientele of the landlords[39] (Rossi Doria 1999: 100).

This event, almost forgotten by the Italian national historical narrative, was an extraordinary example of social engagement. Peasants challenged the government, proposing an idea which was subversive in the Southern Italian context: to substitute the vertical model of clientelism with a horizontal one of a continuous discussion by collective organizations in the political arena (Rossi Doria 1999: 106). The historical re-evaluation of certain events with the active engagement of the government to improve the situation in the labour market together with the redistribution of wealth could potentially generate a revival of social participation and social trust. The lesson of the *Fasci Siciliani* is still valid more than a hundred years on, and proves that the past of a region is more than its reputation of passive behaviour; a reputation which has emerged from a stagnant and unfair society.

7.5   SUMMARY

In this chapter the evidence gathered from the socio-economic model has been paired with an historical analysis to propose a broader theory. It is suggested that the lack of social capital is not dependent upon a deviant historical path. Certain historical events are not an original sin that determines a perpetual absence of social trust and a reduced density of social networks. In reality, the importance of certain historical events is overshadowed by the current socio-economic underperformance of the regions. Social capital sleeps and with it the potential positive influence of regional history.

In the next chapter we will describe how institutions and political culture evolved in two countries tainted by geographical fracture: Italy, which straddles the North European and Mediterranean world, and Belgium, on the division of both Germanic and the Latin world. The recent institutional reforms (more advanced in Belgium than in Italy) and their impact on social capital are explored in the light of their fragmented and chaotic institutional evolution.

NOTES

1. These findings relate also to the traditional debate on the Southern question and Banfield's amoral familism theory. The term *Questione Meridionale* (Southern issue) is used in historic-political language to refer to the socio-economic and cultural differences between the North and the South of Italy and the studies connected with this issue. The long-term permanence of this deep division has been the object of many analyses and studies since the eighteenth century, but the debate increased in importance after Italian unification in 1861. Among the most influential contributions in

the field: Alcaro (1999), Barbagallo, (1990), Cafiero (1996), Cassano (1996), Chiarello (1992), Colajanni (1894), Compagna (1963), De Martino (1959), Donolo (1972), Donzelli (1990), Dorso (1949), Fortunato (1973), Franchetti and Sonnino (1974), Galasso (1965), Gramsci (1952), Nitti (1900), Petrusewicz (1997, 1998), Rossi Doria (1948, 1958, 1967), Salvadori (1977), Salvemini (1958), Turiello (1882), Villari (1961, 1979), Vöchting (1955). For a complete review see Bevilacqua (1993: 137–62).

The debate on the lack of collective action in the South of Italy (Allum 1975; Arlacchi 1980a; 1980b; Blok 1974; Brogger 1971; Caciagli et al. 1977; Catanzaro 1975; 1979; 1980; 1982; 1983; Collida 1978; Donolo 1972; Friedmann 1954a; 1954b; 1974; Graziani and Pugliese 1979; Graziano, 1974; Lopreato 1961; Mazzarone 1978; Moss and Capannari 1959; 1960; 1962; Pitkin 1954; Reyneri 1979; Schneider and Schneider 1976; Scotellaro 1955; Tarrow 1972; 1976; 1979; Wichers 1964) has been popularized by Banfield's amoral familism theory. Many scholars have subsequently discussed this controversial work from a theoretical point of view (Bagnasco 2006; Benigno 1979; Cancian 1961; Catanzaro 1983; 1992; Cerase 1992; Colombis 1974; 1980; 1992; 1997; Davis 1973; Di Gennaro 1992; Gaggio 2007; Giannini and Salomone 1992; Gribaudi 1993; 1997; Kertzer 2007; Marselli 1963; Meloni 1997; Miller 1974; Mingione and Magatti 1997; Muraskin 1974; Piselli 1997; Pizzorno 1971; Pugliese 1992; Santoro 2007; Sciolla 1997; 2001; 2004; Silverman 1968; Trigilia 1992; Turnaturi and Donolo 1988; Viazzo 2007; for a review Blando 2007; Ferragina 2009b; 2010b) and connecting Banfield's criticism to Putnam's theory (Bagnasco 1999; Ramella 1994; 1995; Sciolla and Negri 1996; Tarrow 1996; Trigilia 2001). The interest for amoral familism did not remain confined to Southern Italian specialists, *The Moral Basis of a Backward Society* is a classic of social science that has been analysed in different disciplines, that is, political sociology (Almond and Verba 1963; Putnam 1993), anthropology (Foster 1965), business studies (Carney 2007; Dyer 2006; Bertrand and Schoar 2006), economics (Aghion et al. 2010; Alesina and La Ferrara 2002; Alesina and Giuliano 2010; Alesina and Ichino 2010; Kwon and Arenius 2010; Sabatini 2008; Tabellini 2010), psychology (Triandis 1989); discussed by highly influential works (Adler and Kwon 2002; Coleman 1988; Fukuyama 1995; Inghlehart 1988); and extended to various geographical contexts, as for example, Greece (Mcnall 1976), Spain (Aceves 1971), Mexico (Quigley 1973), South Korea (Kim 1990) Poland (Tarkowska and Tarkowski 1991), Russia (Schrader 2004), South Africa (Moller 2010), and third world countries (Woolcock 1998). For an empirical test of amoral familism theory see Ferragina (2011).

2. Bloch and Febvre will recall this idea creating the so called 'Annals School'. This group of French historians changed completely the sense of historiography. History is a problematic discipline, it has to question the past putting constantly under enquiry all its postulates to reflect upon the other sciences and the evolution of mankind.

3. In the *New Science* (Vico et al. 1968) Vico equated history to natural sciences. History is regulated by universal laws and principles that repeat themselves constantly, constituting the reference point for the birth and the development of nations.

4. Also in Wallonia the absence of social capital is considered one of the main reasons for economic slowdown: 'In the case of Wallonia, it is precisely the lack of such social capital that appears to undermine efforts to regenerate economic growth in the region. Despite the efforts of certain stakeholders at regional and local level, the defensive approach to slowing industrial decline by public investments in "lame-ducks", boosting public sector employment and attracting inward investors to replace the declining large firms already apparent in the early restructuring phases of the 1970s has lingered on into the 1980s and 1990s' (Reid and Musyck 2000: 197).

5. Medium-high social capital levels equate with positive values of the residuals and low levels of social capital equate with negative values.

6. Brussels because of its particular status of capital will not be compared to the other regions.

7. Flanders ranks in 35th position in terms of income inequality, in the 67th position for

labour market participation and has the highest national divergence in the European sample.

8. Also in this case, the social capital score is higher than we would have expected from socio-economic predictors. The North East ranks in 48th position for income inequality level, in 68th position for labour market participation and has a high national divergence.

9. This difference does not exist in the Belgian case.

10. The impact of income inequality and the discussion on the residuals are not described in this section. Income inequalities have been approached previously (Chapters 5 and 6), the implications for the cases are clarified by the general model; and the higher positive residuals of the North East and of Flanders, especially, are discussed in the next section to conclude the historical comparative analysis.

11. According to the Eurostat Regional Statistics (2007) labour market participation rates in the four regions analysed are: Flanders (54.8%), North East (54.67%), Wallonia (51.2) and the South of Italy (41.70%).

12. Flanders (4.3%), Wallonia (10.5%), North East (3.09%) and the South of Italy (10.5%) in 2007 (Eurostat 2007).

13. Flanders 3.4% and Wallonia 26.7% (Estevao 2003), North East 4.3% and the South of Italy 26.8% (Bertola and Garibaldi 2002).

14. On the shadow economy see Schneider's contribution (2005). Italy, after Greece, has the highest share of the shadow economy in Europe (26.2% of the GDP) and Belgium is the first non-Mediterranean country (21.5% of the GDP) in the ranking. The shadow economy and unemployment tend to be positively correlated, as shown in the Italian case by Boeri and Garibaldi (2000). A similar situation takes place in Belgium.

15. An interesting argument has been proposed by Pissarides (1990) and successively re-elaborated for the Italian case by Destefanis and Fonseca (2005). Labour market transactions, high costs and coordination problems originated difficulties in the matching between jobs and workers, creating the existence in the same market of unemployment and vacancies (Destefanis and Fonseca 2005:1). 'This argument is proved by the high difference in the Beveridge curve between the North and the South of Italy' (Destefanis and Fonseca 2005: 11). A similar phenomenon has been detected in Belgium: 'the existence of high and low unemployment areas in the same country suggests poor market efficiency in matching people to jobs' (Estevao 2003: 95).

16. The *Poleis* had a limited participation. Only citizens (a small minority of the inhabitants) had political rights. In medieval towns participation was even more restricted.

17. The fragmentation and social cleavages emerged at the time of municipal towns impacted dramatically on the development of democratic institutions (see next chapter).

18. People moved in big waves where industrialization was taking place. The migration from Flanders was an old phenomenon which intensified during the 1860s and continued with regularity until the 1920s. More than 500,000 Flemish moved into Wallonia, in particular at Liege, Charleroi and Tournai (Quairiaux 2006). In Italy the migration toward the North West after World War II started from the North East and then was followed by massive waves from the South (Bevilacqua 1993: 60).

19. Large estate.

20. At this point in time the possession of the land was not so important any more because with the progressive industrialization of the country the number of people employed in the primary sector drastically declined.

21. In Belgium and Italy the struggle to reunify the countries went under the name of *Renaissance* (1830) and *Risorgimento* (1861) rather than revolution or unification (Tollebeek 1998: 334). The past legacy was used to justify and mobilize the population. Belgium and Italy did not want to appear simple 'parvenu' in the international context (Tollebeek 1998: 335) but showed themselves to the other European powers as young states which possessed an old national history.

22. This negative connotation of Walloon and Southern culture is identified with a sort of Mediterranean spirit. 'The Walloons are slow they take time. The Wallonia constitute

the Mediterranean area of Belgium, one could say the South' (Van Dam and Nizet: 2002: 28). The Mediterranean and the Southern connotations are not physical locations but a mythical entity: 'The South is much more than a geographical area. It is a metaphor which refers to an imaginary and mythical entity, associated with both hell and paradise: it is a place of the soul and emblem of the evil that occurs everywhere, but an emblem that in Italy has been embodied in just one part of the nation's territory, becoming one of the myths on which the nation has been built' (Gribaudi 1997: 84).

23. To Wallonia between the 1860s and the 1910s and to the North West after World War II.

24. The *Third Italy* was different from the industrialized North West (the first Italy: engine of the Italian development till the 1970s) and the Mezzogiorno (the second Italy: poor, backward and desolated).

25. *In Culture, Institutions and Economic Development*, Keating et al. (2003: 82) described this transformation and the use of traditional culture to support economic development: 'For more than a century the image of Flanders was one of rural backwardness. The thousands of poor and "uncivilized" Flemish peasants (thus speaking a Flemish dialect) who emigrated south to work in the Walloon industry did a lot to reinforce that image. For a long time the cultural reference of Flanders, the language, thus denoted low status, referring to backwardness, to "poor Flanders". Today this cultural reference to the nineteenth and the first half of the twentieth century has almost disappeared. The history of Flanders now rather uses historical reference points that relate directly to trade and economy, and to glorious cultural products. The medieval history of the county of Flanders, [. . .] Culture is indeed now seen as an important economic asset.'

26. Wind of the North.

27. During the 2010 regional election the Lega Nord has been the first party in the North East obtaining 36% of the votes.

28. Also in Belgium the Germanic character is opposed to the Latin laziness with similar tones. The renewed image of operosity and productivity of the Flemish is completely accepted by the Walloon who very often consider themselves lazy. In the last century the Walloons were still proud of the position of French language and considered Flemish no more than a collection of dialects spoken by backward peasants. The construction of these images in both cases became possible only with the economic success. The change of these conditions contributed to the redefinition of the stereotypes.

29. Rome the big thief.

30. The leader of the party.

31. As, for example, with the *Cassa del Mezzogiorno* and the creation of industrial poles without any local participation.

32. Meaning an increase of the number of the industrial workers smaller than the augmentation of population.

33. Note of the Belgian Socialist Congress about the *Fasci Siciliani* reported by Colajanni (1894: 28).

34. Nitti noticed that in 1799, 1820, 1848, 1859 and then 1893 the South of Italy was always the first part of the country to react against the bad governmental policy (Nitti 1900: 11).

35. A kind of policeman.

36. 50,000 according to the state, more than 150,000 according to Colajanni (1894: 13–14).

37. The protest has been more successful in the countryside than in Palermo and Catania.

38. Bandits.

39. For example in 1948 in the middle of Calabria (which predominantly voted for the *Democrazia Cristiana*) in the area of Crotone more than 50% of people voted for the popular front rather than the Christian Democrats. In this area the occupation of the land led to violent repressions in which a young pregnant mother was killed. We refer to the facts of Calabricata, and to Giuditta Levato, killed by a landlord during a pacific invasion of the land on 28 November 1946 (Rossi Doria 1999).

8. Fraternal twins: institutional evolution and social capital

In the previous chapter the interaction between socio-economic factors and historical evolution has been discussed, thereby explaining the divergent pattern of Wallonia and the South of Italy. Following on from this approach, the sleeping social capital theory has been illustrated by comparing these two deviant cases with Flanders and the North East of Italy (the control cases). This chapter aims to integrate the comparative historical analysis, taking into account the impact of political organizations and institutional change on social capital. As emphasized by North (1990: VII): history matters because present and future are connected to the past by the continuity and transformation of society's institutions.

Belgium and Italy sit on two important fractures of the European continent; Belgium at the crossroads between the Latin and the Germanic world,[1] and Italy between North European and Mediterranean space. These two fractures have different origins but similar effects on the political culture and institutional development of each country, as demonstrated by the parallel passage from a central to a federal state, through regionalization.

Institutional change in the two countries is discussed starting from the wide historical and social cleavages that traversed the two countries after their unification in the nineteenth century. Their political cultures have been characterized by a high fragmentation of society around vertical groups, the diffusion of a system of relations between formal and informal powers, and a pervasive corruption, which served to smooth out the system and avoid blockages. This resulted in a reduction of the willingness to create formal social networks and a lower level of institutional trust. The proportional redistribution of public resources and the complicated equilibrium established among the *pillars* has been almost exclusively managed by the political parties. They limited the interference of other political actors and became hegemonic by occupying the space normally taken by other secondary groups, thereby reinforcing the lack of horizontal ties in society.

Only the progressive deterioration of the traditional parties' control of social and economic life boosted the process of decentralization (started in the 1970s and speeded up by the scandals of the 1990s). Federalism was conceived as an elixir to heal the two countries: to reduce corruption, to create a more articulated separation of powers, to improve the efficiency of public policy and to increase social participation at the local level. However, the decentralization process does not only have potentially positive effects on the social capital level. The presence of a strong de facto asymmetry might act in an opposite sense, especially if adequate institutional arrangements are not put in place to deal with it.

Belgium constituted an institutional model for Italy from the nineteenth century onward. The Belgian constitution of 1830 was the blueprint for the *Statuto Albertino*.[2] Subsequently, Belgium and Italy moved in parallel, commencing a decentralization process in the 1970s. This process brought (in 1993) a federal reform in Belgium and it is still under way in Italy, where the fiscal and administrative decentralization has not yet been followed by the institutional decentralization and the consequent recognition of the federal status in the constitution.

Then we apply the theory of institutional change formulated by Douglass North together with a problem-solving approach to analyse the development of Belgian and Italian political culture. We argue that a political culture based on the proportional distribution of public resources, without any assessment of efficiency, spread out from the unsolved challenges which had emerged during the unification process. The low level of institutional trust and the weak density of social networks are partially explained by this peculiar political culture and the role assumed by political parties, which occupied all the space normally taken by other secondary groups. The collapse of the old political system fostered decentralization; it is suggested that this process might have positive or negative effects on social capital according to the capacity of the new institutional design which deals with the strong regional asymmetry existent in both countries.

8.1   INSTITUTIONAL CHANGE AND THE PROBLEM-SOLVING APPROACH

The evolution of a society is dictated by the continuous interaction between institutions and organizations: institutions intended as the rules of the game and organizations as the players (North 1990: 3). In Douglass North's words institutions are: 'the structure that humans impose on human interaction and therefore define the incentives that determine the choices that individuals make, that shape the performance of societies and economies over time' (North 1990: 2). Organizations, on the other hand, are a group of individuals bound by some common purpose to achieve objectives (North 1990: 5).

The chapter focuses on political and institutional organizations. This is because the social fragmentation of the two countries has been managed centrally by the elite in power through the expansion of the political, social and economic prerogatives of their political parties. The progressive institutional change, represented by the passage from centralism to federalism and its effect on social capital can only be understood by looking simultaneously at the evolution of these political institutions and organizations.

The development of Belgian and Italian political culture can be illustrated through the lens of the profound social fragmentation existent in the two countries. The presence of dominant vertical groups, the capillary diffusion of a complicated system of formal and informal relationships and a high degree of corruption characterized the development of this political culture. Political parties have been for a long time the main gatekeepers of this institutional structure; they absorbed the shock generated by social fragmentation and monopolized the space between society and the government of the country. In this way, they eroded the role of other secondary groups, reducing horizontal ties and, in the long run, institutional trust.

The choice of individuals to be less involved in secondary groups can be understood by analysing institutional development. Political institutions reduced the incentive to create associations outside the channels provided by political parties and trade unions. The existence of this institutional structure constrained the freedom of choice of individuals, often pushing them to take decisions that cannot be considered rational and efficient in the neo-classical sense of the term. Individuals and organizations developed their own rationality to maximize the use of social networks in the given institutional framework. The consociational democracy is not the most efficient political system, however in many phases of Belgian history it helped political actors to reform institutions and carry on with political and social life, avoiding social unrest.

Institutional constraints and the social norms generated by these constraints changed over time, altering the choice and the opportunities available to individuals and organizations. This is demonstrated by the passage from centralism to federalism. The change has been invoked by political organizations and citizens to increase efficiency and participation,[3] following the Tocquevillian idea that the existence of powerful local organizations enhances the concern among citizens for political and social issues. The corollary of this idea in social capital terms is that the decentralization process will favour social trust and the creation of social networks. However, the situation in Belgium and especially in Italy is more complex (see Section 8.6), because of the existence of a strong de facto asymmetry and a regional dependence.

The institutional reforms, and with them the fixation of the limits for the future choices of individuals and organizations, are a comprehensive outcome of the past. Each institutional evolution is the result of continuous problem solving that engages society and political elites (Haydu 1998: 356); to explain these evolutions the continuities and the constraints across time have to be considered simultaneously. The solutions proposed to deal with the historical and social evolutions often embody new contradictions bringing about new evolutions. There is not a strict path dependency that can explain this evolution; we can only argue that choices taken at a certain point of time contribute to influence social actors in the future.

Belgian and Italian cases can be read according to this common lens: similar historical and social fragmentation contributed to the evolution of similar political institutions and organizations. The proportional distribution of resources operated by political parties heavily conditioned social interactions among individuals and their ability to generate social capital. However, alternative constraints, such as the ethno-linguistic division in Belgium and the impact of the Cold War in Italy, affected institutional change differently. In Belgium, the federal reform was quicker than in Italy, because historically Belgian elites have been 'trained' to find consensual solutions. The different outcomes produced by a similar process show that previous institutional traditions are fundamental in the elaboration and solution of a new problem. On the one hand, Italian and Belgian elites operated similar choices because they judged the previous centralist organization of the state to be a failure. On the other hand, the subsequent advent of federalism and the formulation of new institutional arrangements demonstrate that the alternative constraints faced by Italy and Belgium determined a slightly different problem solving approach.

8.2 SOCIAL CLEAVAGES AND POLITICAL DEVELOPMENT

The social fragmentation of the two countries resulted in a similar political culture and to a certain extent institutional evolution. The key element of this political culture is the logic of proportional distribution of public posts among the members of *pillars* and clienteles. The totalizing role played by political parties to put in place this distribution generated a reaction against clientelism at the beginning of the 1990s; this reaction boosted the decentralization process.

During this transformation, as emphasized in the previous section, political elites had to take into account different past institutional arrangements in their problem-solving exercise. In Belgium the agreements between Socialists and Christian Democrats constantly rescued the country from critical situations,[4] fostering the creation of a consociational democracy. In Italy the impact of fascism with its strong centralism and the strategic position of the country during the Cold War pushed the Christian Democrats to opt for the exclusion of the Communist Party from the government coalitions. This different choice still has important consequences in the institutional process (see Section 8.5).

During the nineteenth century, the Belgian political arena was divided between the Socialists, rooted in industrial Wallonia, and the Christian Democrats, rooted in rural Flanders. Also in Italy after World War II, there was a marked division between the Christian Democratic Party, more successful in the rural areas of the North East and the Mezzogiorno, and the Communist Party, more influential in the industrial cities of the North West and the Centre. In Belgium the political division was super-imposed on the original fracture between the Germanic and the Latin world: in Italy the ideological contrast was more diffused and only par-tially linked to the original fracture between the Mediterranean and the Northern space.

In the two countries, differently from the rest of Europe, the trade union movement was almost equally split between the Christian Democrats and the left wing parties (Seiler 1977: 460). The success of Catholic trade unions was due to the polymorphic character of the Belgian (PSC) and Italian Christian Democratic (DC) parties: they were able to attract at the same time the bourgeoisie and the poor peasants. This diffused inter-class penetration gave the PSC the chance to participate in almost all govern-mental coalitions from the late nineteenth century to the 1990s (Seiler 1977: 460) and to the DC being the dominant party of each governmental coalition from 1948 to 1992.

The division of the political arena generated a strong conflict in society. Despite this ideological and geographical division, in Belgium the conflict resolution was often achieved through consensual agreements. The capac-ity of generating these agreements became the main characteristic of the Belgian model (the consociational model). In Italy a similar mechanism was not developed.[5] The impact of the Cold War[6] generated instead the paradoxical situation of a party (the Communist Party) able to collect more than 30 per cent of the popular vote but constantly sitting on the opposition benches.

The Belgian consociational system evolved through three historical events: the pact of Loppem, the royal and the school questions. The pact of Loppem introduced in 1918 universal suffrage, thanks to the leaders of the three main parties' agreement (the Socialists, the Catholics and the Liberals). This agreement was supported by the coalition between

Catholics and Socialists, generating for the first time a consensus in Flanders and Wallonia (Deschouwer 2006: 897).

The consociational system matured after War World II (Deschouwer 2006: 903) to solve the intricate royal and school questions. The royal question exploded between the Catholics on one side, who defended the return of King Leopold,[7] and the Socialists and Liberals on the other, who were firmly opposed to it. In 1950 a referendum took place with victory for the king's supporters (with 57 per cent of the general vote). However, the king's supporters were a majority only in Flanders: in Wallonia most people followed the indication of Socialists and Liberals against him. The result was accompanied by huge protests in Wallonia. In order to prevent social unrest, the parties and the trade unions agreed on a compromise, which partially went against the results of the referendum. King Leopold was forced to leave the crown to his brother. This decision saved the monarchical regime and also accommodated the Wallonian request (Deschouwer 2006: 897).

The school question proposed an opposite dilemma and enhanced a similar compromise. The Socialists and the Liberals, running a coalition government at the time, tried to reduce the influence of Catholic schools. The huge protests of Catholics resulted once again in compromise. The parties signed an agreement which established a quasi-proportional distribution of the financial resources between the two networks of schools and the setting up of a three-party commission to lead the future of educational policy. (Deschouwer 2006: 897).

These three questions showed that in Belgium a political majority could not impose its will because the opposition always had a relative majority in Flanders or Wallonia. The consociational device and a prudent political leadership were chosen to solve the main systemic crises (Deschouwer 2006: 897). At the same time a pervasive proportional logic of repartition became indispensable to mediate and contain the contrasts among the *pillars* (see next section).

In Italy, the promulgation of the 1948 constitution was also an exercise in compromise. During the war the Communist and the Socialist parties collaborated with the Christian Democrats in drafting the constitution that established the creation of 20 autonomous regions.[8] After the short consensus generated by the post-war period, differently from Belgium, left wing parties were excluded from the coalition governments during the Cold War. As a consequence, the autonomous regions[9] mentioned in the constitution were not created in order to avoid the left wing parties governing the central part of the country (Emilia Romagna, Tuscany and Umbria). The Christian Democrats delayed the decentralization process until the early 1970s.[10] The lack of consensual agreement generated by the

Cold War still impacts on Italian political life. The Italian political elites, facing a fragmentation similar to Belgium, have been historically unable to compromise, and this situation, in the presence of an articulated procedure to modify the constitution, increased the obstacles to setting up the decentralization process.

In both countries a majority of 2/3 of the parliament is required in order to amend the constitution (Dunn 1974: 151). In the Italian case there is an exception to this rule, a confirmative referendum can be proposed to back up a constitutional reform voted by an absolute majority of the parliament. The 2001 constitutional reform passed through this process only with the votes of the centre-left coalition. The subsequent lack of consensus between the two larger political coalitions did not allow full application of the reform. The centre-right coalition, which took power in 2001, put in place the reformed constitution only minimally and proposed its own[11] new agenda. Before we turn to the decentralization process and its effect on social capital, the political culture and the development of party systems will be described in the next two sections.

8.3 POLITICAL CULTURE

Political culture in Belgium and Italy is characterized by at least three common features: the high fragmentation of society around vertical groups,[12] the capillary diffusion of complicated relationships between formal and informal powers and widespread corruption. These three features resulted in a reduction of institutional trust and in the willingness to create formal social networks.[13]

Belgian and Italian societies are rigidly divided into organized communities based on ideological, linguistic, cultural and professional factors – a vertical organization of society that closely resembles the fragmentation of medieval towns (described in the previous chapter). This context favoured the emergence of the principle of proportionality[14] in all spheres of society to regulate the contrast among different pillars. Citizens became perversely linked to the decision makers and for most of the time were only able to access the labour market through their *pillars* or clienteles (Deschouwer 2006: 897). This vertical principle prevailed also within political parties and trade unions (normally generator of horizontal ties), with the creation of internal factions that operated to satisfy the requests of specific *pillars* (or clienteles) in exchange for votes.

The proportional distribution of public posts in Italy was, until the 1992 scandals,[15] almost a legitimate activity. This procedure was named *Manuale Cencelli* (Cencelli's guide) after the high ranking Christian

Democrat civil servant Massimiliano Cencelli who 'theorized' the exact repartition of jobs and political posts.[16] This phenomenon generated a dysfunctional relation between the ministerial cabinet and top tier civil servants. In Belgium the distribution of top positions (director general and secretary general) was decided collectively by the government and at a lower level, civil servant positions were assigned by an unofficial inter-party committee. The quota of nominations was usually fixed in a document annexed to the coalition protocol (De Winter and Dumont 2006: 969) and followed the same logic illustrated for the Italian case.

The functioning of this complicated and delicate system has been smoothed by a diffused corruption. The assignation of public posts was essential for each *pillar* to maintain the control of votes and boost the party's membership.[17] Political control of the civil service created a venue for dubious dependencies between parties, individual administrators and citizens (Maesschalck and Van de Walle 2006: 1007). The middle man in charge of the mediation between parties and voters became progressively a reference point to gain contracts, get permission to open a business, build a house, get a job, and so on. Knowing the right people (especially the right middle man) was the only way to be connected to political parties and to get things done (Peters 2006: 1087). There was no incentive for individuals to organize themselves through alternative forms of participation (see next section).

Politicians balanced corruptive behaviours and informal agreements with their public function,[18] following the idea that there was an optimal level of corruption to achieve better compromise between different political parties and pillars (Peters 2006: 1086). The persistence of this system after World War II and its perverse form of efficiency generated a high tolerance of corruption, and this social acceptance spread even further illicit behaviour. The diffusion of this modus operandi to all society reinforced the pessimistic attitude in regard to the impartiality of institutions and the ethic of politics and politicians. The lack of trust towards institutions can be typified by the popular stereotype of the politicians always being corrupt – almost as if corruption and politics were synonyms.[19]

In the light of social capital theory it is possible to see how corruption became an essential element of Belgian and Italian institutions. The corruption generated by the system legitimized and reinforced a tendency for illicit behaviour in each segment of society, almost as if it were a normal component of the democratic process. Citizens became inured to the system. People understood that the only way to get things done was to be part of this logic of informal and often illicit exchange, and this decline in behaviour reduced willingness to participate in associations and affected the creation of horizontal ties. At the same time, the level of social trust decreased thus generating a diffused pessimism regarding the functioning of institutions.

In the 1990s, this perverse stability collapsed. The structural system of corruption became unsustainable; the inefficiencies generated by the system swamped its benefits. In both countries the answer to the collapse of the previous logic was an acceleration of the decentralization process which had started in the 1970s. The decentralization was idealized, as an elixir to improve public policy efficiency and to restructure the political system, almost as if centralization were the only cause of the diffused corruption. Before turning to the analysis of the decentralization process the role of political parties, the keystone of the political arch, is discussed.

8.4   THE RISE AND FALL OF PARTITOCRACY

Political parties have a structural role as a filter between the needs of citizens and government action; for this reason they have been the most important secondary group in society. Their role in Belgium and Italy has been crucial to counterbalance the huge government instability generated by the social fragmentation described previously and to allow a smooth relation between the different pillars and clienteles. In order to perform this function the parties acquired an overwhelming presence in society, which has often been referred to as partitocracy.[20] In the long run their overarching presence decreased the space for other secondary groups, destroyed horizontal ties and reduced the development of alternative forms of political organization (8.4.1).

The traditional political parties maintained complete control over society until the scandals of the 1990s. These scandals affected particularly the Christian Democratic parties, symbolic of the system in Belgium and Italy, and boosted popular support for new anti-systemic and region-based parties rooted in the wealthiest areas of the two countries. Following their protest, the political system evolved, turning irreversibly toward federalism. In the last 20 years, the reduced role of traditional parties favoured government stability (8.4.3). Despite this change, the so-called 'Copernican Revolution'[21] did not substantially reduce the level of corruption in the two countries (8.4.2).

8.4.1   The Role of Partitocracy

Political parties limited the interference of the other political actors in society to the minimum: voters, party rank-and-file, MPs, individual ministers, civil servants, and even the judiciary were completely controlled by the party's elites (De Winter and Dumont 2006: 958). This situation had a negative effect on the creation and consolidation of formal social networks. Parties colonized the space normally occupied by other secondary groups. The social domination exerted by the parties reinforced the absence of other horizontal organizations.[22] This in turn created incentives only to constitute other political parties, rather than alternative political organizations. As a consequence Belgium and Italy developed the most fragmented party systems in Europe. In Belgium, just to provide an example, from 1969 to 1988 there has been an average of 6.9 parties represented in the parliament (De Winter and Dumont 2006: 958). The totalitarian role of political parties on social and political life was represented by the lack of independence of the MPs and by the influence exerted on the recruitment and promotion processes in the largest companies[23] of the country.

MPs in Italy and Belgium, in contrast to other countries with an established first-past-the-post system, were completely overwhelmed by party dictates. They did not have resources to pursue research and formulate autonomous proposals in parliament and were strongly sanctioned if they did not conform to party decisions during the parliamentary vote (De Winter and Dumont 2006: 967). The MPs' only role was to participate in cultural and social events in their constituency.[24] These activities were encouraged by the parties and considered more rewarding than engagement with their constituency's problems (De Winter and Dumont 2006: 967). The parties controlled also the most important segments of economic life. The managers of the largest companies consulted political parties and trade unions before every recruitment. This influence, of course, was stronger in the case of semi-public companies. Parties interfered at different levels, ranging from the janitor in a public kindergarten to the chairman of the board of the national airline company (De Winter and Dumont 2006).

8.4.2   The Decline of Partitocracy

After the scandals of the 1990s in Belgium a series of reforms, named 'Copernicus reform' were adopted to eradicate the illicit behaviours. The authority of the new managers over the parties' decisions increased considerably, however most of them still have a political pedigree and their board of directors is often tacitly nominated by political parties (De Winter and Dumont 2006: 968). In Italy the situation is similar. The scandals of 1992 generated initial indignation, but afterwards the illicit behaviours regained their central role in the social life of the country.[25]

Despite the pervasiveness of illicit political behaviour, something changed irreversibly in the relation between parties and society. The Christian Democrats, the symbol of the old political system, declined; the PSC, after the dioxin scandal, moved for the first time to the benches of the opposition (Maesschalck and Van de Walle 2006: 1000) and the DC after *Mani Pulite's* operation disappeared from the political panorama; those parties that managed to survive saw their gatekeeper's role reduced drastically. The political strategies of the parties became less important and more focused on presenting media-attractive candidates.[26]

The progressive weakening of the traditional parties has been accompanied by the large affirmation of new region-based anti-system parties (Deschower 2006: 897), such as the *Lega Nord* in the North of Italy and the *Vlaams Blok* in Flanders. These parties were the first to denounce the corrupt system and gained certain credibility for it; they pushed the decentralization process to improve accountability and control. The shake up of the party system during the 1990s presaged a call for the renewal of political culture, especially with regard to MPs' accountability and the de-politicization of public services. However, this increased concern did not lead to fundamental change of the old ways (De Winter and Dumont 2006: 970), and it can be argued that the situation is worsening rather than improving. The persistence of the old ways and the contemporary destruction of political parties are providing more power to informal middle-men and organizations.[27] In the past their role was controlled by the parties, today they are out of control and exert hegemony in society. In the areas where there is low participation in the labour market, as in the South of Italy (see Chapter 7), they have acquired an absolute control of all forms of economic activity.

8.4.3   From Functional Governmental Instability to Stability

The strength of political parties was yoked to the extraordinary governmental instability.[28] A certain degree of continuity was provided by the political longevity of key office holders[29] (prime ministers, foreign affairs and finance ministers). Government instability was a device to accommodate social conflicts and perpetrate the logic of proportional distribution. This instability, together with the continuing role of the parties, helped to deal with deadlocks and political blockages and continuously attributed the right representation to each pillar.

The changes to the party system, brought about by the end of the Christian Democratic domination and the progressive usury of consociational mechanisms resulted in an increasing role for the government and with it major stability. After 1987 governments in Belgium lasted more than three years on average over a four year period mandate (De Winter and Dumont 2006: 959), and in Italy with some exceptions (1994 and 2008) almost all parliamentary majorities, with some small change, lasted for all the mandate. The increased stability put the government in position to substitute the role of the parties, progressively usurping the legislative power (De Winter and Dumont 2006: 965). This stability together with a reduction of power of traditional parties has been one of the main ingredients of the federal reform. This ongoing process, the asymmetric character of the new institutions and their impact on social capital, are the subjects of the next two sections.

8.5   THE LONG ROAD TO FEDERALISM

The creation of a central state had been influenced by the social and historical fragmentation of the two countries during the nineteenth century, a fear of foreign domination and the machinations of a small bourgeois elite, despite proposals to create a federal system to answer the regional diversity of the new countries. The Belgian constitution of 1830 represented a reference model for the *Statuto Albertino*. In both cases according to this initial structure, the centralist institutional framework remained unquestioned for more than a century. Only during the 1970s did new priorities emerge to give momentum to the decentralization process. The scandals of the 1990s and the decline of the traditional party system reinforced popular support for federalization.

However, the pace and depth of the decentralization process have been different in the two countries. In Belgium the federalization process was conceived as a tool to solve the ethno-linguistic question between the French and the Flemish speaking communities and to improve the overall effectiveness of public policy[30] (Swenden et al. 2006: 864; Swenden and Maarten 2006: 888). In Italy the process has been driven by the need to improve the efficiency of public policy and to strengthen the democratic principle with a locally diffused separation of powers (Groppi 2008: 3). The creation of autonomous regions followed the Madisonian idea of the separation of powers and the Tocquevillian vision of increasing social participation in local government and weakening central power.

After clarifying the genesis and the aim of the decentralization process, in the next sections the two elements that comprise the decentralization process in Belgium and Italy are analysed. First, decentralization is happening by disaggregation without following a clear blueprint,[31] and second, there is a strong asymmetry between the different regions with important consequences for social capital.

8.5.1   A Federal Reform by Disaggregation

Belgium and Italy are clear examples of decentralization by disaggregation[32] (Swenden et al. 2006: 864). Belgium needed 18 years to put in place fully operational federal units, and in Italy the constitution has not yet been modified in a federal direction. In both countries all the transformations have been managed by the centre without a direct autonomous expansion of regional competencies[33] (Swenden and Maarten 2006: 880–81).

In Belgium the decentralization process was hindered by at least three factors. Originally the Flemish did not have a recognized language,[34] and only with the advent of the standard use of Dutch did the movement acquire a strong bargaining power at national level. Second, until the 1960s[35] socio-economic cleavages[36] were considered more important than the ethnic question. Finally, the presence of Brussels, originally a Flemish speaking city and then progressively franchized by the economic and political elite, completed a context unfavourable to the reform. The strengthening of the culture and economic position of Flanders and the political scandals accelerated the decentralization process. In 1993 Belgium became a fully fledged federal state.

In Italy the decentralization process encountered more obstacles than in Belgium despite the sudden recognition of regional autonomy in the 1948 constitution. Regions were only paid lip service, because of the Cold War, until the 1970s. Also the activation of the constitutional norms, during the 1970s and the 1980s, did not empower regions and they remained a peripheral factor of Italian political life. The financial and administrative autonomy of regions increased progressively during the 1990s. Despite this fact and the scandals of the 1990s, unlike Belgium, regions are not yet formally represented at national level: Italy remains a regional state in transition.

In Belgium the competencies and self-funding capacity of local authorities (regions and communities) increased dramatically during the 1980s. The Belgian federal model has a unique asymmetry, as a result of the alternative vision of the decentralization process that distinguished Walloons and Flemish. The Walloons after the economic slowdown of the 1960s, supported federalism through regional decentralization. The Flemish, instead, supported cultural autonomy through community decentralization.

The decentralization process was guided from the centre and evolved through a long series of agreements between Walloons and Flemish parties. Federal and regional competences were divided sharply to decrease the number of decisions that the two ethnic groups should take together. With the decentralization process underway Belgium seemed set to exit from the consociational model (Swenden and Maarten 2006: 886).

Decentralization proceeded with the creation in the 1970s of the communities and in the 1980s of the regions and the court of arbitration.[37] The competencies of communities are quite narrow[38] and mainly linked to education policy and linguistic issues. On the other hand, regions have very extensive powers,[39] which increased incrementally with each reform (1980, 1988–89, 1992–93 and 2000s). Regions and communities gained a high financial autonomy; during the 2000s their level of expenditure exceeded 50 per cent of the total public budget[40] (excluding interests on the payment of the debt). Tax-raising autonomy is also larger than in federal countries like Germany and Austria. After 2000, tax-raising reached 20 per cent of the total amount spent by the two institutions.

To sum up, in Belgium the complete separation of competencies (proposed in order to reduce the inefficiencies of consociational democracy and to give large autonomy to the ethno-linguistic groups), may result, if new issues like the royal and school question emerge, in strong intergovernmental tensions with very little mechanism of discussion.[41]

In Italy the process of decentralization was more complicated than in Belgium. After the 1970s the intervention of the state and the tardiness of the constitutional court in enforcing regional law paralysed local legislative activity: for almost 20 years regions remained only a powerless third tier of bureaucracy. The creation of the state-regions conference[42] by the constitutional court changed the situation in conjunction with the 1990s scandals. During this period new laws established a larger autonomy for city councils and counties, according to the principle of subsidiarity fostered by the European Union.

The transfer of administrative functions, the identification of the communitarian role of regions, a new electoral system and the increase of financial autonomies were quickly implemented (Groppi 2008: 10). In 2001, at the end of this intense period of legislative evolution a constitutional reform was approved by the centre-left coalition with the back up of a confirmative referendum.

The reform established the direct election of the president and the autonomy of regional legislation. The competencies of the state, reversing the previous constitutional arrangements, are now mentioned in the constitution,[43] similarly for federal states. Regions have residual competencies: agriculture, industry, trading, tourism, urban planning and social assistance.[44] The clause concerning national interest, which during the 1970s and 1980s had been used to block many laws proposed by the regions (Groppi 2008: 10), disappeared. The reform established also a greater financial autonomy.

Yet despite decentralization, a connection between regional and national reform was not established.[45] The increased regional competencies did not alter the centralist model. The state remained the gatekeeper; regions and local authorities played a decisive role only at administrative level. In addition to this limitation there has been minimal implementation of the reform because the centre-right coalition, opposed to the reform, was in power at the time of activation. This minimal actuation reinforced the traditional role of the central state, in conjunction with the re-affirmation of the principle of national interest by the constitutional court (sentence 303/2003).

The lack of consensus and mechanisms to generate it decreased the efficiency and the impact of the decentralization process. The new centre-right majority followed the same non-consensual path of the centre-left coalition imposing a new reform with an absolute majority. However, this reform was rejected by a referendum in 2006 (Groppi 2008: 12). The failure of this radical design of constitutional reform encouraged the centre-right coalition to approve in 2009 a less ambitious reform, through ordinary law.

The law pledges a stronger fiscal decentralization without changing the institutional framework. Despite the criticisms from the centre-right majority to Prodi's previous plan for decentralization, the 2009 reform is similar to the so called *Bozza Prodi*[46] presented by the centre-left government two years previously (Ferragina 2010c). The reform proposes three main innovations: local authorities can autonomously impose new taxes to finance local needs, a shift from historical[47] to standard costs[48] in the fields of health, education and social assistance, and finally the creation of an equalization fund to re-distribute from the wealthier to the poorer regions in cases of necessity.[49]

The only difference between the law proposed by the centre-right coalition and the 'Bozza Prodi' is the absence of the terms 'solidarity' and 'social inclusion'. This may have important consequences on social capital of the poorest regions (see next section). The absence of the affirmation of values such as inter-regional solidarity and social inclusion, in a law which is only a mere enunciation of principles[50] and in presence of a large socio-economic gap, cannot be ignored.

8.5.2   An Asymmetric Federalism

Italian and Belgian decentralization processes feature many elements of de facto and *de jure* asymmetry.[51] In Belgium the existence of a de facto asymmetry at cultural and socio-economic level resulted in a different vision of federal construction between the Flemish and Walloons.[52] In Flanders the coincidence between the ethno-linguistic community and the geographical region brought about the merger of the two sub-national entities. In the

French speaking world, Wallonia and Brussels[53] regions gained further competences from the French ethno-linguistic community. The French Community has ceded some of its legislative authority to the French community commission in Brussels and Wallonia. The French Community now also lives under the name Communauté Bruxelles-Wallonie, symbolizing the presence of dual identities in French-speaking Belgium. There is no agreement on which principle should prevail in the organization of Belgian federalism. For these reasons, regions and communities do not yet have regional constitutional papers (Swenden and Maarten 2006: 885). The different relation between community and region in Flanders and Wallonia is progressively transforming a de facto into a *de jure* asymmetry.

Also in Italy there is a strong de facto asymmetry, represented by the socio-economic gap between the Centre-North and the South. This gap has been analysed by many social scientists and become famous under the name of *Questione Meridionale*.[54] Together with this de facto asymmetry there is also a *de jure* asymmetry due to the existence of five regions with a special statute. They enjoyed great autonomy before the creation of the other regions in 1970. However, this *de jure* asymmetry, granted for particular cultural (Valle d'Aosta, Trentino Alto Adige contain large language minorities), historical (Friuli-Venezia-Giulia was at the centre of a long contentious issue with Yugoslavia) and geographical (Sardinia and Sicily are two islands) conditions is disappearing as increasing power is attributed to the other regions.

The existence of a strong de facto asymmetry in bipolar contexts suggests a reconsideration of the traditional argument that federalism impacts positively on social capital because it enhances greater local participation (Tocqueville 1961). For this reason, in the next section regional socio-economic divergence and federalism are revisited in the light of social capital theory and the empirical data provided in Chapter 6.

8.6   THE PARADIGM OF REGIONAL DEPENDENCE

Social security in European countries is managed through an inter-personal economic transfer from the wealthiest to the poorest citizens. The existence of a strong de facto asymmetry[55] transforms the interpersonal into an inter-regional redistribution, from Flanders to Wallonia in Belgium and from the Centre-North to the South in Italy (Cantillon et al. 2006; Trigilia 1992).

In Belgium the largest transfer from Flanders to Wallonia is operated through the benefits for people of working age. The percentage of population that does not participate in the labour market or is unemployed is largest in Wallonia (see previous chapter). This situation raised a contrast at the federal level between the Flemish, who promote the federalization of social security arguing that the existence of these inter-regional transfers explains the inability of Walloons to catch up with the Flemish, and the Walloons, who argue that the split of social security would irreversibly lead to more poverty and inequality in Wallonia and Brussels, and eventually in the whole country (Cantillon et al. 2006: 1043). The existence of two constitutional arrangements, the need for a majority in both regions to reform regional and community competencies and the alarm bell procedure, guarantees the maintenance of the federal financing of social security.

In Italy the asymmetry between the Centre-North and the South is stronger than in Belgium (see Section 7.2). However, in the new federal reform voted in 2009, in contrast to Belgium, there are no institutional arrangements to protect national solidarity. There is the risk that decentralization pushed from the centre without the provision of institutional counter-powers to the regions would reduce the social security transfers to the southern part of the country and result in deteriorating socio-economic conditions.

At a general level, a potential deterioration of labour market conditions and an increase of income inequality due to the reduction of transfers from the wealthiest to the poorest regions would probably reduce social capital (as shown by the empirical model in Chapter 6). In this scenario, the positive effects generated by increased accountability and more efficient local governance boosted by the decentralization process may be curtailed by the deterioration of socio-economic conditions if some institutional counter-power is not offered to the weakest regions. In asymmetric countries, federalism can contribute to social capital creation only if the solidarity principle is re-affirmed in conjunction with the attribution of a certain institutional power at national level to regions.[56]

The concern for national solidarity in Italy is even more important, if the historical evolution of public expenditure for infrastructures is considered. Nitti (1900) showed how after unification, the money for infrastructures and public services flowed from the poorest to the richest part of the country. More than a century later the large socio-economic gap persists.[57] If the expenditure of the enlarged public sector is considered, the state invested between 1996 and 2007 (Table 8.1), an average of €14,349 per citizen in the Centre-North and only €10,195 in the South (Various 2008: 133).

The relative disadvantage is stronger if the expenditure of public companies, which do most of the infrastructural investments (roads, railways, energy, communication), is analysed. During the period 1996–2007 only

*Table 8.1   Distribution of the expenditure of the enlarged public sector:
years 1996–2007 (average proportions of the total Italian
expenditure)*

Macro-area	Population (%) (percentuale)	GDP (%) (percentuale)	Total public expenditure (percentuale)
Centro-nord	64.1	75.9	71.5
Mezzogiorno	35.9	24.1	28.5
Italy	100	100	100

Source: Ferragina 2010c.

*Table 8.2   Public national companies. Investments for the South in
percentage of the national value: years 1996–2007*

Company	1996 (%)	2007 (%)
ANAS	31.3	51.5
Ferrovie	29.5	21.0
ENEL	35.6	27.6
Aziende ex IRI	24.0	13.4
ENI	34.9	36.3
Poste	6.6	27.6

Source: Ferragina 2010c.

ANAS[58] invested more in the South than in the North, and ENI[59] had a similar level of per capita expenditure. All the others (former IRI, post office, railways and ENEL) invested less (per capita) in the South than in the North (Table 8.2). In particular railways and former IRI invested much less than the percentage of the GDP per capita produced by the South of Italy (Table 8.2).

In the light of these data and the historical analysis of the previous chapter, we can argue that the South is structurally underfunded and that the lack of socio-economic development generated is not due to innate cultural incapacity. The annual report of the department for development and economic cohesion[60] confirms how dystonic the debate on federalism is: 'the current debate on the administrative decentralization and fiscal federalism is not always based on correct empirical evidence and above all a correct use of the information available' (Various 2008: 137).

In Italy, since 2001, the expenditure and decentralization of fiscal policies is greater than in federal countries (Table 8.3). After 2007 the local

Table 8.3   Tax collected by the local administrations as a percentage of the total

Year	Germany	Austria	Spain	United Kingdom	Italy
1995	12.9	15.8	12.3	4.4	9.5
2000	8.5	14.9	12.6	4.6	15.6
2006	11.8	14.1	11.9	5.4	18.3

Source: Ferragina 2010c.

administrations collected more than 30 per cent of tax, and for the first time the money collected has been greater than the expenditure (Ferragina 2010c). After the decentralization of the financing and administrative competence, the debate should focus on institutional reform. This reform should guarantee social security transfers from the North to the South, provide a larger share of financing for infrastructures in the South, and establish a constitutional guarantee, on the model of the Belgian constitution, for the regions to defend their prerogatives. Only in these conditions could the Mezzogiorno enhance the virtuous cycle of social capital creation discussed in the previous chapter and realized by Flanders (see Section 7.3).

8.7   SUMMARY

The historical analysis undertaken in the previous chapter has been completed by the discussion of the evolution of political institutions and organizations. A problem-solving approach has been applied to Belgian and Italian cases to explain how political institutions and organizations impacted on the social capital level and how institutional transformations may affect it in the future.

In both cases, historical cleavages and social fragmentation have been handled through the development of an institutional system based on the proportional distribution of public resources among the elites in power and their clienteles. This distribution resulted in the total colonization of the relationship between individuals and the state by the political parties. The high level of corruption generated to make the system work and the lack of incentive to create secondary associations (apart from political parties) to deal with political and social issues, has eroded social trust and formal social networks. The collapse of this party system, when the costs of the system overcame the benefits, was accelerated during the decentralization process of the 1990s. Belgium, thanks to the consociational device, reformed the institutions into a federal direction in 1993; Italy, in the absence of the consociational device, remained a regional state with a federal vocation.

Federalism has been conceived in both countries as an elixir to increase accountability and local participation in the political process. According to the Tocquevillian idea, this should increase social capital in the future.[61] Despite the importance of this shift and, potentially, the positive effects of federalism on social capital, the absence of the national solidarity principle and of an adequate institutional balance between central state and regions in the new reform, may negatively impact on the socio-economic conditions of the Mezzogiorno. The reduction of social transfers from the Centre-North to the South may worsen labour market conditions and increase inequalities.

These two factors, empirically observed in Chapter 6, may in turn reduce social capital. In the future, federalism can enhance social capital in the South of Italy only if social security remains in the hands of the federal state. In Belgium, Walloons can defend their prerogatives constitutionally through the alarm bell procedure and the veto power of the regions. In Italy the absence of institutional mechanisms to support the regional prerogatives at national level leaves the poorest regions without protection. Decentralization can enhance its full potential in terms of social capital creation only if the progressive construction of vertical subsidiarity is accompanied by a certain level of horizontal solidarity among the regions. Therefore, the decentralization, in a strong de facto asymmetrical context, should not be extended to social security financing.

This consideration brings us back to Tocqueville's words and the empirical results of the general model. Social capital can increase if the prerogatives of local authorities are reinforced but at the same time the socio-economic gap is reduced. Carlo Cattaneo, the father of the Italian federal movement, was non-coincidentally inspired by Tocqueville's writings. The Lombard writer never conceived federal reform in Italy as a means to enhance local interests over national solidarity (Cattaneo 1966) and his thoughts can be read in the light of social capital theory. The federal principle, inspired by the will to enhance institutional freedom, efficiency and regional autonomy, cannot be counterposed to the idea of interpersonal and inter-regional solidarity. A state in which there are not sufficient institutional checks and balances to guarantee the fusion between the efficiency of federal arrangements and inter-regional solidarity is destined to isolation, and separation, and with it the destruction of social capital.

In the last two chapters we have proposed an in-depth historic-institutional analysis of two deviant cases to complete the socio-economic model (presented in Chapter 6). We argued that historical and institutional development cannot be treated as a simple independent variable of a quantitative model, but has to be analysed simultaneously with socio-economic factors to understand their impact on social capital. In the previous chapter through the *sleeping social capital theory*, we suggested that 'history cannot be blamed' for the lack of social capital in Wallonia and the South of Italy. Moreover the role of a glorious past cannot be enacted if there are not sufficient socio-economic conditions, notably a certain level of labour market participation and redistribution of income in society.

In this chapter we connected the lack of social capital to institutional development in Belgium and Italy. In particular, Wallonia and the South of Italy are influenced by a strong dependence from the most developed areas of the country. In this respect, the decentralization process (conceived as an answer to this asymmetrical situation, to improve the efficiency of public policy and increase transparency and participation) has been implemented as a fundamental step to radically change the institutional evolution of the two countries. However, this process (which is following a general European tendency, discussed in Chapter 3) cannot generate an increase of social capital without the action of a parallel central social security system designed to support labour market participation, economic redistribution and a reduction of regional differences.

NOTES

1. The interest of the 'Belgian scar' has been well described by Armstrong Kelly (1969: 344): 'History has left three vertical areas of scar tissue on the continent of Europe. [. . .] The central scar, though, is the most fascinating. It is the scar that reproduces the central kingdom of Charlemagne's succession, the zone in which the Teutonic and Gallo-Roman culture have millennially clashed.'
2. The *Statuto Albertino* was the constitution approved by the Kingdom of Piedmont in 1848. The project of Italian unification started from this state. The first Italian constitution of 1861 is largely inspired by 1848 principles.
3. In the Belgian case federalism has been invoked also from the Flemish movement for ethno-linguistic reasons.
4. The school and the royal questions.
5. At the end of the 1970s some faction of the Christian Democrats tried to establish a compromise with the Communist Party. The so called *compromesso storico* (historical compromise) failed after the killing of Aldo Moro, leader of the Christian Democrats, by the extreme left group *Brigate Rosse*. The former members of the Communist Party entered in the ministerial cabinet for the first time only in 1996.
6. For the particular geographical position of the country at the border of the NATO treaty bloc.
7. Accused of collaborationism during the Nazi occupation.
8. Five with a larger autonomy, the so-called: *regioni a statuto speciale* (translated as 'regions with special constitutional arrangements').

9. Apart from the five with special constitutional arrangements.
10. They changed their position only when the Communist Party condemned the Soviet invasion of Czechoslovakia in 1968.
11. Which was refused by another referendum in 2006.
12. In Belgium this phenomenon took the name of *pillarization*.
13. These are two of the three dimensions to measure social capital used in the study (see Chapter 2).
14. This had an impact on the formation of the consociational model illustrated in the previous section.
15. The *operazione mani pulite* (translated as 'operation clean hands') launched by a pool of prosecutors and judges of Milan's court involved thousands of entrepreneurs and politicians. In 1992 the Christian Democrats and the Socialist party (which together were able to collect almost 50% of the popular vote) disappeared from the political scene.
16. Each role was weighted qualitatively, for example each minister was valued as two and a half vice-ministers, and then assigned according to the electoral weight of the party or the faction (Venditti 1981).
17. Party memberships were counted before each congress and new government formation.
18. In a famous speech at the chamber on 3 July 1992, Craxi asked all parties to assume the responsibility for the scandals and find a political solution to them. In this speech corruption and collusion with informal powers are described as part of the political system and not the act of single people.
19. According to the interviews collected by Van Dam and Nizet (2002: 52) there is not a country in Europe where the lack of trust and respect for political institutions is as high as in Belgium. People tend to perceive the existence of corruption at every level also when there is no proof of it. This sentiment is more diffused in Wallonia, but is rapidly increasing also in the Flanders (Billiet et al. 2006: 926–7).
20. 'The main particularity of party government in Belgium, which like Italy is often labelled as partitocracy, is the overwhelming role played by organized political parties' (De Winter and Dumont 2006: 957).
21. Term used only in Belgium.
22. The absence of groups able to create horizontal ties does not mean that in these countries there was not an associative life. The church, for example, plays an important role in both countries; however the other large organizations followed the vertical logic described in the previous sections.
23. Privately or publicly owned.
24. Such as inaugurating buildings, distributing prizes at schools, attending festivities, dedications, vernissages (private inaugurations) balls, receptions, openings of commercial and cultural initiatives, sports manifestations, fairs, funerals and weddings.
25. Ministers and important public officers have been accused of corruption in recent years.
26. They invested in pretty women, well-assimilated candidates of foreign origin and increasingly children of famous of politicians, most of them lacking in experience or in simple political skills (De Winter and Dumont 2006: 968).
27. Including organized crime in Italy.
28. De Winter and Dumont pointed out that Italy and Belgium were pathological cases of executive instability in the European context (2006: 959).
29. 'Looking at the political personnel in the executive, Huyse found much more stability. Although there were 13 cabinets between 1944 and 1961, there were only eight prime ministers, four ministers of Foreign Affairs and seven Ministers of Finance. This is an indicator of the fact that individual members of the political elite did play a crucial role in keeping the Belgian system on the tracks' (Deschouwer 2006: 896).
30. The decentralization process together with the rules established in the Maastricht treaty contributed to reduce the distributive prerogative of the federal state and signed the end of the 'waffle-iron politics' with a decrease of public debt in 2005 below 100% of the GDP (it was 135% in the early 1990s) (Swenden and Maarten 2006: 888).

31. The methodology pursued to reform has been quite different. In Belgium through a large consensus and in Italy through a struggle between the centre-left and centre-right coalitions.
32. Historically this pattern has been followed more by regional countries rather than federal states.
33. Differently from Spain that is the other case of federalism by disaggregation.
34. Their language was only a collection of dialects.
35. Before the collapse of the Walloon economy.
36. Such as the already mentioned school and royal questions.
37. Which progressively became almost a constitutional court to deal with the issues between the central state and regions/communities.
38. The main competence of the community is to manage education and linguistic issues. The community has some residual power also on health policy and assistance to individuals and all international treaties on domestic matters. In Flanders, as mentioned, the community and the region have been merged.
39. The competences of regions are: employment policy, public investment, economic development, housing policy and structural planning, scientific research, transport policy, inter-municipal cooperation for provision of utilities, transport, road construction and waterways, aspects of foreign trade, energy and most of agricultural policy, foreign policy (including treaties) in all spheres of domestic competence.
40. The spending autonomy grew progressively from 8% of the public budget in 1980 to more than 50% in the year 2000.
41. 'The Belgian unitary state combined the absence of unilateral venues to achieve policy outcomes with strong pressures to conclude mutually acceptable compromises. In the federal system these two characteristics have been watered down, thereby reducing Belgium's capacity to cope with outstanding conflictual issues' (Swenden and Maarten 2006: 890–91).
42. The state-regions conference is a forum for discussion between the central government and the regions. Its objective is to create fair cooperation between central and local administrations.
43. These competences are quite extensive: penal and civil law, environment, competition and the minimum guarantee of civil and social services.
44. There is another set of concurrent competences in which the state dictates the principles and disciplines the regions.
45. There has been no modification of the chambers and no constitutionalization of the state-regions conference (Groppi 2008: 10).
46. Draft.
47. The financing of social expenditure from the state was based on the expenses of the previous year without any accountability.
48. Calculated by a governmental commission which should consider the different needs of each territory.
49. This fund will be monitored by the central state to answer to the regional requests.
50. The reform does not propose quantifications of the standard costs or strict principles for the equalization fund.
51. On one hand, the term asymmetric federalism refers to cultural, socio-economic and political party differences between the federated entities and the centre; this is called de facto asymmetry. On the other, the term asymmetry is used to describe a situation in which some federal entity gained greater self-governing powers than others, this is called *de jure* asymmetry (Swenden 2002: 67).
52. As we have discussed previously, Flemish nationalism has been driven by cultural and linguistic concerns which brought about the original creation of communities. On the other hand Walloon nationalism has been driven only by socio-economic concern. This gave rise to the creation of the autonomous regions (Swenden and Maarten 2006: 880–81).
53. Brussels is predominantly a French-speaking city.

54. The socio-economic gap between the South and the North of Italy is stronger than in Belgian regions.
55. This de facto asymmetry is determined by three conditions: social risks are unequally redistributed between the regions, the capacity to contribute to the collective schemes of social security and income tax differs strongly between the regions and there is a different degree of tax evasion (Cantillon et al. 2006: 1037).
56. The vagueness of the law voted in 2009 makes difficult the formulation of a precise judgement. In the absence of quantifications (that is, the transfers from a region to another, the quantification of standard costs) we can only deal with the principles highlighted in the reform.
57. In terms of growth rates, secondary education achievements, poverty concentration, exclusion of the weaker categories, disparity in the structure of social assistance. For a detailed analysis of the divergence between the North and the South of the country in relation to these aspects see Ferragina (2010c: 15–20).
58. The company that manages the highway system.
59. Oil and gas company.
60. The report is redacted by the same government that proposed the fiscal federalism in 2009.
61. This pattern seems plausible in Belgium. On the other hand we argued that in the South of Italy the situation is different.

9. Conclusion

Social capital is a new concept widely used in the literature to revitalize an old sociological debate: the necessity of strong secondary groups, informal ties and trust in order to guarantee the stability of society and the functioning of political institutions during the process of modernization (see Chapter 1; Ferragina 2010a). On this basis, we defined and measured social capital as a multi-dimensional concept constituted by three dimensions: informal social networks, formal social networks and social trust.

The informal social networks dimension captures Tönnies' *Gemeinschaft* and Durkheim's idea of *Mechanic* solidarity, and it has been measured by evaluating the intensity of family and friendship ties. The formal social networks dimension captures Tönnies' *Gesellschaft* and Durkheim's idea of formal solidarity, and it has been measured by evaluating the density of membership and participation in formal associations. The social trust dimension captures the idea that the correct functioning of a modern society is based on the existence of a conducive environment, and it has been measured by evaluating the extent to which citizens trust one another, their institutions and how much they engage in the political debate (for an accurate discussion see Chapters 2 and 4).

The founding fathers of sociology made a distinction between formal and informal social networks, by emphasizing that the modernization of society was generating a fast shift from the community based forms of solidarity to less bonding ties, as represented by formal associative networks. These two dimensions form a sort of micro-social sphere in which individuals interact amongst themselves. Gorz (1992) complemented this discussion, defining social trust as a macro-social sphere intimately related to the individual's interaction and the general structure of society. High scores in this dimension suggest the existence of an environment conducive to the participation of each individual.

Putnam (1993) popularized the concept, transforming this old theoretical debate into of one of the hottest topics in social science (see Chapter 1). He proposed an historical explanation for the present lack of social capital in the South of Italy, arguing that this was due more to the absence of medieval towns during the twelfth and thirteenth centuries (and the presence of the authoritarian rule of the Normans) than the longstanding socio-economic underdevelopment (see Chapter 7). This conclusion raised a heated debate on the determinants of social capital.

As highlighted in the introduction, the main criticism to Putnam's seminal work concentrated on: (1) the lack of concern for the structural socio-economic conditions, notably income inequality, and (2) the excessive determinism of the historical analysis. The historical evolution of Southern society was reduced to a sort of 'original sin', and events of 800 years ago were considered the main determinants for the present lack of collective action, associative participation and ultimately the cause of institutional ineffectiveness. In the book we integrated the insights of these two criticisms and proposed an innovative cross-regional analysis of 85 European regions (Chapter 3), linking together the socio-economic (Chapters 4, 5 and 6) and the historic-institutional analyses (Chapters 7 and 8) to explore the determinants of social capital.

The socio-economic determinants of social capital, that is, income inequality, labour market participation, national divergence and economic development, have been tested through a series of Ordinary Least Square (OLS) regression models (Chapter 6). Despite explaining more than 60 per cent of the variance of social capital across European regions, this methodology did not allow us to consider the influence of social change over time and its impact on the institutional design of each region and nation (see Chapters 1, 7 and 8). For this reason, we argued that to investigate the determinants of social capital, one has to integrate the synchronic and the diachronic perspectives under the guidance of a methodological framework able to put these two approaches in continuity. Hence, the comparative historical analysis has been undertaken starting from the results gathered from the regression model. Paraphrasing Collingwood, we matched the two analyses exercising a 'disciplined imagination' to reconstruct the original path of two deviant cases and developing some general conclusion on social capital theory.

We acknowledge that a comparative historical analysis is never neutral and can result in different interpretations of the same historical events, however unlike Putnam, we have 'disciplined our historical imagination': looking at two deviant cases from the general pattern (identified by the regression model), and exploiting the comparative research design, matching the two deviant cases with two control cases (see Chapter 6).

The residuals of the regression analysis indicate that Wallonia and the South of Italy are different from the other European regions. This is because they have extremely poor social capital scores, but at the same time they display positive residuals (exactly like regions with social capital largely above the average). In simple words, if the present socio-economic conditions of Wallonia and the South of Italy are considered, social capital scores should be even lower than currently detected. This finding: (1) suggests that Wallonia and the South of Italy are different from the other regions analysed, where the socio-economic conditions would predict a higher social capital in the regions above average and a lower social capital in the regions below; and (2) challenges Putnam's analysis, suggesting an alternative explanation for the lack of social capital in the South of Italy[1] (and Wallonia).

9.1 THE CONTRIBUTION

The book investigated the main determinants of social capital with an innovative research design. Specifically it contributes to the literature in four ways:

1. categorizing 85 European regions according to the density of formal social networks, informal social networks and social trust (Chapter 4);
2. explaining the variance of social capital across 85 European regions, relying on socio-economic factors, that is, income inequality, labour market participation, national divergence and economic development (Chapters 5 and 6);
3. proposing an innovative research design linking the socio-economic and historical-institutional analyses (on the basis of the residuals of the regression model, Chapter 6); and
4. proposing a comparative historical analysis of two deviant cases and elaborating the *sleeping social capital theory* (Chapters 7 and 8).

9.1.1 The Categorization of European Regions

Regions have been categorized according to the different scores in the three social capital dimensions, namely informal social networks, formal social networks and social trust (Chapter 4). As previously highlighted these three dimensions relate directly to sociological theory, and in particular to Tönnies, Durkheim and Weber's seminal contributions. It has been argued that this categorization is a useful device to check the consistency of the measurement with the previous literature and to detect whether the regional and national classification diverge (Chapter 4).

Only in Austria, Greece, Ireland and Sweden (see Table 4.4), all regions are classified in the same category of the country, while in the other cases one or more regions have different characteristics from the rest of the nation. For example, in Belgium (the cleavage between Flemish and Walloon), in Italy (where the North Eastern part diverges considerably from the other regions), in France, Spain and Portugal (where the capitals and some other regions have different characteristics from the rest of the country), in Germany (where the Eastern land have different characteristics from the rest of the country), and in the United Kingdom (where Scotland, Northern Ireland, Wales and the North are substantially different from the regions located in the South).

On these bases we grouped 85 European regions in seven clusters: the Synergic Regions, the Nordic Regions, the Network Based Regions, the Formally Jointed Regions, the Trust Based Regions, the Formally Jointed Regions and the Disjointed Regions.

1. The Synergic Regions display scores above the European average for all three dimensions. In these regions, individuals tend to participate in associative life, spend time with their family and friends and trust their fellow countrymen and institutions. The positive interaction between these three dimensions supports the functioning of political institutions and constitutes an environment that enhances a large social participation, contributing to a healthy civic and social life. This model is prevalent among Scandinavian regions (see Table 4.3).
2. The Nordic Regions display formal social networks and social trust scores above the European average but informal social networks below average. In these regions, individuals privilege formal interactions and trust other people and institutions. The presence of a dense network of formal associations and generous welfare state provisions is concomitant to the weakness of informal ties (see Fukuyama 1995; Etzioni 1995). This group includes Dutch, Belgian, Finnish, Danish, German and Austrian regions (see Table 4.3).
3. The Network Based Regions display informal and formal social networks scores above the European average but social trust below average. In these regions individuals are very active in their individual sphere however their general level of trust is quite low. They share geographical proximity and a residual social security system and reversely from the Nordic group the structure of the welfare state seems to give incentive to the creation of formal and informal networks rather than contributing to social and institutional trust (see Table 4.3).
4. The Informally Jointed Regions display only formal social network scores above the average. In these regions the modernization process did not significantly erode communitarian ties, and at the same time did not support the development of formal social networks and social trust. This group includes Mediterranean and British regions (see Table 4.3), in particular the presence of 11 Mediterranean (Greek, Spanish, Portuguese and French) regions calls to mind the amoral

familism hypothesis formulated by Banfield (1958). According to him, informal social networks (in particular the relation with the immediate family) are so strong that they destroy all forms of formal associations and trust in institutions (for an empirical test see Ferragina 2011).

5. The Trust Based Regions display only social trust scores above the average. In these regions formal and informal social networks are underdeveloped but individuals seem to trust each other and their institutions. There are only seven regions in this group (see Table 4.3): five German Land and two large cities (Paris and London). Four German Land included in this cluster were part of East Germany, this largely confirms the analysis of Völker and Flap (2001). They argued that the legacy of communism explains the presence of a high level of social trust, in contexts where people had a weak 'micro-sphere' of bridging and bonding ties.

6. The Formally Jointed Regions display only formal social networks above the average. In these regions formal social networks have replaced community-based ties during the process of modernization, however the level of social trust did not increase in parallel (as in the Nordic regions). This group includes only two regions: the North East of Italy and the Nord of France (Table 4.3).

7. The Disjointed Regions display scores below the European average for all three dimensions. In these regions formal and informal social networks are extremely weak and there is a complete lack of social trust. The Disjointed group includes Italian, French, German, Portuguese, Spanish, Belgian and British regions. This is the most heterogeneous category, including 21 regions below the European average (see Table 4.3).

9.1.2 Three Socio-Economic Factors Explaining the Variance of Social Capital

In Chapter 5 we illustrated at the theoretical level why income inequality, labour market participation, national divergence and economic development should largely explain the variance of social capital across European regions. The impact of these predictors on social capital and its three dimensions were empirically tested using a series of OLS regressions and evaluating their semistandardized and maximum impact coefficients (Chapter 6).

The baseline model explains 64 per cent of the variation of social capital across European regions (Table 6.1, column 1), showing that income inequality, labour market participation and national divergence have a significant impact while economic development does not. This surprising result – it has been often argued in the literature that economic development is an important predictor of social capital – has been tested more accurately by dropping the other independent variables of the model in rotation. By doing so, we observed that economic development seems to impact on social capital only if income inequality and labour market participation are not considered in the predictive model. Hence, we concluded that the explanatory power of the level of economic development has been over-emphasized in the literature because other important variables have been omitted in the predictive models (Chapter 6).

More broadly, our findings suggest that a reduction of income inequality and national divergence and increasing participation in the labour market would be conducive to the creation of social capital among European regions. The level of income inequality seems to be the most relevant explanation when the whole sample of regions is considered simultaneously, while national divergence has a stronger explanatory power for the regions ranked above the average and labour market participation for those below the average.

In order to gain more insights on the impact of each predictor on social capital, we also tested the effect of the four independent variables on the three dimensions of social capital. In the case of formal social networks, income inequality, labour market participation and national divergence explain 60 per cent of the variation across European regions (Table 6.1, column 2). The direction of the effect is the same measurement for social capital, however the magnitude of the effect is rather different. The level of income inequality is by far the most important predictor followed by labour market participation and the national divergence (which impacts only marginally).

In the case of informal social networks the model explains only 44 per cent of the variation across European regions, and only two predictors, namely the national divergence and the level of income inequality, play a significant role (Table 6.1, column 3). The direction of the effect remains the same for the national divergence (a lower divergence predicts higher scores of informal social networks) while it reverses for the level of income inequality. A decrease of income inequality has a negative impact on the density of informal social networks of each region.

These findings suggest that when income inequality increases within a region, people tend to react against the higher incertitude by strengthening their safety nets, that is, the bonding relationships with family and friends. This finding seems to confirm communitarian theories (Fukuyama 1995; Etzioni 1995), redistributive policy tends to destroy spontaneous reciprocity and strong ties. Hence, the reduction of income inequality proposes a trade off between the positive effect generated on formal social networks (and social trust, as we will see below) and the negative effects on informal social networks.

In the case of social trust the model explains 62.8 per cent of the variance (Table 6.1, column 4). Only income inequality and labour market participation have a significant effect on the variation of social trust among European regions. As for formal social networks, a reduction of income inequality has a stronger effect than an increase of participation in the labour market, while unlike the previous case, the national divergence does not have a significant effect.

To sum up, the empirical evidence, gathered from the analysis of the socio-economic predictors of social capital and its dimensions, suggests that income inequality, labour market participation and national divergence accurately explain the variance of social capital across Europe. In particular a reduction of income inequality would strongly favour a positive variation of formal social networks and social trust in society, while a stronger national cohesion would support the strengthening of informal ties. At the general level, the effects have the same directionality: an increase of income inequality and national divergence are negatively correlated to social capital and its dimensions, while an increase of labour market participation has a positive effect. The only remarkable exception is the positive correlation between an increase of income inequality and informal social networks. This confirms the argument proposed by the communitarians that emphasized how redistributive policy might destroy reciprocity and strong ties.

However, the positive effect of a decrease in income inequalities on formal social networks and social trust would be much stronger than the negative effect on informal social networks. The positive effect of these two dimensions is so strong, that despite the negative effect on one dimension, the level of income inequality remains the main predictor of social capital. The discussion amongst socialists, libertarians and communitarians concerning the relation between income inequality and social capital is perhaps an ideological battleground (for the opposite effect of income redistribution on formal and informal ties), but offers an empirical buttress to the notion of income redistribution if the primary aim of policy makers is to increase social capital.

The impact of labour market participation and national divergence, unlike income inequality, is unidirectional for all social capital dimensions. An increase of labour market participation and a decrease of national divergence would positively contribute to participation in formal and informal networks and would support stronger trust in European regions. This is confirmation of Gorz's (1992) hypothesis that a growing participation in the labour market reinforces the micro- and macro-social spheres (see Chapter 5). The problem remains how to generate an increasing participation in the labour market under the current economic climate. In this regard two potential solutions have been discussed (see Chapter 5): on one hand to pursue a more efficient activation policy (implemented almost everywhere in European regions), or on the other, more radical, to foster work sharing through the institutionalization of part-time work (as in the Dutch case) or providing a basic income, reducing the relation between income earned and the guarantee of basic social services for each citizen.

It would be interesting, from a social capital perspective, to observe at the empirical level the potential effects of the measures suggested by the *Boisonnat Commission* (see Chapter 5), to increase the opportunity to undertake less profitable economic activities and to spend more time participating in voluntary and communitarian activities in the micro-sphere, without the exclusion of individuals from the formal labour market. However, such a measure would require a decided shift in our society and economic system from a world based on competition and productivity to another kind of world based on participation in secondary groups and solidarity.

The idea of solidarity is central also to discuss the relation between national divergence and social capital. A stronger redistribution among regions of the same country, based on inter-individual solidarity, may increase social capital. We argued in Chapter 8, referring to the Belgian and Italian cases, that in a context of growing decentralization (see Chapter 3) the central management of social security would guarantee the provision of a similar level of basic social services also in regions that were economically poor and dependent (see Chapter 8), generating a positive impact on the level of social capital. This would connect transparency and local engagement fostered by the federal system, with economic redistribution and a reduction in national divergence guaranteed by the centralization of the social security system.

9.1.3   Linking Socio-Economic and Historical Institutional Comparative Analyses

The socio-economic model has been also exploited to select few cases for the historic-institutional analysis. The integration between the synchronic and diachronic perspectives has been undertaken, evaluating the residual of the regression model rather than simply observing at the theoretical level commonalities and differences among European regions (see Chapters 1 and 6). This methodological device made it possible to overcome the selection bias problem (Skocpol 1979) and contributed to the investigation of Putnam's historical explanation starting right from the structural socio-economic conditions of European regions.

Putnam explained the absence of participation and social trust in the Mezzogiorno referring to historical events that took place during the twelfth and thirteenth centuries. However, his historical claims were simply juxtaposed to the present lack of social capital but not directly connected to the socio-economic analysis (Lupo 1993; Tarrow 1996). As already emphasized in Chapter 7, different from the American scholar, the historical and institutional evolutions of the Mezzogiorno has been inter-preted starting from the socio-economic model and proposing a compara-tive historical analysis (exploiting the similarity with the Walloon case). The comparison between deviant (Wallonia and the South of Italy) and regular cases enabled a refinement of the general findings gathered from the socio-economic model (Lijphart 1971).

At the general level, we observed in the regression model that income inequality, labour market participation and national divergence would predict a lower level of social capital for the regions ranked above the average in the social capital ranking and vice versa. We suggested that this finding is explained by the positive reinforcing effect of well func-tioning institutions and by the consolidation, over a period of time of social participation and trust in contexts where these elements of social capital are already strong (Rothstein 2001). Reversely, where social capital scores are below the average, the negative reinforcing effect is explained by the bad functioning of institutions, the presence of a non-conducive environment, and the absence of social trust over a period of time (Woolcock 1998).

Furthermore, we argued that the cases in which social capital is largely below the average but the residuals are positive are particularly interest-ing when exploring the impact of historical and institutional evolution on social capital, because the socio-economic model indicates that social capital should be even lower than detected. We suggested (Chapters 6 and 7) that in these cases the impact of historic-institutional evolutions on social capital could be investigated, comparing them with two regular cases located in the same country.

On these bases we challenged Putnam's theory from a comparative perspective, arguing that in the Mezzogiorno and Wallonia the adverse socio-economic conditions seem to curtail the creation of social capital and are not conducive to enhance a rediscovery of their glorious past, which would be functional to the creation of regional solidarity and greater social capital. Therefore, starting from the comparison between Wallonia and the South of Italy with Flanders and the North East of Italy we proposed an alternative historical explanation to Putnam: the *sleeping social capital theory*.

9.1.4   Why does Social Capital Sleep?

The findings of the regression model fundamentally challenged Putnam's historical explanation of the lack of social capital in the South of Italy and offered an interesting puzzle that we have disentangled from a comparative perspective (see Chapter 7). We have argued that Putnam's work, nourished by doctrines like the 'end of history' (Fukuyama 1992) was largely deterministic, and proposed the dismissal of more articulated historical interpretations.

This determinism has reduced Southern Italian history as being a negative path to modernity; only the Italian regions that experienced the development of medieval towns during the twelfth and thirteenth centuries have got high levels of social capital today, the others 'are condemned' by the prevalence of the authoritarian rule of the Normans more than 800 years ago.

However, from a purely historical perspective, the medieval town is not unanimously considered to be a symbol of freedom, creation of horizontal ties and embryo of democratic life. In *Making Democracy Work*, Putnam disregarded the division within municipal towns and their dearth of civic participation by his simplistic over-generalizations using the experience of few areas in North Central Italy, ignoring the existence of important towns in the South (Chapter 7).

To this more complicated historical picture we have added the result of the regression model, which indicated that social capital in the South of Italy and Wallonia should be much lower than currently detected according to their socio-economic condition. Hence, we unfolded Putnam's theory by undertaking a comparative analysis between these two deviant cases and two regular cases located in the same country, namely Flanders and the North of Italy.

We have argued that the historical legacy does not have a negative effect on the present lack of social capital in Wallonia and the South of Italy, but that the potentially positive effect of the historical legacy is currently curtailed by the poor socio-economic conditions, notably by the high level of income inequality and the low level of labour market participation. This historical interpretation was driven by the comparison with Flanders and the North East of Italy.

In a sense, the value of the historical legacy for present socio-economic development is similar to the 'appropriable social capital' theorized by Coleman (1990) at the individual level. Using the example of the Korean students, Coleman argued that the construction of a secret network of people (at a time in which the appreciation for the authoritarian government was rapidly declining among the population) as a means of organizing the democratic revolt was the result of a process of socialization that took place during their childhood (with the involvement in the local churches).

The relation between historical evolutions and the socio-economic variables has similar characteristics at the macro level. Only after reaching a sufficient level of labour market activity and income redistribution (this is comparable to the growing unpopularity of the authoritarian government) can the memory of historical events of social engagement become fully appropriable by the population (this is comparable to the participation in the local churches during childhood), leading to the development of innovative forms of social participation (this is comparable to the construction of the secret circles that enhanced the democratic revolt). This process increases social capital even further if socio-economic development is matched by the revival of the unique historical legacy of the area. The reconstruction of this unique past can rapidly become a source of pride for the entire area, contributing in turn to an increasing intra-regional solidarity, and with it enhancement of social networks and social trust.

The Flemish case (and also to a lesser extent that of the North East of Italy) illustrates this process well. We have argued in Chapter 7 that the socio-economic improvements that took place in the nineteenth century were matched by the revival of the glorious Flemish traditions of the thirteenth and fourteenth centuries. The increase of social capital generated by the reduction of income inequality and the increasing participation in the labour market due to the economic development was multiplied by the reconstruction of Flemish identity and pride. This pride and self-confidence has, in turn, increased the feeling of solidarity within the region and contributed to generate a level of social capital, which is hardly explicable by the single socio-economic predictors (Flanders is the European region with the highest positive residual).

We suggested, in the divergent cases, that the value of the historical legacy is affected by the poor present socio-economic conditions. Social capital sleeps, not because of the absence of certain clearly defined historical steps as suggested by Putnam, but because socio-economic underdevelopment profoundly depressed the self-pride of Southern Italians and Walloons.

The biased and simplistic interpretations of Southern Italian and Walloon history (see Chapter 7) will be discarded only when their socio-economic conditions reach a sufficient level, enacting a cycle similar to Flanders and the North East of Italy. Stronger redistribution, an increase of labour market participation accompanied by a simultaneous process of 'reinvention of the past' could enhance a positive cycle of social capital increase in both areas. As stated in Chapter 7, the historical legacy in these two areas should not be seen as the root of the present lack of social capital but as a potential element for improvement. An important moment of social engagement also existed in the history of these two areas; the imagery of Walloons and Southern Italians should be nourished by these almost forgotten examples of collective history (as for example, the *Fasci Siciliani* described in Chapter 7) rather than the prevailing idea that the historical legacy of these areas is simply an original sin, a burden to carry through the process of modernization.

The historical analysis is completed by the comparison of the Belgian and Italian institutional evolutions. Their institutional evolutions have been analysed through a problem-solving approach: a certain amount of corruption, the proportional distribution of resources in every field, and the total control of social life (with the consequent reduction of social capital) have been used functionally to dealing with the geographical and cultural fractures that historically traversed the two countries.

However, the growing costs of such a system fostered a process of rapid decentralization after the 1970s. Federalism became associated with efficiency, conflict resolution and the intensification of political participation (in accordance with Tocqueville's classic argument). However the establishment of fully-fledged federalism, which extends also to social security, in asymmetric countries (like Belgium and Italy) may negatively impact on social capital by increasing income inequality and national divergence. Starting from Cattaneo's and Tocqueville's studies, we argued that the decentralization process could generate greater social engagement (increasing social capital) only if the social security system, operating redistribution at the individual and at the regional level, would remain centrally managed. This conclusion assumes a general value in Western Europe where the decentralization process is taking place in the context of increasing regional inequalities (see Chapter 3).

9.2   MEMBERSHIP UNLIMITED

As previously discussed, social capital has been used empirically to discuss issues that have been the focus of sociology for almost two centuries. Putnam's original formulation and measurement went back to the relation between the modernization of society, the disaggregation of secondary groups and institutional evolutions. He proposed a radical shift from the idea that social disaggregation is dependent upon structural changes and collective responsibilities, to the idea that culture and history are the key factors to explain this evolution (Putnam's theoretical argument is in line with a more general shift from socio-economic to cultural history, see Viazzo 2007).

Cultural mindsets and historical evolutions matter and can enhance structural patterns that are difficult to overcome (Putnam 1993). However Putnam's historical vision is deterministic. Are Southern Italians really to be considered incapable of increasing their involvement in the micro- and macro- social spheres because of the absence of medieval towns more than eight centuries ago (Putnam 1993)?

Putnam's historical vision is influenced heavily by communitarian theories. It is not coincidental that the word *comuni* (medieval towns) has the same Latin root of the word community. The existence of medieval towns in the North represents the focal point, the main difference with the un-civic South. A coincidental communitarian awakening alongside an increased ability to make free choices puts together contrary philosophical visions (communitarianism and libertarianism), and should support the strengthening of participation in society.

The results gathered from the empirical study do not support Putnam's conclusion; equality, involvement in paid work and interregional solidarity seem to play a large role in explaining the variation of social capital. The empirical evidence supports the idea instead, that only a more collective vision of society can counterbalance the dominant individualism, and contribute to increase social capital. Jordan emphasized how individualism cannot support the creation of authentic secondary spaces in society, simply because there are no projects that can be exclusively considered at the individual level:

> We can also recognize immediately that there is really no such thing as an individual project, however we may strain to think of one. Poets need publishers and readerships, marathon runners need competitors and stewards, even hermits need people to get away from and pleasures to give up. [. . .] The most universal projects [. . .] are explicitly shared with chosen others, and the relations they establish are integral to the projects themselves. (Jordan 1992: 160.)

The creation of secondary spaces and the reinforcement of those that already exist require a new redistributive impulse that can only be guaranteed by public powers, allowing everybody, especially the weaker categories of society[2] to be part of this collective project. The development of the micro-sphere through participation in associations and the time spent to consolidate informal networks has to be complemented by a renewed engagement in the macro-social sphere, the main 'place' in which people can rethink the configuration of our society.

Social scientists, in this context, should reconsider the role of history in conjunction with quantitative analysis. However, this re-visitation of the role of history does not mean it should be treated as a linear variable of an empirical model or should justify deterministic claims supported by quantitative synchronic analyses. Social scientists should use history, instead, to illuminate social evolutions of a specific area exerting a 'disciplined imagination' (Collingwood et al. 1999) in combination with quantitative analysis, respecting historical complexity, non-linearity and its contradictory patterns.

In this work we refuted a dialectic that prescribes the turning out of a set of historical steps (according to the model of the developed countries) to achieve a certain aim such as the increase of social capital. 'The end of history' cannot be found; the reality of the European continent is too pervaded by contradictory turning points to give confirmation of the fact that social scientists are absolutely right. In spite of the work of Putnam and Fukuyama, history is endless and a rich source of surprises (Tollebeek 1998: 353).

The *Fasci Siciliani* movement (Section 7.4), an almost unknown episode of social engagement and social capital creation at the end of the nineteenth century in Sicily, an area passive and deprived in collective action (according to Putnam's theory), demonstrated that thousands of Sicilian peasants were certainly not a dependent variable of history. Their culture and mindset cannot be prescribed by Putnam and Banfield's theories; their exercise of will to change their society cannot be forgotten in order to produce a polished and linear model that explains the present lack of social capital according to an original sin (like the absence of medieval towns in the South of Italy in the twelfth and thirteenth centuries).

These dominant paradigms that consist of the imposition of the winner's version of history,[3] as the only path to modernity, pervade our research, our lecture theatres and our vision of the world.[4] I hope with this work to have demonstrated that it is possible to combine quantitative research and a re-visitation of a consolidated bias without falling into deterministic analysis.

Thompson ([1991]1963), in the first chapter of *The Making of the English Working Class*, distinguished the London Corresponding Society[5] from the other social movements that were developing at the beginning of the nineteenth century because it opposed itself to the 'notion of exclusiveness', which preserved hereditary elites or powerful property groups. According to the society, the only way to promote democracy and social improvement was to enable everybody to join their association, and they emphasized the principle of unlimited membership at their first meeting.

This principle seems a paradoxical concept with which to conclude a book on the determinants of social capital.[6] However, the empirical evidence collected in this work (quantitative and historical), points in this direction. The only way to increase social capital in European regions is to develop an efficient connection between participation in the micro-social sphere and the involvement in the macro-social sphere, reinforcing collective values to counterbalance the dominant individualism. 'To throw open the door to propaganda and agitation in this *unlimited way* implied a new notion of democracy, which cast aside ancient inhibitions and trusted to self-activating and self-organizing processes among people' (Thompson 1991 [1963]: 24), supported by larger economic equality, and a redistribution of work opportunities, to regenerate the secondary space devoted to private and public engagement.

NOTES

1. All theoretical generalizations and empirical results proposed in the book and summarized in the next section are valid under a certain number of assumptions. First of all, this research is not immune from two intrinsic problems of every comparative analysis based on standardized surveys: the failure to satisfy the conditions of exchangeability and identification and the possibility that interviewees interpreted the questionnaires differently, as a result of their cultural and geographical background (see Chapter 2).
    Also the comparative historical analysis presents two strong theoretical assumptions (Skocpol 1979). The first is that we cannot control for the potential impact of other variables (other than historic and institutional evolutions) on social capital in the comparison. The second is that we assumed that Walloon and Southern Italian historic-institutional evolutions are completely independent. In reality these two regions probably had connections and relations at different levels (cultural, historical and institutional). Nevertheless, despite the existence of these limitations, the integration of two methods supported the combination of the strength of the quantitative approach and the in-depth historical-institutional analysis, providing a solid empirical basis to the deductive and inductive reasoning undertaken to discuss the research puzzle (see Chapter 1).
2. Women, young people and immigrants.
3. The economically developed North over the poor South of Italy and the advanced Flanders over the depressed Wallonia.
4. In the famous book *The Whig Interpretation of History*, Sir Herbert Butterfield (1931) criticized the description of history as a line of progression toward the glorious present.
5. A society created to defend the rights of workers (see Thompson [(1991)1963]; Chapter 1).
6. We have clarified in the introduction how social capital theorists emphasized the importance of the creation of exclusive social networks to generate social capital.

Bibliography

Abbott, A. (1990) Conceptions of Time and Events in Social Science Methods. *Historical Methods*, 23, 140–50.

Aceves, J. (1971) *Social Change in a Spanish Village*, London, Schenkman.

Adler, P.S. & Kwon, S.W. (2002) Social Capital: Prospects for a New Concept. *The Academy of Management Review*, 27, 17–40.

Adorno, T.W. (1950) *The Authoritarian Personality*, New York, Harper.

Adorno, T.W. & Horkheimer, M. (1979) *Dialectic of Enlightenment*, London, Verso.

Aghion, P., Algan, Y., Cahuc, P. & Shleifer, A. (2010) Regulation and Distrust. *The Quarterly Journal of Economics*, 125, 1015–49.

Aguilera, M.B. (2002) The Impact of Social Capital on Labor Force Participation: Evidence from the 2000 Social Capital Benchmark Survey. *Social Science Quarterly*, 83, 853–74.

Akaike, H. (1973) Information Theory and an Extension of the Likelihood Ratio Principle. In Petrov, B.N. & Csaki, F. (eds) *Second International Symposium of Information Theory*. Budapest, Akademinai Kiado, 267–81.

Akerlof, G. (1980) A Theory of Social Custom, of which Unemployment may be one Consequence. *The Quarterly Journal of Economics*, 94, 749–75.

Alcaro, M. (1999) *Sull'Identità Meridionale*, Turin, Einaudi.

Alderson, A.S. & Nielsen, F. (2002) Globalization and the Great U-Turn: Income Inequality Trends in 16 OECD countries. *American Journal of Sociology*, 107, 1244–99.

Alesina, A. & Giuliano, P. (2010) The Power of Family. *Journal of Economic Growth*, 15, 93–125.

Alesina, A. & Ichino, A. (2010) *L'Italia Fatta in Casa*, Milan, Mondadori.

Alesina, A. & La Ferrara, E. (2002) Who Trusts Others. *Journal of Public Economics*, 85, 207–34.

Allum, P. (1975) *Potere e Società a Napoli nel Dopoguerra*, Turin, Einaudi.

Almond, G.A. & Verba, S. (1963) *The Civic Culture: Political Attitudes and Democracy in Five Nations*, Princeton, Princeton University Press.

Andersen, T.M. & Svarer, M. (2007) Flexicurity – Labour Market Performance in Denmark. *CESifo Economic Studies*.

Anderson, B.R. (1983) *Imagined Communities: Reflections on the Origin and Spread of Nationalism*, London, Verso.

Anderson, J.J. (1990) Skeptical Reflections on a Europe of Regions: Britain, Germany and the ERDP. *Journal of Public Policy*, 10, 417–47.

Anderson, P. (1964) Origins of the Present Crisis. *New Left Review*, 35, 2–42.

Anderson, P. (1974) *Passages from Antiquity to Feudalism*, London, Verso.

Argyle, M. (1992) Benefits Produced by Supportive Relationship. In Veil, H. & Baumann, U. (eds) *The Meaning and Measurement of Social Support.* New York, Hemisphere Publishing Corp, 13–32.

Aristotle (1997) *Politics*, Oxford, Oxford University Press.

Arlacchi, P. (1980a) Mafia e Tipi di Società. *Rassegna Italiana di Sociologia*, 1, 3–49.

Arlacchi, P. (1980b) *Mafia, Contadini e Latifondo nella Calabria Tradizionale*, Bologna, Il Mulino.

Aron, R. (1967) *Les Étapes de la Pensée Sociologique*, Paris, Gallimard.

Arrow, K.J. (1972) Gifts and Exchanges. *Philosophy and Public Affairs*, 1, 343–62.

Atkinson, A.B. (1970) On the Measurement of Inequality. *Journal of Economic Theory*, 2, 244–70.

Atkinson, A.B. (1999) Is Rising Inequality Inevitable? A Critique of the Transatlantic Consensus. *WIDER Annual Lectures 3*. Oslo.

Atkinson, A.B. (2003) Income Inequality in OECD Countries: Data and Explanations. *CESifo Conference on Globalisation, Inequality and Well-Being.* CESifo Working Paper No. 881.

Atkinson, A.B., Rainwater, L. & Smeeding, T.M. (1995) *Income Distribution in OECD Countries: Evidence from the Luxembourg Income Study*, Paris, Organisation for Economic Cooperation and Development.

Bache, I. & Jones, R. (2000) Has EU Regional Policy Empowered the Regions? A Study of Spain and the UK. *Regional and Federal Studies*, 10, 1–20.

Bagnasco, A. (1977) *Le Tre Italie*, Bologna, Il Mulino.

Bagnasco, A. (1999) *Tracce di Comunità*, Bologna, Il Mulino.

Bagnasco, A. (2006) Ritorno a Montegrano. In Banfield, E.C. (ed.) *Le Basi Morali di una Società Arretrata.* Bologna, Il Mulino, 9–31.

Banfield, E.C. (1958) *The Moral Basis of a Backward Society*, Glencoe Ill, Free Press.

Barbagallo, F. (1990) Il Mezzogiorno come Problema Attuale. *Studi Storici*, 3, 585–96.

Barber, B. (1983) *The Logic and Limits of Trust*, New Brunswick, Rutgers University Press.

Barbier, J.C. & Ludwig-Mayerhofer, W. (2004) Introduction. The Many Worlds of Activation. *European Societies*, 6, 423–36.

Barnes, J.A. (1954a) *Politics in a Changing Society*, Oxford, Oxford University Press.

Barnes, J.A. (1954b) Class and Committees in a Norwegian Island Parish. *Human Relations*, 7, 39–58.

Barrington Moore, J. (1966) *Social Origins of Dictatorship and Democracy. Lord and Peasant in the Making of the Modern World*, London, Allen Lane.

Barro, R. & Sala-i-Martin, X. (1992) Convergence. *The Journal of Political Economy*, 100, 223–51.

Becker, G.S. (1996) *Accounting for Tastes*, Cambridge MA, Harvard University Press.

Bell, D. (1962) America as a Mass Society. In Bell, D. (ed.) *The End of Ideology*. New York, Collier Books, 21–38.

Bendix, R. (1964) *Nation-Building and Citizenship. Studies of Our Changing Social Order*, New York, Wiley.

Benigno, F. (1989) Famiglia Mediterranea e Modelli Anglosassoni. *Meridiana*, 6, 29–61.

Benjamin, W. (1965) Book Review of the Civic Culture: Political Attitudes and Democracy in Five Nations. *The Journal of Politics*, 27, 206–209.

Berkowitz, S.D. (1982) *An Introduction to Structural Analysis. The Network Approach to Social Research*, Toronto, Butterworths.

Berlin, I. (1978) Corsi e Ricorsi. *The Journal of Modern History*, 50, 480–89.

Bertola, G. & Garibaldi, P. (2002) The Structure and History of Italian Unemployment. *CESifo Working Paper No. 907.*

Bertrand, M. & Schoar, A. (2006) The Role of Family in Family Firms. *The Journal of Economic Perspectives*, 20, 73–96.

Beugelsdijk, S. & Van Schaik, T. (2005a) Differences in Social Capital between 54 Western European Regions. *Regional Studies*, 39, 1053–64.

Beugelsdijk, S. & Van Schaik, T. (2005b) Social Capital and Growth in European Regions: An Empirical Test. *European Journal of Political Economy*, 21, 301–24.

Bevilacqua, P. (1993) *Breve Storia dell'Italia Meridionale dall'Ottocento a Oggi*, Rome, Donzelli.

Bevir, M. (2005) *New Labour: A Critique*, London, Routledge.

Billiet, J., Maddens, B. & Frognier, A. (2006) Does Belgium (still) Exist? Differences in Political Culture between Flemings and Walloons. *West European Politics*, 29, 912–32.

Blando, A. (2007) Il Ritorno di Banfield. *Meridiana*, 59–60, 307–23.

Bloch, M. (1954) *The Historian's Craft*, Manchester, Manchester University Press.

Blok, A. (1974) *The Mafia of a Sicilian Village, 1860–1960: A Study of Violent Peasant Entrepreneurs*, Oxford, Basil Blackwell.

Boeri, T. & Garibaldi, P. (2000) Shadow Unemployment in a Depressed Labor Market. *Le Nuove Frontiere della Politica Economica Conference.* Rome.

Boeri, T. & Garibaldi, P. (2005) Shadow Sorting. *NBER Chapters.* National Bureau of Economic Research.

Boldrin, M., Canova, F., Pischke, J.S. & Puga, D. (2001) Inequality and Convergence in Europe's Regions: Reconsidering European Regional Policies. *Economic Policy*, 16, 207–53.

Bonnell, V. (1980) The Uses of Theory, Concepts and Comparison in Historical Sociology. *Comparative Studies in Society and History*, 22, 156–73.

Borzel, T.A. (2002) *States and Regions in the European Union*, Cambridge, Cambridge University Press.

Bott, E. (1957) *Family and Social Network. Roles, Norms, and External Relationship in Ordinary Urban Families*, London, Tavistock Publications Limited.

Boudon, R. (1998) Limitations of Rational Choice Theory. *The American Journal of Sociology*, 104, 817–28.

Bourdieu, P. (1980) Le Capital Social. *Actes de la Recherche en Science Sociale*, 31, 2–3.

Bourdieu, P. (1986) The Forms of Capital. In Richardson, J.G. (ed.) *Handbook of Theory and Research for the Sociology of Education.* New York, Greenwood Press, 241–58.

Bourdieu, P. & Passeron, J.C. (1970) *La Reproduction. Eléments pour une Théorie du Système d'Enseignement*, Paris, Editions de Minuit.

Bourguignon, F. (1979) Decomposable Income Inequality Measures. *Econometrica*, 47, 901–20.

Bourne, A.K. (2003) The Impact of European Integration on Regional Power. *JCMC*, 41, 597–620.

Bowles, S. & Gintis, H. (2002) Social Capital and Community Governance. *The Economic Journal*, 112, 419–36.

Brehm, J. & Rahm, W. (1997) Individual-Level Evidence for the Causes and Consequences of Social Capital. *American Journal of Political Science*, 41, 999–1023.

Breiman, L. (1992) The Little Bootstrap and other Methods for Dimensionality Selection in Regression: X-Fixed Prediction Error. *Journal of the American Statistical Association*, 87, 738–54.

Brenner, N. (2004) *New State Spaces. Urban Governance and the Rescaling of Statehood*, Oxford, Oxford University Press.

Brenner, N. (2009) Open Questions on State Rescaling. *Cambridge Journal of Regions, Economy and Society*, 2, 123–39.

Brezzi, P. (1959) *I Comuni Medioevali nella Storia d'Italia*, Turin, ERI-Edizioni Rai Radiotelevisione Italiana.

Brinton, C. (1938) *The Anatomy of Revolution*, New York, W.W. Norton.

Brogger, J. (1971) *Montevarese: A Study of Peasant Society and Culture in Southern Italy*, Bergen, Universitetsforlaget.

Brook, K. (2005) Labour Market Participation: The Influence of Social Capital. *Labour Market Trends.* Office for National Statistics.

Brown, H.P. (1991) *Egalitarianism and the Generation of Inequality*, Oxford, Clarendon Press.

Bullain, I. (1998) Autonomy and the European Union. In Suski, M. (ed.) *Autonomy: Applications and Implications*. Netherlands, Kluwer Law International, 343–56.

Burt, R.S. (1992) *Structural Holes: The Social Structure of Competition*, Cambridge MA, Harvard University Press.

Butterfield, H. (1931) *The Whig Interpretation of History*, London, Bell.

Caciagli, M. (1977) *Democrazia Cristiana e Potere nel Mezzogiorno*, Firenze, Guaraldi.

Cafiero, S. (1996) *Questione Meridionale e Unità Nazionale. 1861–1995*, Rome, La Nuova Italia Scientifica.

Calhoun, C. (1998) Explanation in Historical Sociology: Narrative, General Theory, and Historically Specific Theory. *The American Journal of Sociology*, 104, 846–71.

Calvo-Armengol, A. & Jackson, M.O. (2004) The Effects of Social Networks on Employment and Inequality. *American Economic Review*, 94, 426–54.

Cancian, F. (1961) Southern Italian Peasant: World View and Political Behaviour. *Anthropological Quarterly*, 34, 1–18.

Cantillon, B., Maesschalck, V.D., Rottiers, S. & Verbist, G. (2006) Social Redistribution in Federalised Belgium. *West European Politics*, 29, 1034–56.

Carney, M. (2007) Minority Family Business in Emerging Markets. *Family Business Review*, 20, 289–300.

Cartocci, R. (2007) *La Mappa del Tesoro. Atlante del Capitale Sociale in Italia*, Bologna, Il Mulino.

Cassano, F. (1996) *Il Pensiero Meridiano*, Bari, Laterza.

Catanzaro, R. (1975) Potere e Politica Locale in Italia. *Quaderni di Sociologia*, 24, 273–322.

Catanzaro, R. (1979) Le Cinque Sicilie. Disarticolazione Sociale e Struttura di Classe in un' Economia Dipendente. *Rassegna Italiana di Sociologia*, 20, 7–35.

Catanzaro, R. (1980) *Partecipazione, Potere e Sviluppo*, Catania, Pellicano Libri.

Catanzaro, R. (1982) Note sulla Carenza di Conflittualità e di Azione Collettiva nel Mezzogiorno. *Inchiesta*, 57, 39–48.

Catanzaro, R. (1983) Struttura Sociale, Sistema Politico e Azione Collettiva nel Mezzogiorno. *Stato e Mercato*, 8, 271–315.

Catanzaro, R. (1992) Dall'Irresponsabilità allo Spirito di Rapina. Note in Merito al Sistema Politico Locale nel Mezzogiorno. In Cerase, P. (ed.) *Dopo il Familismo Cosa? Tesi a Confronto sulla Questione Meridionale negli Anni '90*. Milan, Franco Angeli, 46–55.

Cattaneo, C. (1966) *I Problemi dello Stato Italiano*, Milan, Mondadori.

Cerase, P. (1992) *Dopo il Familismo Cosa? Tesi a Confronto sulla Questione Meridionale negli Anni '90*, Milan, Franco Angeli.

Champernowne, D.G. (1974) A Comparison of Measures of Inequality of Income Distribution. *The Economic Journal*, 84, 787–816.

Chiarello, F. (1992) La Questione Meridionale come Questione Meridionale. In Cerase, P. (ed.) *Dopo il Familismo Cosa? Tesi a Confronto sulla Questione Meridionale negli Anni '90*. Milan, Franco Angeli, 113–25.

Clarke, K.A. (2001) Testing non Nested Models of International Relations: Reevaluating Realism. *American Journal of Political Science*, 45, 724–44.

Clarke, K.A. (2003) Nonparametric Model Discrimination in International Relations. *Journal of Conflict Resolution*, 47, 72–93.

Clarke, K.A. (2005) The Phantom Menace: Omitted Variable Bias in Econometric Research. *Conflict Management and Peace Science*, 22, 341–52.

Colajanni, N. (1894) *In Sicilia, gli Avvenimenti e le Cause*, Rome, Perino.

Coleman, J.S. (1988) Social Capital in the Creation of Human Capital. *American Journal of Sociology*, 94, S95–S120.

Coleman, J.S. (1990) *Foundations of Social Theory*, Cambridge MA, Harvard University Press.

Collida, A.B. (1978) *L'Economia Italiana tra Sviluppo e Sussistenza*, Milan, Franco Angeli.

Collingwood, R.G., Dray, W. & Dussen, W.J. (1999) *The Principles of History: And Other Writings in Philosophy of History*, Oxford, Oxford University Press.

Colombis, A. (1974) Organizzazione Sociale e Familismo Amorale a Chiaromonte. Critica della Tesi di E.C. Banfield da Parte di un Familista. *Sociologia dell'Organizzazione*, 4, 437–88.

Colombis, A. (1980) Ricerca Sociale Concetti ed Ideologie. Con Particolare Riferimento alle Aree Interne, Montane, Depresse. *Basilicata*, 24, 65–75.

Colombis, A. (1992) L'Invenzione del Familismo Amorale. In Cerase, P. (ed.) *Dopo il Familismo Amorale Cosa? Tesi a Confronto sulla Questione Meridionale negli Anni '90.* Milan, Franco Angeli, 201–12.

Colombis, A. (1997) Invece del Familismo: La Famiglianza. In Meloni, B. (ed.) *Famiglia Meridionale senza Familismo.* Catanzaro, Meridiana Libri, 382–408.

Commissariat Général du Plan (1995) Le Travail dans 20 Ans. Paris, Odile Jacod/La Documentation Française.

Compagna, F. (1963) *La Questione Meridionale*, Milan, Garzanti.

Cook, D.R. & Weisberg, S. (1982) *Residuals and Influence in Regression*, New York, Chapman & Hall.

Costa, D.E. & Kahn, M.E. (2003) Understanding the American Decline in Social Capital, 1952–1998. *Kyklos*, 56, 17–46.

Cox, D.R. (1961) Tests of Separate Families of Hypotheses. *Proceedings of the Fourth Berkeley Symposium*, I, 105–23.

Crainz, G. (1999) Campagne e Movimenti Contadini tra Crisi Agraria e Grande Guerra. In Rossi Doria, A. (ed.) *La Fine dei Contadini.* Soveria Mannelli (CZ), Rubbettino Editore, 47–67.

Cusack, T. (1999) Social Capital, Institutional Structures, and Democratic Performance: A Comparative Study of German Local Governments. *European Journal of Political Research*, 35, 1–34.

Dalton, H. (1920) The Measurement of Inequality of Incomes. *The Economic Journal*, 30, 348–61.

Davis, J. (1973) *Land and Family in Pisticci*, London, New York, Athlone Press and Humanities Press.

De Graaf, N.D. & Flap, H.D. (1988) 'With a Little Help from my Friends': Social Resources as an Explanation of Occupational Status and Income in West Germany, The Netherlands, and the United States. *Social Forces*, 67, 452–72.

De Martino, E. (1959) *Sud e Magia*, Milan, Feltrinelli.

De Winter, L. & Dumont, P. (2006) Do Belgian Parties Undermine the Democratic Chain of Delegation? *West European Politics*, 29, 957–76.

Delfosse, P. (1994) La Terre Contre l'État? Pouvoir d'État et Résistances Traditionnelles en Belgique (1851–1929). *Le Mouvement Social*, 166, 53–90.

Deschouwer, K. (2006) And the Peace Goes on? Consociational Democracy and Belgian Politics in the Twenty-First Century. *West European Politics*, 29, 895–911.

Destefanis, S. & Fonseca, R. (2005) Matching Efficiency and Labour Market Reform in Italy. A Macroeconomic Assessment. *CELPE discussion papers 93.* University of Salerno.

Di Gennaro, G. (1992) Oltre il Familismo. Vecchi e Nuovi Limiti allo

Sviluppo del Mezzogiorno. In Cerase, P. (ed.) *Dopo il Familismo Cosa? Tesi a Confronto sulla Questione Meridionale negli Anni '90*. Milan, Franco Angeli, 179–200.

Dika, S. & Singh, K. (2002) Applications of Social Capital in Education Literature: A Critical Synthesis. *Review of Educational Research*, 72, 31–60.

Donolo, C. (1972) Sviluppo Ineguale e Disgregazione Sociale nel Meridione. *Quaderni Piacentini*, 47, 121–8.

Donzelli, C. (1990) Mezzogiorno tra Questione e Purgatorio. Opinione Comune, Immagine Scientifica, Strategie di Ricerca. *Meridiana*, 9, 13–55.

Dorso, G. (1949) *L'Occasione Storica*, Turin, Einaudi.

Dunford, M. (1993) Regional Disparities in the European Community: Evidence from REGIO Databank. *Regional Studies*, 27, 727–43.

Dunn, J.J. (1974) The Revision of the Constitution in Belgium: A Study in the Institutionalization of Ethnic Conflict. *The Western Political Quarterly*, 27, 143–63.

Durkheim, E. (1893) *De la Division du Travail Social*, Paris, PUF.

Durlauf, S.N. (2002) On the Empirics of Social Capital. University of Wisconsin, Department of Economics, Unpublished Paper.

Dyer, W.G. (2006) Examining the 'Family Effect' on Firm Performance. *Family Business Review*, 19 (4), 253–73.

Eisenstadt, S.N. (1963) *The Political Systems of Empires*, New York, Free Press.

Esping-Andersen, G. (1990) *The Three Worlds of Welfare Capitalism*, Cambridge, Polity.

Esping-Andersen, G., Gallie, D., Hemerijck, A. & Myles, J. (2002) *Why We Need a New Welfare State*, Oxford, Oxford University Press.

Estevao, M. (2003) Regional Labor Market Disparities in Belgium. *Reflects et Perspetives*, XLII, 95–114.

Etzioni, A. (1995) *The Spirit of Community: Rights, Responsibilities, and the Communitarian Agenda*, London, Fontana.

Eurobarometer (2005) Social Capital. Special Eurobarometer 223.

Eurobarometer (2006) European Social Reality. Special Eurobarometer 273.

European Parliament (1988) Resolution on Community Regional Policy and the Role of the Regions. In European Parliament (ed.) *19.12.1988, No C 326*. Official Journal of the European Communities (OJEC).

Eurostat (2005) Regional Statistics.

Eurostat (2007) Regional Statistics.

Eurostat (2009) Labour Market Statistics.

EVS (1990) European Value Survey.

EVS (1999–2000) European Value Survey.

Ezcurra, R. & Rapun, M. (2006) Regional Disparities and National Development Revisited: The Case of Western Europe. *European Urban and Regional Studies*, 13, 355–69.

Fernandez, R.M., Castilla, E.J. & Moore, P. (2000) Social Capital at Work: Networks and Employment at a Phone Center. *American Journal of Sociology*, 105, 1288–356.

Ferragina, E. (2009a) *Capitale Sociale e Riforma del Welfare. La Terza via dell'Europa*, London, Turin, OMP.

Ferragina, E. (2009b) The Never-Ending Debate about the Moral Basis of a Backward Society: Banfield and Amoral Familism. *Journal of the Anthropological Society of Oxford*, 2, 141–60.

Ferragina, E. (2010a) Social Capital and Equality: Tocqueville's legacy. *The Tocqueville Review*, XXXI, 73–98.

Ferragina, E. (2010b) Le Teorie che non Muiono Mai sono quelle che Confermano le Nostre Ipotesi di Base. *Meridiana*, 65, 265–87.

Ferragina, E. (2010c) Capitale Sociale e Mezzogiorno. *Società e Impresa, Capitale, Coesione Sociale e Cultura d'Impresa, Field Conference*. University of Cosenza.

Ferragina, E. (2011) Il Fantasma di Banfield: Una Verifica Empirica della Teoria del Familismo Amorale. *Stato e Mercato*, 92, 283–312.

Ferragina, E. & Seeleib-Kaiser, M. (2011) Welfare Regime Debate: Past, Present, Futures? *Policy and Politics*, 39, 4, 583–611.

Ferrera, M. (1993) *Modelli di Solidarietà*, Bologna, Il Mulino.

Ferrera, M. (1997) *Le Trappole del Welfare State*, Bologna, Il Mulino.

Field, A. (2005) *Discovering Statistics Using SPSS. Second Edition*, Thousand Oaks, Sage.

Fine, B. (1999) The Developmental State is Dead. Long Live Social Capital? *Development and Change*, 30, 1–19.

Fine, B. (2008) Social Capital in Wonderland. The World Bank Behind the Looking Glass. *Progress in Development Studies*, 8, 261–9.

Fingleton, B. (1999) Estimates of Time to Economic Convergence: An Analysis of Regions of the European Union. *International Regional Science Review*, 22, 5–34.

Fortunato, G. (1973) *Il Mezzogiorno e lo Stato Italiano*, Firenze, Vallecchi.

Foster, G.M. (1965) Peasant Society and the Image of Limited Good. *American Anthropologist*, 67, 293–315.

Fourier, J. (1836) *La Fausse Industrie Morcelée Répugnante et Mensongère et l'Antidote, l'Industrie Naturelle, Combinée, Attrayante, Véridique Donnant Quadruple Produit*, Paris, Anthropos.

Franchetti, L. & Sonnino, S. (1974) *Inchiesta in Sicilia*, Firenze, Vallecchi.

Freeman, L.C. (1976) A Bibliography of Social Networks. Monticello IL, Council of Planning Librarians.

Freitag, M. (2006) Bowling the State Back in: Political Institutions and the Creation of Social Capital. *European Journal of Political Research*, 45, 123–52.

Friedmann, F.G. (1954a) The World of 'la Miseria'. *Partisan Review*, 20, 218–31.

Friedmann, F.G. (1954b) The Peasant: A Symposium Concerning the Peasant Way and View of Life. *Mimeographed.*

Friedmann, F.G. (1974) *Osservazioni sul Mondo Contadino dell'Italia Meridionale*, Milan, Franco Angeli.

Fukuyama, F. (1992) *The End of History and the Last Man*, London, Penguin.

Fukuyama, F. (1995) *Trust: The Social Virtues and the Creation of Prosperity*, New York, Free Press.

Fukuyama, F. (2000) Social Capital and Civil Society. *IMF Conference on Second Generation Reforms*. Washington DC, IMF Institute and the Fiscal Affairs Department.

Gaggio, D. (2007) Come Ripensare il Ruolo della Cultura nella Storia Economica? *Contemporanea*, 10, 709–14.

Galasso, G. (1965) *Mezzogiorno Medievale e Moderno*, Turin, Einaudi.

Geertz, C. (1973) *The Interpretation of Cultures*, New York, Basic Books, inc.

Giannini, M. & Salomone, A. (1992) Il Familismo tra Amoralità e Sviluppo Meridionale. In Cerase, P. (ed.) *Dopo il Familismo Cosa? Tesi a Confronto sulla Questione Meridionale negli Anni '90.* Milan, Franco Angeli, 63–9.

Giblin-Delvallet, B. (2004) Lille Métropole. Une Eurométropole en Devenir? *Vingtième Siècle. Revue d'histoire*, 81, 69–80.

Giddens, A. (1979) *Central Problems in Social Theory*, London, Macmillan.

Giddens, A. (1998) *The Third Way. The Renewal of Social Democracy*, Cambridge, Polity Press.

Gilbert, N. (2004) *Transformation of the Welfare State. The Silent Surrender of Public Responsibility*, New York, Oxford University Press.

Gilbert, N. & Van Voorhis, R. (2001) *Activating Unemployed: A Comparative Appraisal of Work-Oriented Policies*, Rutgers, NJ, Transaction Publishers.

Gini, C. (1912) *Variabilità e Mutabilità*, Bologna, P.Cappuccini.

Gini, C. (1921) Measurement of Inequality of Incomes. *The Economic Journal*, 31, 124–6.

Goldstone, J.A. (1998) Initial Conditions, General Laws, Path

Dependency, and Explanation in Historical Sociology. *The American Journal of Sociology*, 104, 829–45.

Goldthorpe, J.H. (1991) The Uses of History in Sociology: Reflections on some Recent Tendencies. *The British Journal of Sociology*, 42, 211–30.

Goldthorpe, J.H. (1997) Current Issues in Comparative Macrosociology: A Debate on Methodological Issues. *Comparative Social Research*, 16, 1–26.

Gorz, A. (1988) *Métamorphoses du Travail. Quête du sens. Critique de la Raison Economique*, Paris, Editions Galilée.

Gorz, A. (1992) On the Difference between Society and Community, and Why Basic Income Cannot by Itself Confer Full Membership of Either. In Van Parijs, P. (ed.) *Arguing for Basic Income. Ethical Foundations for a Radical Reform.* London, Verso, 178–84.

Gorz, A. (1997) *Misères du Présent, Richesses du Possible*, Paris, Editions Galilée.

Gorz, A. (1999) *Reclaiming Work. Beyond the Wage-Based Society*, Cambridge, Polity Press.

Goul Andersen, J., Clasen, J., Van Oorschot, W. & Halvorsen, K. (2002) *Europe's New State of Welfare: Unemployment, Employment Policies and Citizenship*, Bristol, The Policy Press.

Gramsci, A. (1952) *La Questione Meridionale*, Rome, La Rinascita.

Granovetter, M.S. (1973) The Strength of Weak Ties. *The American Journal of Sociology*, 78, 1360–80.

Granovetter, M. (1985) Economic Action and Social Structure: The Problem of Embeddedness. *The American Journal of Sociology*, 91, 481–510.

Graziani, A. & Pugliese, E. (1979) *Investimenti e Disoccupazione nel Mezzogiorno*, Bologna, Il Mulino.

Graziano, L. (1974) Clientelismo e Sviluppo Politico: Il Caso del Mezzogiorno. In Graziano, L. (ed.) *Clientelismo e Sviluppo Politico*. Milan, Franco Angeli, 333–62.

Gribaudi, G. (1993) Familismo e Famiglia a Napoli e nel Mezzogiorno. *Meridiana*, 17, 9–42.

Gribaudi, G. (1997) Images of the South: the Mezzogiorno as Seen by Insiders and Outsiders. In Lumley, R. & Morris, J. (eds) *The New History of the Italian South. The Mezzogiorno Revisited*. Exeter, University of Exeter Press, 83–113.

Grootaert, C. & Van Bastelaer, T. (2002a) *The Role of Social Capital in Development*, Cambridge, Cambridge University Press.

Grootaert, C. & Van Bastelaer, T. (2002b) *Understanding and Measuring Social Capital. A Multidisciplinary Tool for Pratictioners*, Washington, The World Bank.

Groppi, T. (2008) L'Evoluzione della Forma di Stato in Italia: Uno Stato Regionale senz' Anima? *La Costituzione Ieri e Oggi*. Accademia Nazionale dei Lincei.

Gustafson, B. & Johansson, M. (1999) In Search of Smoking Guns: What Makes Inequality Vary over Time in Different Countries? *American Sociological Review*, 64, 585–605.

Haas, E.B. (1975) *The Obsolescence of Regional Integration Theory*, Berkeley CA, Center for International Studies.

Hall, P.A. (1999) Social Capital in Britain. *British Journal of Political Science*, 29, 417–61.

Halvorsen, R. & Jensen, P.H. (2004) Activation in Scandinavian Welfare Policy. *European Societies*, 6, 461–83.

Hanifan, L. (1916) The Rural School Community Center. *Annals of the American Academy of Political Science*, 67, 130–38.

Haydu, J. (1998) Making Use of the Past: Time Periods as Cases to Compare and as Sequences of Problem Solving. *The American Journal of Sociology*, 104, 339–71.

Helliwell, J.F. & Putnam, R.D. (1995) Economic Growth and Social Capital in Italy. *Eastern Economic Journal*, 21, 295–307.

Hendry, D.F. & Richard, F. (1982) On the Formulation of Empirical models in Dynamic Econometrics. *Journal of Econometrics*, 20, 3–33.

Hepburn, E. (2008) The Rise and Fall of a 'Europe of the Regions'. *Regional and Federal Studies*, 18, 537–55.

Hooghe, L., Schakel, A.H. & Marks, G. (2008a) Appendix A: Profiles of Regional Reform in 42 Countries (1950–2006). *Regional and Federal Studies*, 18, 183–258.

Hooghe, L., Schakel, A.H. & Marks, G. (2008b) Appendix B: Country and Regional Scores. *Regional and Federal Studies*, 18, 259–74.

Inglehart, R. (1988) The Renaissance of Political Culture. *The American Political Science Review*, 82, 1203–30.

Inglehart, R. (1999) Trust, Well-Being and Democracy. In Warren, M. (ed.) *Democracy and Trust*. Cambridge, Cambridge University Press.

Jackman, R. & Miller, R. (1996) A Renaissance of Political Culture? *American Journal of Political Science*, 40, 632–59.

Jacobs, J. (1961) *The Death and Life of Great American Cities*, London, Cape.

Jesuit, D.K. (2008) Subnational Analyses Using Luxembourg Income Study (LIS) Data Archive. *LIS Working Paper, No. 494.*

Jesuit, D.K., Rainwater, L. & Smeeding, T.M. (2002) Regional Poverty within the Rich Countries. *LIS Working Paper, No. 318.*

Jesus Velasco, G. (2004) Seymour Martin Lipset: Life and Work. *The Canadian Journal of Sociology*, 29, 583–601.

Jordan, B. (1992) Basic Income and the Common Good. In Van Parijs, P. (ed.) *Arguing for the Basic Income. Ethical Foundations for a Radical Reform*. London, Verso.

Kawachi, I., Kennedy, B., Lochner, K. & Prothrow, D. (1997) Social Capital, Income Inequality and Mortality. *American Journal of Public Health*, 87, 1491–8.

Keating, M. (2008) A Quarter Century of the Europe of the Regions. *Regional and Federal Studies*, 18, 629–35.

Keating, M., Loughlin, J. & Deschouwer, K. (2003) *Culture, Institutions and Economic Development: A Study of Eight European Regions*, Cheltenham, UK and Northampton, MA, USA, Edward Elgar.

Kelly, G.A. (1969) New Nationalism in an Old World. *Comparative Politics*, 1, 343–65.

Kertzer, D.I. (2007) Banfield, i Suoi Critici e la Cultura. *Contemporanea*, 10, 701–709.

Kim, D. (1990) The Transformation of Familism in Modern Korean Society. *International Sociology*, 5, 409–25.

King, G., Keohane, R.O. & Verba, S. (1994) *Designing Social Inquiry: Scientific Inference in Qualitative Research*, Princeton, Princeton University Press.

Kiser, E. & Hetcher, M. (1991) The Role of General Theory in Comparative Historical Sociology. *The American Journal of Sociology*, 97, 1–30.

Kiser, E. & Hetcher, M. (1998) The Debate on Historical Sociology: Rational Choice Theory and Its Critics. *The American Journal of Sociology*, 104, 785–816.

Knack, S. (2002) Social Capital and the Quality of Government: Evidence from the States. *American Journal of Political Science*, 46, 772–85.

Knack, S. & Keefer, P. (1997) Does Social Capital Have an Economic Pay-Off? A Cross Country Investigation. *Quarterly Journal of Economics*, 112, 1251–88.

Knox, A., Savage, M. & Harvey, P. (2006) Social Networks and the Study of Relations: Networks as Method, Metaphor and Form. *Economy and Society*, 35, 113–40.

Kohler-Koch, B. (1996) Catching up with Change: The Transformation of Governance in the European Union. *Journal of European Public Policy*, 3, 359–80.

Kuznets, S. (1955) Economic Growth and Income Inequality. *The American Economic Review*, 45, 1–28.

Kwon, S.W. & Arenius, P. (2010) Nations of Entrepreneurs: A Social Capital Perspective. *Journal of Business Venturing*, 25, 315–30.

La Porta, R., Lopez de Silanes, F., Schleifer, F. & Vishny, R. (1999) The Quality of Government. *Journal of Law and Economics*, 15, 222–8.

Langer, S. & Knauth, K. (1942) *Philosophy in a New Key: A Study in the Symbolism of Reason, Rite, and Art*, Cambridge MA, Harvard University Press.

Lasswell, H. (1948) *Power and Personality*, New York, Norton.

Laumann, E.O. (1973) *Bonds of Pluralism: The Form and Substance of Urban Social Networks*, New York and Chichester, Wiley.

Lemann, N. (1996) Kicking in Groups. *Atlantic Monthly*, 277, 22–6.

Lijphart, A. (1971) Comparative Politics and the Comparative Method. *The American Political Science Review*, 65, 682–93.

Lijphart, A. (1975) The Comparable-Cases Strategy in Comparative Research. *Comparative Political Studies*, 8, 158–77.

Lin, N. (2000) Inequality in Social Capital. *Contemporary Sociology*, 29 (6), 785–95.

Linden, H.V. (1920) *Belgium: the Making of a Nation*, Oxford, Clarendon Press.

Lipset, S.M. (1958) A Sociologist Looks at History. *The Pacific Sociological Review*, 1, 13–17.

Lipset, S.M. (1960) *The Political Man. The Social Bases of Politics*, New York, Doubleday & Company, Inc.

Lipset, S.M. (1996) *American Exceptionalism. A Double-Edged Sword*, New York, W.W. Norton and Company.

LIS (2000) Luxembourg Income Study.

Lopreato, J. (1961) Social Stratification and Mobility in a South Italian Town. *American Sociological Review*, 26, 585–96.

Loury, G.C. (1977) A Dynamic Theory of Racial Income Differences. In Wallace, P.A. & LaMond, A. (eds) *Women, Minorities and Employment Discrimination*. Lexington MA, Lexington Books, 153–86.

Lupo, S. (1993) Usi e Abusi del Passato. Le Radici dell'Italia di Putnam. *Meridiana*, 18, 151–68.

Machiavelli, N. & Inglese, G. (1995) *Il Principe*, Turin, G. Einaudi.

Maesschalck, J. & Van de Walle, S. (2006) Policy Failure and Corruption in Belgium: Is Federalism to Blame? *West European Politics*, 29, 999–1017.

Magrini, S. (1999) The Evolution of Income Disparities among the Regions of the European Union. *Regional Science and Urban Economics*, 29, 257–81.

Magrini, S. (2004) Regional (Di)Convergence. In Henderson, V. & Thisse, J. (eds) *Handbook of Urban and Regional Economics, Vol. IV*. Amsterdam, North Holland, 2741–96.

Mahler, V.A. (2002) Exploring the Subnational Dimension of Income Inequality: An Analysis of the Relationship between Inequality and Electoral Turnout in the Developed Countries. *International Studies Quarterly*, 46, 117–42.

Mahoney, J. & Rueschemeyer, D. (2003) Comparative Historical Analysis: Achievements and Agendas. In Mahoney, J. & Rueschemeyer, D. (eds) *Comparative Historical Analysis in the Social Sciences.* Cambridge MA, Cambridge University Press, 3–38.

Mallows, C.L. (1973) Some Comments on CP. *Technometrics*, 15, 671–6.

Marselli, G.A. (1963) American Sociologists and Italian Peasant Society: With the Reference to the Book of Banfield. *Sociologia Ruralis*, 3, 319–38.

Marshall, T.H. (1950) *Citizenship and Social Class and Other Essays*, Cambridge, Cambridge University Press.

Marshall, T.H. (1963) *Sociology at the Crossroads and other Essays*, London, Heinemann.

Mazzarone, R. (1978) Studiosi Americani in Basilicata negli Anni Cinquanta. *Basilicata*, 22, 45–8.

McNall, S.G. (1976) Barriers to Development and Modernization in Greece. *Annals of the New York Academy*, 268, 28–42.

Meloni, B. (1997) Introduzione. In Meloni, B. (ed.) *Famiglia Meridionale senza Familismo.* Catanzaro, Meridiana Libri, IV–LXIII.

Mill, J.S. (1882) *A System of Logic, Ratiocinative and Inductive: Being Connected View of the Principle of Evidence and the Methods of Scientific Investigation*, New York, Harper & Brothers Publisher.

Miller, A.J. (1984) Selection of Subsets of Regression Variables. *Journal of the Royal Statistical Society. Series A (General)*, 47, 389–425.

Miller, R.A. (1974) Are Familists Amoral? *American Ethnologist*, 1, 515–35.

Mingione, E. & Magatti, M. (1997) Strategie Familiari e Sviluppo: Una Comparazione Nord-Sud. In Meloni, B. (ed.) *Famiglia Meridionale Senza Familismo.* Catanzaro, Meridiana Libri, 137–58.

Mitchell, C.J. (1969) *Social Networks in Urban Situations*, Manchester, Manchester University Press.

Moller, V. (2010) Strengthening Intergenerational Solidarity in South Africa. *Journal of International Relationships*, 8, 145–60.

Montesquieu, C. (1914) *The Spirit of Laws*, London, G. Bell & Sons Ltd.

Moravcsik, A. (1993) Preferences and Power in the European Community: A Liberal Intergovernmentalist Approach. *Journal of Common Market Studies*, 34, 473–524.

Moss, L.W. & Cappannari, S.C. (1959) A Sociological and Anthropological Investigation of an Italian Rural Community. *IVth World Congress of Sociology, International Sociological Association.* Milan.

Moss, L.W. & Cappannari, S.C. (1960) Patterns of Kinship, Comparaggio and Community in a Southern Italian Village. *Anthropological Quarterly*, 33, 24–32.

Moss, L.W. & Cappannari, S.C. (1962) Estate and Class in a South Italian Hill Village. *American Anthropologist*, 64, 287–300.

Muller, E.N. & Seligson, M.A. (1994) Civic Culture and Democracy: The Question of Causal Relationships. *The American Political Science Review*, 88, 635–52.

Munshi, K. (2003) Networks in Modern Economy: Mexican Migrants in the U.S. Labor Market. *The Quarterly Journal of Economics*, 118, 549–99.

Muraskin, W. (1974) The Moral Basis of a Backward Sociologist: Edward Banfield, the Italians, and Italian-Americans. *The American Journal of Sociology*, 79, 1484–96.

Nisbet, R.A. (1969) *The Quest for Community*, New York, Oxford University Press.

Nitti, F.S. (1900) *Nord e Sud, Prime Linee di una Inchiesta sulla Ripartizione Territoriale delle Entrate e delle Spese dello Stato in Italia*, Turin, Roux e Viarengo.

North, D.H. (1990) *Institutions, Institutional Change and Economic Performance*, Cambridge, Cambridge University Press.

O'Connel, M. (2003) Anti 'Social Capital': Civic Values versus Economic Equality in the EU. *European Sociological Review*, 19, 241–8.

OECD (2001) *The Contribution of Human and Social Capital to Sustained Economic Growth and Well-being. International Symposium Report*, Paris, OECD.

Olson, M. (1982) *The Rise and Decline of Nations: Economic Growth, Stagflation, and Social Rigidities*, New Haven, Yale University Press.

Ostrom, E. & Ahn, T.K. (2003) *Foundations of Social Capital*, Cheltenham, UK and Northampton, MA, USA, Edward Elgar.

Paine, T. (1974) Agrarian Justice. In Foner, P.F. (ed.) *The Life and Major Writings of Thomas Paine*. Secaucus NJ, Citadel Press, 605–23.

Paldam, M. (2000) Social Capital: One or Many? Definition and Measurement. *Journal of Economic Surveys*, 14, 629–53.

Paxton, P. (1999) Is Social Capital Declining in the United States? A Multiple Indicator Assessment. *American Journal of Sociology*, 105, 88–127.

Peters, G.B. (2006) Consociationalism, Corruption and Chocolate: Belgian Exceptionalism. *West European Politics*, 29, 1079–92.

Petrakos, G., Rodríguez-Pose, A. & Rovolis, A. (2005) Growth, Integration and Regional Inequality in Europe. *Environment and Planning*, 37, 1837–55.

Petrusewicz, M. (1997) The Demise of Latifondo. In Lumley, R. & Morris, J. (eds) *The New History of the Italian South. The Mezzogiorno Revisited*. Exeter, University of Exeter Press, 20–41.

Petrusewicz, M. (1998) *Come il Meridione Divenne una Questione. Rappresentazioni del Sud Prima e Dopo il Quarantotto*, Soveria Mannelli (CZ), Rubbettino.

Pico Della Mirandola, G. (1994) Oration on the Dignity of Man. Available at http://www.cscs.umich.edu/~crshalizi/Mirandola/.

Piketty, T. (1999) Can Fiscal Redistribution Undo Skill-Biased Technical Change? Evidence from the French Experience. *European Economic Review*, 43, 839–51.

Pirenne, H. (1963) *Early Democracies in the Low Countries: Urban Society and Political Conflict in the Middle Ages and the Renaissance*, New York, Harper & Row.

Piselli, F. (1997) L'Approccio di Rete negli Studi sulla Famiglia. In Meloni, B. (ed.) *Famiglia Meridionale senza Familismo*. Catanzaro, Meridiana Libri, 409–32.

Pissarides, C.A. (1990) Unemployment and the Persistence on Employment Shocks, papers 377, London School of Economics, Centre for Labour Economics.

Pitkin, D.S. (1954) *Land Tenure and Family Organisation in an Italian Village*, Cambridge MA, Harvard University Press.

Pizzorno, A. (1971) Amoral Familism and Historical Marginality. In Dogan, M. & Rose, R. (eds) *European Politics: A Reader*. Boston, Little Brown.

Pizzorno, A. (1999) Perché si Paga il Benzinaio. Nota per una Teoria del Capitale Sociale. *Stato e Mercato*, 57, 373–93.

Polanyi, K. (1957) *The Great Transformation*, Boston, Beacon Press.

Portes, A. (1998) Social Capital: Its Origins and Applications in Modern Sociology. *Annual Review of Sociology*, 24, 1–24.

Przeworski, A. & Teune, H. (1970) *The Logic of Comparative Social Inquiry*, New York, Wiley.

Pugliese, E. (1992) Famiglia, Occupazione e Mercato del Lavoro. In Cerase, P. (ed.) *Dopo il Familismo Cosa? Tesi a Confronto sulla Questione Meridionale negli Anni '90*. Milan, Franco Angeli, 84–104.

Putnam, R.D. (1993) *Making Democracy Work: Civic Traditions in Modern Italy*, Princeton, Princeton University Press.

Putnam, R.D. (1995) Bowling Alone: America's Declining Social Capital. *Journal of Democracy*, 6, 65–78.

Putnam, R.D. (2000) *Bowling Alone: The Collapse and Revival of American Community*, New York, Simon & Schuster.

Quadagno, J. & Knapp, S.J. (1992) Have Historical Sociologists Forsaken Theory? Thoughts on the History/Theory Relationship. *Sociological Methods Research*, 20, 481–507.

Quariaux, Y. (2006) *L'Image du Flamand en Wallonie*, Brussels, Labor.

Quigley, C. (1973) Mexican National Character and Circum-Mediterranean Personality Structure. *American Anthropologist*, 75, 319–22.

Radcliffe-Brown, A.R. (1940) On Social Structure. *The Journal of the Royal Anthropological Institute of Great Britain and Ireland*, 70, 1–12.

Ragin, C. (1987) *The Comparative Method: Moving Beyond Qualitative and Quantitative Strategies*, Berkeley, University of California Press.

Ramella, F. (1994) Gruppi Sociali e Cittadinanza Democratica. L'Associazionismo nella Letteratura Sociologica. *Meridiana*, 20, 93–133.

Ramella, F. (1995) Mezzogiorno e Società Civile: Ancora l'Epoca del Familismo Amorale. *Il Mulino*, 3, 471–80.

Reid, A. & Musyck, B. (2000) Industrial Policy in Wallonia: A Rupture with the Past. *European Planning Studies*, 8, 183–200.

Renan, E. (1882) Qu'est-ce qu'une Nation? Available at http://www.bmlisieux.com/archives/nation04.htm.

Reyneri, E. (1979) *La Catena Migratoria: Il Ruolo dell'Emigrazione nel Mercato del Lavoro di Arrivo e di Esodo*, Bologna, Il Mulino.

Rokkan, S. (1964) Book Review of The Civic Culture: Political Attitudes and Democracy in Five Nations. *The American Political Science Review*, 58, 676–9.

Rose, N. (2000) Community, Citizenship, and the Third Way. *American Behavioural Scientist*, 43 (9), 1395–411.

Rossi Doria, A. (1999) *La Fine dei Contadini*, Soveria Mannelli (CZ), Rubbettino Editore.

Rossi Doria, M. (1948) *Riforma Agraria e Azione Meridionalista*, Bologna, Edizioni Agricole.

Rossi Doria, M. (1958) *Dieci Anni di Politica Agraria nel Mezzogiorno*, Bari, Laterza.

Rossi Doria, M. (1967) Il Mezzogiorno Agricolo e il suo Avvenire 'l'Osso e la Polpa'. *Nord e Sud nella Società e nell'Economia Italiana Oggi. Atti del convegno promosso dalla fondazione Einaudi.* Turin, Einaudi.

Rothstein, B. (2001) Social Capital in the Social Democratic Welfare State. *Politics and Society*, 29, 206–40.

Rothstein, B. & Stolle, D. (2003) Introduction: Social Capital in Scandinavia. *Scandinavian Political Studies*, 26, 1–26.

Rothstein, B. & Uslaner, E. (2006) All for all: Equality and Social Trust. *Center for European Studies, Working paper series No. 117.*

Russell, B. (1918) *Roads to Freedom: Socialism, Anarchism and Syndacalism*, London, George Allen & Unwin.

Sabatini, F. (2008) Social Capital and the Labour Market. *MPRA Munich Personal RePEc Archive.*

Salvadori, M. (1977) *Il Mito del Buongoverno. La Questione Meridionale da Cavour a Gramsci*, Turin, Einaudi.

Salvemini, G. (1958) *Scritti sulla Questione Meridionale (1896–1955)*, Turin, Einaudi.

Santoro, M. (2007) Dall'Ethos all'Habitus (Ovvero Perché a Montegrano c'è Sempre Qualcosa da Fare). *Contemporanea*, 10, 695–701.

Sartori, G. (1970) Concept Misformation in Comparative Politics. *The American Political Science Review*, 64, 1033–53.

Sartori, G. (2009) Chance, Luck, and Stubbornness, an Autobiographical Essay. In Collier, D. & Gerring, J. (eds) *Concepts and Method in Social Science: The Tradition of Giovanni Sartori*. New York, Routledge, 331–40.

Scheepers, P., Grotenhuis, M.T. & Gelissen, J. (2002) Welfare States and Dimensions of Social Capital: Cross-national Comparisons of Social Contacts in European Countries. *European Societies*, 4, 185–207.

Schneider, G., Plumper, T. & Baumann, S. (2000) Bringing Putnam to the European Regions: on the Relevance of Social Capital for Economic Growth. *European Urban and Regional Studies*, 7, 307–16.

Schneider, J. & Schneider, P.T. (1976) *Culture and Political Economy in Western Sicily*, New York, Academic Press.

Schneider, J.A. (2005) Getting Beyond the Training vs. Work Experience Debate: The Role of Labor Markets, Social Capital, Cultural Capital, and Community Resources in Long-Term Poverty. *Journal of Women, Politics & Policy*, 27, 41–53.

Schrader, H. (2004) Social Capital and Social Transformation in Russia. *JEEMS*, 4, 391–410.

Schwarz, G. (1978) Estimating the Dimension of a Model. *Annals of Statistics*, 6, 461–4.

Sciolla, L. (1997) *Italiani. Stereotipi di Casa Nostra*, Bologna, Il Mulino.

Sciolla, L. (2001) Familismo. *Il Mulino*, 4/01, 653–9.

Sciolla, L. (2004) *La Sfida dei Valori*, Bologna, Il Mulino.

Sciolla, L. & Negri, N. (1996) L'Isolamento dello Spirito Civico. In Sciolla, L. & Negri, N. (eds) *Il Paese dei Paradossi. Le Basi Sociali della Politica in Italia*. Rome, La Nuova Italia Scientifica.

Scotellaro, R. (1955) *Contadini del Sud*, Bari, Laterza.

Seiler, D. (1977) Clivages, Régions et Science Politique: Application d'un Schéma d'Analyse aux Cas de la Suisse et de la Belgique. *Canadian Journal of Political Science/Revue Canadienne de Science Politique*, 10, 447–72.

Sherif, M., Harvey, O.J., White, B., Hood, W. & Sherif, C. (1988) *Intergroup Conflict and Cooperation: The Robber's Cave Experiment*,

Normans Institute of Groups Relations, University of Oklahoma, reprinted by Wesleyan University Press.

Silverman, S. (1968) Agricultural Organisation, Social Structure and Values in Italy: Amoral Familism Reconsidered. *American Anthropologist*, 70, 1–20.

Sims, C.A. (1980) Macroeconomics and Reality. *Econometrica*, 48, 1–48.

Skocpol, T. (1979) *States and Social Revolutions. A Comparative Analysis of France, Russia and China*, Cambridge MA, Cambridge University Press.

Skocpol, T. (1984) Sociology's Historical Imagination. In Skocpol, T. (ed.) *Vision and Method in Historical Sociology*. Cambridge MA, Cambridge University Press.

Skocpol, T. (1996) Unravelling from Above. *The American Prospect*, 25, 20–25.

Skocpol, T., Ganz, M. & Munson, Z. (2000) A Nation of Organisers: The institutional Origins of Civic Voluntarism in the United States. *American Political Science Review*, 94, 527–46.

Smidt, C.E. (2003) *Religion as Social Capital: Producing the Common Good*, Waco, Baylor University Press.

Smith, D. (1991) *The Rise of Historical Sociology*, Cambridge, Polity Press.

Smith, S.S. & Kulynich, J. (2002) It May be Social, But Why is it Capital? The Social Construction of Social Capital and the Politics of Language. *Politics & Society*, 30, 149–86.

Smyrl, M.E. (1997) Does European Community Regional Policy Empower the Regions? *Governance*, 10, 287–309.

Somers, M. (1998) 'We're No Angels': Realism, Rational Choice, and Relationality in Social Science. *The American Journal of Sociology*, 104, 722–84.

Stein, C. (1955) Inadmissibility of the Usual Estimator for the Mean of a Multivariate Normal Distribution. *Proceedings of the Third Berkeley Symposium on Mathematical Statistics and Probability*, 1, 197–206.

Stein, M.R. (1960) *The Eclipse of Community: An Interpretation of American Studies*, Princeton, Princeton University Press.

Sudgen, R. (2000) Team Preferences. *Economics and Philosophy*, 16, 175–204.

Swenden, W. (2002) Asymmetric Federalism and Coalition-Making in Belgium. *Publius – The Journal of Federalism*, 32, 67–87.

Swenden, W., Brans, M. & De Winter, L. (2006) The Politics of Belgium: Institutions and Policy under Bipolar and Centrifugal Federalism. *West European Politics*, 29, 863–73.

Swenden, W. & Maarten, T.J. (2006) 'Will it Stay or Will it Go?' Federalisation and the Sustainability of Belgium. *West European Politics*, 29, 877–94.

Tabellini, G. (2010) Culture and Institutions. *Journal of the European Economic Association*, 8, 677–716.

Tamilina, L. (2008) Welfare States and Social Trust: 'Crowding-Out' Dilemma. In Falcone, R., Barber, S.K. & Singh, M.P. (eds) *Trust in Agent Society*. Berlin, Springer-Verlag, 112–34.

Tarkowska, E. & Tarkowski, J. (1991) Social Disintegration in Poland. *Telos*, 89, 103–108.

Tarrow, S. (1972) *Partito Comunista e Contadini nel Mezzogiorno*, Turin, Einaudi.

Tarrow, S. (1979) *Tra Centro e Periferia*, Bologna, Il Mulino.

Tarrow, S. (1996) Making Social Science Work across Space and Time: A Critical Reflection on Robert Putnam's Making Democracy Work. *American Political Science Review*, 90, 389–97.

Thompson, E.P. (1991 [1963]) *The Making of the English Working Class*, Harmondsworth, Penguin.

Thomson, I.T. (2005) The Theory that Won't Die: From Mass Society to the Decline of Social Capital. *Sociological Forum*, 20, 421–48.

Tilly, C. (1964) *The Vendée: A Sociological Analysis of the Counter-Revolution of 1793*, Cambridge MA, Harvard University Press.

Tilly, C. (1978) *From Mobilization to Revolution*, Reading MA, Addison-Wesley.

Tilly, C. (1984) *Big Structures, Large Processes, Huge Comparisons*, New York, Russell.

Tocqueville, A.D. (1904) *L'Ancien Régime et la Révolution*, Oxford, Oxford University Press.

Tocqueville, A.D. (1961) *De la Démocratie en Amérique*, London, Macmillan & Co Ltd.

Tollebeek, J. (1998) Historical Representation and the Nation-State in Romantic Belgium. *Journal of the History of Ideas*, 59, 329–53.

Tönnies, F. (1955) *Community and Association*, London, Routledge.

Torfing, J. (1999) Workfare with Welfare: Recent Reforms of the Danish Welfare State. *Journal of European Social Policy*, 1, 5–28.

Triandis, H. (1989) The Self and Social Behaviour in Differing Cultural Contexts. *Psychological Review*, 96, 506–20.

Trigilia, C. (1992) *Sviluppo Senza Autonomia. Effetti Perversi delle Politiche nel Mezzogiorno*, Bologna, Il Mulino.

Trigilia, C. (2001) Social Capital and Local Development. *European Journal of Sociology Theory*, 4, 427–42.

Turiello, P. (1882) *Governo e Governati in Italia*, Bologna, Zanichelli.

Turnaturi, G. & Donolo, C. (1988) Familismi Amorali. In Donolo, C. & Fichera, F. (eds) *Le Vie dell'Innovazione.* Milan, Feltrinelli, 164–85.

Uslaner, E.M. (2000–2001) Producing and Consuming Trust. *Political Science Quarterly* 115, 569–90.

Van Dam, D. & Nizet, J. (2002) *Wallonie, Flandre: des Regards Croisés,* Brussels, De Boeck.

Van Oorschot, W. & Arts, W. (2005) The Social Capital of Welfare State: the Crowding out Hypothesis Revisited. *Journal of European Social Policy,* 15, 5–26.

Van Oorschot, W., Arts, W. & Gelissen, J. (2006) Social Capital in Europe: Measurement and Social and Regional Distribution of a Multifaceted Phenomenon. *Acta Sociologica,* 49, 149–67.

Van Parijs, P. (1992) *Arguing for Basic Income. Ethical Foundations for a Radical Reform,* London, Verso.

Various (1981) *Storia D'Italia Vol. 4. Comuni e Signorie. Istituzioni, Società e Lotte per l'Egemonia,* Turin, UTET.

Various (2008) Rapporto Annuale Dipartimento per lo Sviluppo e la Coesione Economica sugli Interventi nelle Aree Sottoutilizzate.

Venditti, R. (1981) *Il Manuale Cencelli. Il Prontuario della Lottizzazione Democristiana. Un Documento sulla Gestione del Potere,* Rome, Editori Riuniti.

Viazzo, P.P. (2007) Revocare l'Ostracismo? L'Antropologia di Fronte a un Classico Ripudiato. *Contemporanea,* 10, 714–19.

Vico, G., Bergin, T.G. & Fisch, M.H. (1968) *The New Science of Giambattista Vico,* Ithaca, Cornell University Press.

Villari, P. (1961) *Il Sud nella Storia d'Italia,* Bari, Laterza.

Villari, P. (1979) *Le Lettere Meridionali ed Altri Scritti sulla Questione Sociale in Italia,* Napoli, Guida.

Vöchting, F. (1955) *La Questione Meridionale,* Napoli, Iem.

Völker, B. & Flap, H. (2001) Weak Ties as a Liability: The Case of East Germany. *Rationality and Society,* 13, 397–428.

Vuong, Q. (1989) Likelihood Ratio Tests for Model Selection and Non-Tested Hypotheses. *Econometrica,* 57, 307–33.

Weber, M. (1946) The Protestant Sects and the Spirit of Capitalism. In Gerth, H.H. & Wright, M.C. (eds) *From Max Weber.* New York, Oxford University Press, 302–46.

Weber, M. (1961) Types of Social Organisation. In Parson, T., Shils, E. & Naegele, K.D. (eds) *Theories of Society.* New York, Glencoe Free Press.

Wellman, B. & Leighton, B. (1979) Networks, Neighborhoods, and Communities. *Urban Affairs Quarterly,* 14, 363–90.

Werbner, R.P. (1984) The Manchester School in South-Central Africa. *Ann. Rev. Anthropol.,* 157–85.

Whyte, W.H. (1956) *The Organization Man*, New York, Simon and Schuster.

Wichers, A.J. (1964) Amoral Familism Reconsidered. *Sociologia Ruralis*, 4, 168–81.

Wilensky, H.L. (1975) *The Welfare State and Equality: Structural and Ideological Roots of Public Expenditure*, Berkeley, University of California Press.

Williamson, J.G. (1965) Regional Inequality and the Process of National Development: A Description of Patterns. *Economic Development and Cultural Change*, 13, 1–84.

Winstanley, G. (1649) *The True Levellers Standard Advanced*, London, available at http://www.kingston.ac.uk/cusp/Lectures/Hill.htm.

Woolcock, M. (1998) Social Capital and Economic Development: Toward a Theoretical Synthesis and Policy Framework. *Theory and Society*, 27, 151–208.

Woolcock, M. & Narayan, D. (2000) Social Capital: Implications for Development Theory, Research and Policy. *The World Bank Research Observer*, 15, 225–51.

Yver, G. (1968) *Le Commerce et les Marchands dans l'Italie Méridionale au XIIIe & au XIVe Siècle*, New York, Burt Franklin.

Zak, P.J. & Knack, S. (2001) Trust and Growth. *The Economic Journal*, 111, 295–321.

Index